JACKALS

The Stench of American Fascism

ALEX CONSTANTINE

Jackals: The Stench of American Fascism
Copyright © 2016 Alex Constantine. All Rights Reserved.

References to Internet websites (URLs) were accurate at the time of writing. Neither the author nor Trine Day is responsible for URLs that may have expired or changed since the book was prepared.

Published by:
Trine Day LLC
PO Box 577
Walterville, OR 97489
1-800-556-2012
www.TrineDay.com
publisher@trineday.net

Library of Congress Control Number: 2015949160

Jackals: The Stench of Facsism/Constantine, Alex
—1st ed.
p. cm.
Epub (ISBN-13) 978-1-63424-016-1
Kindle (ISBN-13) 978-1-63424-017-8
Print (ISBN-13) 978-1-63424-015-4
1. United States -- Politics and government -- 2001-2009. 2. United States -- Politics and government -- 1945-2001. 3. Fascism. 4. Conspiracies -- United States -- History I. Title

First Edition
10 9 8 7 6 5 4 3 2 1

Printed in the USA
Distribution to the Trade by:
Independent Publishers Group (IPG)
814 North Franklin Street
Chicago, Illinois 60610
312.337.0747
www.ipgbook.com

For the "Disappeared"

CONTENTS

INTRODUCTION

TERROR ON THE RIGHT

*America has long been an exporter of terrorism, according
to a secret CIA analysis released Wednesday by the Web
site WikiLeaks. And if that phenomenon were to become a
widely held perception, the analysis said, it could damage
relations with foreign allies and dampen their willingness
to cooperate in 'extrajudicial' activities, such as the rendition and interrogation of terrorism suspects.*
– Washington Post, August 25, 2010

A "Wink and Nod" from the CIA

The Knights Templar of the corporations at the Central
Intelligence Agency have a long history of striking alliances with political undesirables of all kinds, from the
post-WW II recruitment of Nazis to secret liaisons with Middle Eastern terrorists. One example bridging both camps was
the Agency's tie to Black September, the Palestinian paramilitary group named after the "era of regrettable events" that began on September 16, 1970, when Jordan's King Hussein declared military rule culminating in the deaths and expulsions
of thousands of Palestinians in response to a PLO coup plot.

Black September kidnapped and murdered eleven Israeli
athletes during the 1972 Summer Olympics in Munich. The
PLO at that time was considered the most formidable terrorist
threat to Israel, led by Yasser Arafat, who had a "wink-and-
nod understanding with the CIA," as the *Washington Post* reported on November 12, 2004.

1

For 30 years, Arafat "allowed his top intelligence officers to maintain regular contact with the agency – even as he publicly continued his defiant and ultimately fruitless quest for a Palestinian state." The CIA's relationship with Arafat began a year before the conflict in Jordan, when the Agency made contact with Ali Hassan Salameh, also known as Abu Hassan, a Fatah recruit and Black September's chief of operations.

In classified CIA cable traffic, Salameh was code-named "MJTRUST/2."

The *Post*'s David Ignatius reported that Robert Ames, a CIA case officer, made contact with Hassan with encouragement from Yassar Arafat, who sought an open channel with American intelligence. Ames continued to interact with Hassan in the spring of 1970, when they met in Kuwait. Ignatius:

> A senior CIA officer later that year tried to recruit Abu Hassan by offering him a large payment in Rome. The Palestinian angrily refused, insisting he was not an American agent. The botched recruitment was followed by years of bloody turmoil. King Hussein expelled PLO guerrillas from Jordan in September 1970; Arafat responded by creating a secret terrorist wing, known as Black September – with America's former contact, Abu Hassan, as one of its key operatives.

A covert "understanding" was struck between the killer and the CIA, represented by Ames, at a meeting held at the Waldorf-Astoria in November 1974. Arafat was there for a United Nations visit. The alliance was cemented during the 1975-76 civil war in Lebanon, with Arafat's guerillas providing security for U.S. diplomats in West Beirut.

Was a friendly wink-and-nod the extent of CIA complicity?

Fraternal facial gestures aside, a few years before this report, on September 16, 2001, Ignatius wrote:

> Even after Munich, the CIA worked to maintain its intelligence link to Salameh. Ames sent the Palestinian this message in September 1973, using a simple code for the

CIA, the PLO and Israel: "My company is still interested in getting together with Ali's company. The southern company [Israel] has investigated. I've seen a lot of their files, and they know about our contacts."

The Black September leader wasn't the only terrorist in the clan to act on hostility towards the Israelis. Hassan Salameh, Ali's father, was a central figure in the Palestinian struggle – a loyal aide to Haj Amin al-Husseini, the Grand Mufti of Jerusalem (1921–1948), the notorious Nazi collaborator. Following the collapse of a pro-Nazi uprising in Iraq in 1941, Haj Amin and Hassan Salameh fled to Nazi Germany. Salameh took a German wife, was trained in paramilitary operations by Hitler's Army. He returned to Palestine in October 1944 as a guerilla fighter embroiled in Operation ATLAS, a joint Nazi-Palestinian plot to poison the drinking water of Tel Aviv and kill the city's 160,000 Jewish residents. The operation failed. Salameh was seriously wounded and fled to Jerusalem to have his injuries treated by a physician in Qula.

These ties survived the collapse of the Reich: Haj Amin's granddaughter subsequently married Abu Hassan, and *New York Times* reporter Elliott A. Green describes an enduring postwar Nazi connection:

> One of the Nazis who met Haj Amin el-Husseini in the years of Nazi triumphs was one Franois Genoud ... founder and militant of the pre-war Swiss Nazi party, the National Front. He met Husseini in 1936 in the Middle East and once again in Berlin in 1943, while he was an agent of the Abwehr (German intelligence agency) and while Husseini, the British-appointed Mufti of Jerusalem, was urging on the Holocaust and recruiting Arabs and other Muslims into the Nazi service. Genoud met him several times in Beirut after the war, until the Mufti died in 1974. Meanwhile, unrepentant, veteran Nazi Genoud got a management position with the Red Cross in Brussels, and later (1958) opened a bank in Geneva called the Banque Commerciale Arabe (backed by Syrian funds). Through his connections in Cairo, a postwar sanctuary

for sundry Nazi war criminals, he met leaders of the Algerian FLN and was later invited to run a bank in newly independent Algeria, the Banque Populaire Arabe.... He counted among his friends Wadi Haddad and Ali Hassan Salameh, PLO master terrorists who accomplished airliner hijackings and other high-profile terrorist acts.

On January 5, 1997, the *Philadelphia Inquirer* published its own independent investigation of Genoud, reporting that the CIA and State Department also gave a wink-and-nod to the Swiss banker and his closest Nazi/terrorist cronies:

> By 1955, Genoud had used his wartime contacts to become an adviser, researcher and banker to the cause of Arab nationalism. Along with Reichenberg in Tangiers and Cairo, Genoud set up AraboAfrika, an import-export company that served as a cover for the dissemination of anti-Jewish and anti-Israeli propaganda and the delivery of weapons to the Algerian National Liberation Front (FLN). Genoud made investments for Hjalmar Schacht, the former Nazi Reichsminister of Finance, president of the Reichsbank and a key postwar intermediary between Germans and Arabs. Numerous former Third Reich officials gained refuge in the Arab world, including Eichmann's deputy, Alois Brunner, who for years was protected by Hafez el-Assad in Damascus.

The CIA financed Brunner and his fellow Nazis in postwar Egypt. And in 1956, William Porter of the American embassy in Rabat briefed the State Department that Genoud, then living at Frankfort/Main in Germany, "purporting to represent the Hjalmar Schacht interests, called at the Embassy this week to discuss ... massive investments" in Morocco:

> The crux of the proposition made to the Moroccan Government by Mr. Genoud and his associates,' says the once-classified document obtained by the *Inquirer* under the Freedom of Information Act, 'involves the sale by the United States – through a long-term, low-interest loan – of 55 mil-

lion dollars' worth of agricultural surpluses to the Schacht group, which would dispose of them in Western Europe and utilize the counterpart for investment in Morocco in the form of equipment and technicians. "Genoud said the Moroccans were keenly interested in securing Schacht's collaboration," according to the document, "partly because of the esteem in which he is held in the Arab world generally, but also because the Moroccans tend to admire the philosophies for which he stands." Porter reported that the embassy did not encourage Genoud, and did not think the Schacht plan would benefit the United States.

More is to be learned about Genoud's contacts with the Americans. The State Department has yet to declassify 16 documents relating to Genoud; 29 other documents relating to his application for a visa or permit to enter the U.S. remain classified.

Neocon Noir

At a December 11, 2011 town hall meeting in New Hampshire, GOP presidential candidate Mitt Romney reminisced about his Mormon missionary days in France, sharply critiqued the records of Newt Gingrich and Barack Obama, and generally appeared to be gathering no moss at the podium ... until someone from the audience asked if he supported the efforts of some Washington politicians to strike the MEK (the Mojahedin-e-Khalq, an Iranian dissident group) from the State Department's list of terrorist organizations.

Romney appeared to be stunned by the question.

"I have not heard of the MEK," he responded, "so I can't possibly tell you whether I support the MEK. I'll take a look at the issue."

"If Romney has never truly heard of the MEK," a reporter for the *Mother Jones* website quipped a day later, "he won't have to go far to learn more – his own special advisor on foreign policy, Mitchell Reiss, is a leading advocate for the group."

Reiss, the president of Washington College, called the previous spring for deletion of the MEK from the terrorist list, stating: "For the United States this is a case where American interests of opposing the regime in Tehran are entirely consistent with American values of freedom and democracy."

In October, he addressed a MEK policy meeting. But Reiss wasn't the only Republican of note to openly support the organization. Andrew Card, John Bolton, Rudolph Guliani and Tom Ridge have all appealed publicly to remove the MEK from the list.

Another prolific neocon opinion-shaper is Michael Ledeen, a former advisor to the NSC and State Department, most widely known as a player in the Iran contra scandal. His bona fides include a stint as an American Enterprise Institute "Freedom Scholar," and a contributing editor at the National Review. Ledeen often writes commentary for the Wall Street Journal, appears regularly on Fox News and a slew of right-wing talk radio programs. But on these occasions, Ledeen doesn't discuss his past as an Italian military intelligence and "risk-assessment" officer with ties to SISME – a clutch of right-wing Italian terrorists.

Jim Lobe, journalist and bureau chief of the Inter Press Service, writes that Ledeen had hard-right connections in Italy, "including alleged ties to the P2 Masonic lodge that rocked Italy in the early 1980s."

In 1981, he returned to Washington and was appointed as an "anti-terrorism" advisor to Secretary of State Al Haig.

Another influential tutor of the neo-conservative movement is Eliot Cohen – another Mitt Romney advisor. The Nation's Max Blumenthal reports that Cohen "rose through the ranks of the Republican foreign policy elite as a protégé of Paul Wolfowitz, the former Assistant Secretary of Defense who is credited with playing a central role in the push for invading Iraq." In 1990, Wolfowitz arranged a position for Cohen "working beside him on the policy planning staff of the Office of the Secretary of Defense. Three years later ... he began using his influence to propel Cohen's career."

In 1997, "Wolfowitz and Cohen joined forces to form the Project for a New American Century, a neoconservative umbrella group that served as the key non-governmental vehicle for promoting the case for invading Iraq after 9/11."

In the beginning of the GW Bush presidency was the word ... of neocons. Terrorism and war are centerpieces of neoconservative preoccupation, and the media are all too often their willing perception management playthings. Who doesn't recall with considerable shock and awe the steady, decisive, ubiquitous drumbeat that issued from the media in the buildup to the Iraq war?

A few years later, it was evident that America had bought itself another reeking quagmire. The neocons went back to work to resell a lucrative war to a civilian population that was having its doubts.

In 2007, PBS aired a neoconservative propaganda series with direct ties to the administration, *America at a Crossroads*. Segments included the hour-long, painfully jingoistic *"The Case for War: In Defense of Freedom,"* a celebration of the invasion of Iraq scripted and narrated by Richard Perle, a fixture at the American Enterprise Institute (a CIA/military intelligence front), former assistant secretary of defense under Reagan, chairman of Bush's Defense Policy Board Advisory Committee.

The program depicted opponents of the war as borderline personalities and "conspiracy theorists" in a sad state of mental disarray.

And this was *public* television – commercial media were even more cynical in their collusion with the Bush administration.

General Paul E. Vallely – a Fox News analyst who once co-authored a research paper, *From Psyop to MindWar: The Psychology of Victory*, with San Francisco Satanist Michael Aquino – was given generous airtime from 2001 to 2007 to promote the war and defend the administration with shaggy-dog apologias. (General Vallely is a psyop specialist who claims that the U.S. lost the Vietnam War because the media were polluted with "enemy propaganda" that undermined civilian confidence in the military.) CBS gave a soapbox to Air

Force General Joseph W. Ralston, vice-chairman of the Cohen Group, a consulting firm named after former Secretary of Defense William Cohen with a client roster that includes Lockheed-Martin and other oversized military contractors. Over at CNN, retired Army general James Marks from McNeil Technologies was retained as military analyst, 2004-2007. In the 2012 presidential race, Marks went on to become a national security advisor for Mitt Romney.

The presence of Pentagon generals in the media – nine of them writing pro-war editorials for the *New York Times* alone – was arranged by former Hill & Knowlton general manager and Assistant Secretary of Defense (under Rumsfeld) Torie Clarke, a senior advisor to Comcast and an on-air commentator at ABC. Clarke has served as press secretary to Senator John McCain. In 1982, she was a press assistant to then Vice President George H.W. Bush. Clarke's bio notes that she is "best known to the public as the chief spokesperson for the Pentagon on 9/11 and the beginning of the Iraq war," architect of the media embedding program in Iraq.

> As Assistant Secretary of Defense for Public Affairs, Ms. Clarke was at her desk in the Pentagon's outer ring when the World Trade Center was attacked on September 11, 2001. From those first moments on 9/11, to embedding correspondents with military units in Operation Iraqi Freedom – a program she conceived, designed and ran – Ms. Clarke has played a leading role in shaping the public's understanding of the war on terrorism. As press secretary for President George H.W. Bush's 1992 re-election campaign, Ms. Clarke witnessed history from the vantage point of Air Force One.

Clarke's media manipulations did much to divide America into seething media tribes, each with its own set of second-hand talking points on war and terror.

She was also the catalyst for the rise of General David Petraeus, who was guided in Iraq by Cohen and other leading neoconservatives. Clarke's pool of military analysts constituted an unparalleled, five-plus year psyop surge. David Barstow at the *New York Times* wrote in 2008, "When David H Petraeus was appointed the commanding general in Iraq in January 2007, one of his early acts was to meet with the [Pentagon's retired military] analysts."

One of those "analysts" was retired US Army General Jack Keane, a "patron" to David Petraeus in his ascent through the ranks – currently a senior advisor at Kohlberg, Kravis, Roberts, and a director of General Dynamics. Also Frederick Kagan from the American Enterprise Institute, the brains behind the "surge" strategy and a well-known neoconservative "intellectual."

Soon, across the channel spectrum, the press was singing his praises.

But Tom Engelhardt, a progressive critic of the war, wrote in October: "Here's the strange thing when you look more carefully at Petraeus' record (as others have indeed done over these last years), the actual results – in Iraq, not Washington – for each of his previous assignments proved dismal. What the record shows is a man who, after each tour of duty, seemed to manage to make it out of town just ahead of the posse, so that someone else always took the fall."

On his stint in Mosul, former ambassador Peter Galbraith offered a sober counterpoint to the sighs of admiration in the mass media:

> As the American commander in Mosul in 2003 and 2004, he earned adulatory press coverage ... for taming the Sunni-majority city. Petraeus ignored warnings from America's Kurdish allies that he was appointing the wrong people to key positions in Mosul's local government and police. A few months after he left the city, the Petraeus-appointed local police commander defected to the insurgency while the Sunni Arab police handed their weapons and uniforms over en masse to the insurgents.

Regarding Petraeus, the media typically say one thing, reality says another. Mosul became an epicenter of insurgency in Iraq because General Petraeus handled matters there in a ham-handed manner. After Mosul, his objective was to train the Iraq army to be self-sufficient. Rod Nordland, who wrote a glowing cover story about the general for *Newsweek* in 2004, had second thoughts in 2007:

> [Petraeus] rose to fame not by his achievements but by his success in selling them as achievements. He's first of all a great communicator ... Training the Iraqi military and shifting responsibility to them was the mantra Petraeus sold to hundreds of credulous reporters and hundreds of even more credulous visiting CODELs (congressional delegations)... By the time he left, the training program was clearly on its way to spectacular failure. By the end of last year that had become received wisdom; it became convenient for the brass to blame the fiasco on the politically less popular and media-friendless General George Casey. Entire brigades of police had to be pulled off the street and retrained because they were evidently riddled with death squads and in some cases even with insurgents. The Iraqi army was all but useless, a feeble patient kept on life support by the American military.

The unreported failures of General David Petraeus reflect the "guidance" he received from neocons like Eliot Cohen and Fred and Kimberly Kagan. Their foreign policy failures are now "our" failures, and not even all the King's neocons can sanitize them.

After the Broadwell affair hit the front pages, the media tried to break his fall. A reporter at NPR enthused that Washington insiders are "in awe of him." But the real Petraeus was catching up with his public image, already tarnished by a routine sex scandal. And America has so much more to learn about the man behind the Madison Avenue gloss. Once again, conservatives will find that they have been wallowing in a world of illusion, but will go on to create more geopolitical disasters. The media will fall in line. Everyone will forget that the addled "conspiracy theorists" dismissed by Richard

Perle were right all along. And more sacrificial victims of a war-profiteering "Complex" will fatten the bottom line. All that it will take is another Torie Clarke.

Financial Terrorism

Conservatives, always quick to point the finger elsewhere, have themselves engaged repeatedly in the systematic use of terror in many forms. To wit: A 2005 BBC report characterized Senator Joseph McCarthy's extreme anti-communist antics as a "reign of terror." Another was financial. In the 1980s, S&Ls across the country were driven into insolvency. And, once again, the Central Intelligence Agency was situated at the heart of it. Many of the thrifts were systematically looted by the CIA and Mafia, as reported by Pizzo and Fricker, et al. in *Inside Job*, a book the corporate press did not consider newsworthy. In October 2008, Robert Sherrill, an exception based on hindsight, recalls:

> In *Inside Job*, Pizzo, Fricker and Muolo write that toward the end of their long investigation they began to pick up reports of C.I.A. involvement. Experts had wondered how so many billions of dollars could just vanish from the thrift industry without a trace. If some of that money were channeled into the contra pipeline or used to serve other legal or illegal covert purposes, that could certainly be one answer.

Deregulation of the S&L industry "created enough chaos to accommodate just about anyone's purposes. And taking out loans from federally insured institutions, giving the money to the contras, and letting federal insurance pick up the losses does have the flavor of what Ollie North might think was a 'neat idea.'"

Sherrill conjectures that the reason CIA ties to the collapse of the S&Ls "have been treated so lightly is that the only attention they stirred in Congress was a ridiculously inept 'investigation' by a subcommittee headed by that unscrupulous boob Frank Annunzio ... known to have had his hand out to the thrift lobby over the years."

If the fall of the go-go thrifts in the '80s taught us anything, it is that the CIA is busily engaged in corporate looting. Taken collectively, they serve as an example of an unknown number of targeted banking establishments and Wall Street firms.

Twenty years later, the implosion of Fannie Mae brought revived financial mass anxiety. The presence of ultra-conservative Nixon-aide/Marriott/Carlyle Group exec Fred Malek (a key advisor to Sarah Palin) on Fannie Mae's auditing committee was a glaring red flag.

The fall of the mortgage giant was not the result of poor judgment or incompetence. The subprime mortgage crisis that rocked its foundations was as deliberate as any Hole-in-the-Wall Gang bank heist.

Ask Nye Lavalle, a wealthy Floridian who set out to expose rampant mortgage fraud before it turned endemic. The *New York Times* reported on February 4, 2012 that after losing the family home to foreclosure, "under what he thought were fishy circumstances, Mr. Lavalle, founder of a consulting firm called the Sports Marketing Group, began a new life as a mortgage sleuth. In 2003, when home prices were flying high, he compiled a dossier of improprieties on one of the giants of the business, Fannie Mae."

Lavalle's report reads like "a blueprint of today's foreclosure crisis." Years before the economic crisis peaked, Lavalle exposed loan-servicing brokers in league with Fannie Mae who

> ... routinely filed false foreclosure documents." Years before a recessionary tide submerged the mortgage market, he discovered that the electronic mortgage registry was "playing fast and loose with the law – something that courts have belatedly recognized, too. You might wonder why Mr. Lavalle didn't speak up. But he did. For two years, he corresponded with Fannie executives and lawyers. Fannie later hired a Washington law firm to investigate his claims. In May 2006, that firm, using some of Mr. Lavalle's research, issued a confidential 147-page report corroborating many of his findings. And there, apparently, is where it ended.

To confirm that looting was afoot at Fannie Mae, one had to look no further than the audit committee where we found Fred Malek, Richard Nixon's "Jew counter" – a select group of directors who failed miserably at spotting irregularities. These dancing partners were paid huge sums in inflated director salaries to look the other way. (In the past, Chicago's Arthur Andersen LLP, formerly one of the "Big Five" accounting firms, performed the same invaluable service for corrupt corporations, but lost its license in 2002 when its collaborative role in investment fraud became obvious in the case of Enron.)

The collapse of the country's largest banks certainly injected fear straight to the hearts of the recession-strapped.

Little Hitlers

Conservatives who rattle on obsessively about the threat of Muslim extremism are usually mute as regards the murderous chaos instigated by far-right extremists like OK City bomber Timothy McVeigh; Kevin William Hardham, the 36-year-old Army field artillery veteran who planted a bomb along the Martin Luther King Day unity parade route in Spokane, Washington in 2011; Pittsburgh cop killer and white supremacist Richard Paplowski; neo-Nazi Keith Luke of Brockton, Massachusetts, arrested after shooting and killing three immigrants from Cape Verde; anti-government militiaman Joshua Cartwright, who murdered a pair of sheriff deputies in Okaloosa County, Florida in 2009, after they attempted to arrest him on a domestic violence charge; The "Sons of the Gestapo," who derailed a passenger train in Arizona on October 5, 1995, leaving one dead and 70 injured; Christian Identity anti-Semite Eric Robert Rudolph, the Atlanta Olympics bomber opposed to the "Satanic New World Order" who killed one and injured 100 in on July 27, 1996; Todd Vanbiber from the Tampa contingent of the National Alliance, arrested on April 23, 1997 after accidently setting off pipe bombs meant for Disney World to distract attention from a series of planned bank robberies; far-right anti-government tax protesters who, in May 1997, set the IRS building ablaze in Colorado Springs, resulting in $2.5

million in damages; former Aryan Nations member Buford
Furrow, who opened fire at a Jewish community center in August 1999, wounding five, drove off to the San Fernando Valley
and murdered Filipino mailman Joseph Ileto, then surrendered
to authorities, declaring that the violence was a "wake-up call to
America to kill Jews…"

Or James Von Brunn, the white supremacist who entered
the U.S. Holocaust Memorial Museum in Washington, D.C.
on June 10, 2009 and shot a security guard. Von Brunn hailed
from the beating heart of the American far-right that gestated
around two of its most prominent leaders, the China Lobby's
General Albert C, Wedemeyer and Liberty Lobby/Institute of
Historical Review/*Spotlight* founder Willis Carto.

In the '80s and '90s, Von Brunn worked at Noontide Press,
a spin-off of Carto's Holocaust-denying Institute of Historical
Review. In his 1999 book, *Kill the Best Gentiles*, van Brunn
wrote that poor, suffering Caucasians endure "today on the
world stage a tragedy of enormous proportions: the calculated
destruction of the White Race and the incomparable culture
it represents." Europe, he claimed, "is now over-run by hordes
of non-Whites and mongrels." Van Brunn's book is dedicated
to leading domestic white supremacists, including Revilo Oliver and Wilmot Robertson.

An autobiographical note posted on Von Brunn' website
claims that he "first … learned how Jews had destroyed Europe
and were now destroying America" from Lieutenant General
Pedro del Valle – identified in ADL intelligence files immediately after WW II as a Nazi collaborator. I first wrote about Del
Valle in *Virtual Government* (Feral House, 1997) after combing
through the ADL accounts of his submerged history:

> Among their contacts in the United States, the Nazi 'elite'
> could rely on the generous assistance of a well-connect-
> ed patron, Pedro Del Valle, who went on to become a
> vice president of ITT. In 1954, Del Valle, a retired Ma-
> rine Corps lieutenant general, was soundly defeated in
> his run for the Republican gubernatorial nomination.

His campaign was spiced with public endorsements of a foaming anti-Semitic tract, *Know Your Enemy*.

Twenty years later, Del Valle and ITT consultant John McCone, formerly a CIA director, threw in to overthrow Allende in Chile's 1970 elections. ITT funneled $350,000 into [opposition campaign coffers], and when the brutal dictatorship of Pinochet was installed, the communications conglomerate conspired with other "conservative" companies to pirate the country's natural resources.

Corporate-Sponsored Death Squads

By and large, the press ignores the cries in resource-rich hot spots like Chile, where American economic interests prevail with an assist from the CIA. But The Company and ITT weren't the sole sponsors of Operation Condor – Pepsico has a long history of involvement in international parapolitics, including narco-terrorism (the soft drink bottler, journalist Alfred McCoy reported decades ago in *The Politics of Heroin in Southeast Asia,* operated an opium refinery in Laos for the CIA during the Vietnam War period – with the lobbying assistance of Richard Nixon preceding his ascension to the presidency), and played a decisive role in the rise of Pinochet.

The *Observer* reports that the September 1973 coup that culminated in the death of Chile's President-elect Salvador Allende, "using CIA sub-machine guns and ammo, was the direct result of a plea for action a month earlier by Donald Kendall, chairman of PepsiCo, in two telephone calls to the company's former lawyer, President Richard Nixon." Kendall arranged a meeting between the owner of Pepsi's Chilean bottling plant and the NSC's Henry Kissinger – "Hours later, Nixon called in his CIA chief, Richard Helms, and, according to Helms's handwritten notes, ordered the CIA to prevent Allende's inauguration."

J. Patrice McSherry, in *Predatory States* (Rowman & Littlefield, 2005), notes that the objective of state terrorism is to defang the opposition, and "impose silence and political paralysis, thereby consolidating existing power relations ..."

The proximate end is to instill terror in society, the ultimate end is control. Condor's targets were persons who espoused political, economic, and social programs at odds with the ideologies and plans of the military dictatorships, their elite allies, and their sponsors in Washington. Through the use of terror, the military states sought to extinguish the aspirations for social justice and deeper democracy held by millions of people during the 1960s and 70s. The evidence suggests that Operation Condor, and the generalized repression of the Cold War years in Latin America, represented a military "solution" to an age-old problem: the distribution of power and wealth. ...

Corporate influence on American foreign policy escalated in the dawn of the twentieth century, and depended on right-wing autocrats around the globe to maintain stability, anti-Bolshivism, and, McSherry observes, "openness to U.S. capitalist expansion." Industry "increasingly sought raw materials and markets in Latin America.... The early part of the twentieth century was marked by U.S. intervention in much of Central America and the Caribbean (Cuba, Nicaragua, Honduras, Puerto Rico, the Dominican Republic, and elsewhere)."

In keeping with U.S. policy, the military installed proxy leaders and trained armies to hold "insurgents" in check:

> A series of pro-U.S. autocrats ruled for decades. The pattern of U.S. interventionism in Central America and the Caribbean in the twentieth century illuminated Washington's urge to control these regions and incorporate them within the U.S. political economy. Even during Franklin Delano Roosevelt's "Good Neighbor" period the U.S. government maintained supportive relations with such dictators as Anastasio Somoza in Nicaragua and Jorge Ubico in Guatemala, ruthless men who willingly protected U.S. investments and generally accepted U.S. political orientations.

After WW II, U.S. foreign policy in developing countries relied less on military force and increasingly on parapolitical operations:

By the 1960s, U.S. covert operations reached Brazil, Chile, and Uruguay, among other South American countries. The Cold War ideological focus on the evils of communism ... provided a rationale for the pursuit of U.S. economic interests in the developing world. U.S. foreign policy during the Cold War was more than an anti-Soviet project. It was an expansionist effort to globalize the U.S. sphere of influence and expand U.S. hegemony, spreading free market capitalism ... The CIA introduced members of Brazilian death squads to military and police officers in Uruguay, Chile, and Argentina, establishing links among them and diffusing the methods of terror, and encouraged them to track political opponents across borders. Brazil, acting in alliance with Washington, offered training in repressive methods to its neighbors.

In Equador, a special "security council" was mustered under a secret contract signed in 2006 – GESPETRO, short for *Grupo Especial de Seguridad Petrolera* (Special Group on Oil Security) – that drew on local military rule to protect its interests.

The multinational role in paramilitary atrocities seldom surfaces in the corporate press, but in recent years has given rise to jarring headlines: "**SHELL ADMITS IMPORTING GUNS FOR NIGERIAN POLICE**" (*Observer*, January 28, 1996); "**Coke Supports Death Squads against Columbia Trade Union**" (*NewsOnline*, April 22, 2004); "**Multinationals Implicated in Deaths by Brazil's Dictatorship**" (re: General Motors, Chrysler and VW – *Brazzil Magazine*, May 26, 2005); "**Congressman Alleges US Corporations Financing Right-Wing Militias**" (*The Daily Background*, June 29, 2007); "**Lawyer for Chiquita in Colombia Death Squad Case May be Next U.S. Attorney General**" (*Huffington Post*, November 6, 2008); "**Drummond Paid Colombian Paramilitaries**" (*Colombia Reports*, March 16, 2011; "**Shell Oil Using Death Squads for Torture, Forced Labor**" (CNN, February 28, 2012); "Bain's Birth by Death Squads: Romney scrutinized over investments from Salvadoran families that ran a corrupt government, 12 years of murderous civil war and death squads" (*In These Times*, September 12, 2012*).*

NIXON'S JACKALS

THE BIRTH OF A SECRET DOMESTIC CIA DEATH SQUAD COMMANDEERED BY THE WHITE HOUSE

On December 22, 1974, the *New York* Times published a report by investigative journalist Seymour Hersh: "Huge C.I.A. Operation Reported in U.S. Against Antiwar Forces, Other Dissidents in Nixon Years." Secretary of State Henry Kissinger met with President Gerald Ford to discuss the muck dripping from Hersh's rake. Kissinger informed the chief executive that the story was "just the tip of the iceberg." Should other operations be exposed, he croaked, *"blood will flow."*

Perception management tactics were employed. The country's leading newspapers and magazines basted Hersh on a spit of slander. The *Washington Post* and *Newsweek* went so far as to impugn his sanity and shred his bizarre "conspiracy theories" out of hand. *Time* magazine argued that the "sensitive and dedicated public servants" of the CIA, lashed to their constitutional mast, would never wade into the seditionist waters detailed in the article.

Hersh revealed that the CIA had conducted a massive spying and covert operations program on domestic soil under the code-name MHCHAOS. The story prompted the Church and Pike hearings of 1975, confirming his allegations.

Kissinger was correct: the spying scandal was the tip of the iceberg. But after the Congressional probes of the 1970s, Operation CHAOS would be memorialized in history books as a domestic *spying* scandal. The mysterious "other operations" that Kissinger mentioned remained classified. CIA Director Richard Helms was convicted for lying to Congress, the Agency was deeply embarrassed, but Kissinger remained a revered political Madonna in the nation's media.

Blood did not flow, after all – or *did* it?

Senator Frank Church, reportedly constrained by limitations beyond his control, narrowed the scope of his investigation to surveillance and backed off from more serious allegations. Domestic murder plots, for instance. The "sensitive and dedicated public servants" of the Agency had *indeed been involved* in political assassinations, according to Timothy S. Hardy at the Center for the Study of Intelligence in a secret report dated July 2, 1996, since declassified: "Although the Commission had become aware of the assassination stories early in its work, it had not been pushed to explore this area until it was well along in probing the domestic activities that had originally led to its formation."

Regardless of political motives behind the exclusion of domestic political murder in the Church Committee's final report – "and such motivations did exist," Hardy mused vaguely – the problem was that by June 1975, "the scheduled deadline, already extended several months," the Church Committee was "still far from completing this aspect of its inquiries." Congressional Pandoras of the '70s never opened the box marked "MURDER." No time for that. Besides, "whatever credibility the Rockefeller Commission could muster would have been sapped by a premature publication of preliminary findings in this highly sensitive area."

MHCHAOS was supposedly terminated by William Colby, Helms's successor, in 1974. But in the real world, the Rockefeller Commission reported a year later, the Operation's massive "files and computerized index are *still intact*."

The secret database on hundreds of thousands of Americans was stored on "Hydra," an IBM 360/67 boasting remote input and retrieval capabilities.

The retention of the CIA's database on dissidents should have been the tip-off that CHAOS was far from dead. In 1974,

MHCHAOS was rebranded as the Agency's International Terrorism Group (ITG). The transition was cosmetic, however, a dab of bureaucratic lip-gloss: "Worried that the inspector general might discover MHCHAOS and expose it," Angus Mackenzie wrote in *Secrets: The CIA's War at Home*, Helms mustered Colby, CHAOS director Richard Ober and Deputy DCI Thomas Karamessines for "a meeting on December 5, 1972. Helms emphasized the importance of running a cleaner, less dubious-looking operation."

Helms was determined that Operation CHAOS survive congressional and journalistic incursions. The solution was a single emotive word: *"Terrorism."* Helms ordered that the CIA's covert war on left-wing dissidents be described within the Agency as *an offensive against terrorism*, and CHAOS/TGI director Richard Ober "identified with the subject of terrorism inside the Agency as well as in the intelligence community."

And so the first "war on terrorism" was born.

The intent of the shell game was to spiff up the Agency's image, MacKenzie notes, "on the assumption that 'terrorists' were more believable as a genuine threat than 'dissidents.' But there was in fact to be *little change in targets.*" MHCHAOS in counter-terrorist drag "continued to hold dissidents in its sights, specifically radical youths, Blacks, women, and antiwar militants. The label 'international terrorist' was designed to replace 'political dissident' as the ongoing justification for illegal domestic operations."

Congressional investigators of the 1970s were unaware that, at a secret 1968 meeting of CIA officials and Wall Street operatives held at the Council on Foreign Relations, it was decided that the Agency's operations had already become too public. Thereafter, "sensitive" jobs would be delegated to "private organizations, many of the personnel of which would be non-U.S. ... particularly *third country nationals.*"

This proposal to grant foreign nationals a license to kill was officially sanctioned in 1969, when Richard Nixon appointed Franklin Lindsay, OSS veteran, CIA operative and CEO of the Rockefeller-financed Itek Corporation, to lead an advisory panel on revamping the Agency. Lindsay had attended the CFR meeting. Many of the proposals drafted in 1968, according to researcher Peter Dale Scott in a short essay, "CIA, DEA, and Their Assassination Capacity," were

> ... implemented by successive CIA directors, most notably the recommendation that the aging CIA bureaucracy had become too large and should be dramatically cut back. In the context of this reversion to 'unofficial cover,' the March 1972 Helms injunction against assassination seems to have been a case of carefully locking the door of an already empty stable. Nine months earlier Lucien Conein, the CIA's case officer in the Diem assassination and a high level contact with the heroin trafficking Corsican Mafia, resigned from CIA, to be brought back at the suggestion of his old OSS colleague Howard Hunt into the White House narcotics effort. There, Conein (by his own admission) supervised a special unit which would have the capacity to assassinate selected targets in the narcotics business.

To researchers of CIA history, Lucien Conein in a known quantity. But Franklin Lindsay's past – particularly his collaboration with Nazis after WW II and a CIA assassination program code-named Operation Ohio – is relatively obscure.

After the war, Lindsay was Frank Wisner's deputy at the Office of Policy Coordination (OPC) – the Nazi-recruiting arm of the Central Intelligence Agency under Allen Dulles. The cutthroats of Operation Ohio, wartime Ukranian collaborators of the Waffen SS, engaged in mob-style murders. Over 20 assassinations in the Mittenwald misplaced persons camp near Munich were carried out under Ohio, funded by the Nazi-recruiting Army Counter-Intelligence Corps and CIA. This death squad went on to engage in violence against Soviet spies and double agents on the American payroll. When publicly exposed, the double agent murders were explained as factional violence among rival Ukranian émigré organizations.

"We were just out of World War Two, and we were using those [wartime] tactics," Lindsay, who oversaw the OPC's Eastern European operations, explained years later. "In my case, I had operated only in wartime conditions. Given the feeling that we were very near war at that time, one tended to operate in the same way." Lindsay, however, rejects the term assassination as a description of CIA/OPC practice during his tenure there."

In a January 1962 *Foreign Affairs* article, Lindsay actually argued that terrorism is necessary to defend a population against communist indoctrination tactics: "Communists go far beyond political indoctrination," he explained. "Once they have a fanatically dedicated minority, they begin the application of systematic terror to ensure that the masses of the people will be brought under, and kept under, complete Communist control." Therefore, America's "freedom fighters" had no recourse but to "organize the civil population into a tightly disciplined force, and, through propaganda and police activities, try to break the grip exercised by the adversary." Liberating a population from communist domination, he wrote, is accomplished through *terror*: "[W]hen two forces are contending for the loyalty of, and control over, the civilian population, the side which uses violent reprisals most aggressively will dominate most of the people, even though their sympathies may lie in the other direction."

When WW II ended, Lindsay and Dulles served on the staff of the congressional committee that approved the Marshall Plan. Nixon served on that committee as well, so he knew the prominent death squad leader and counter-terror terrorist well. The primary recommendations of the CIA reorganization working group chaired by Lindsay were codified by Richard Helms before he was forced from the DCI's office and replaced by William Colby.

The use of foreign nationals in Nixon-era black bag operation was obvious. H.R. Haldeman wrote *in The Ends of Power*: "I was puzzled when [Nixon] told me, 'Tell Ehrlichman this whole group of Cubans [Watergate Burglars] is tied to the Bay of Pigs.' After a pause I said, 'The Bay of Pigs? What does that have to do with the Watergate Burglary?' But Nixon merely said, 'Ehrlichman will know what I mean,' and dropped the subject."

From its inception, Operation 40 recruited professional hit men. The group was led by Nixon and they were indeed Bay of Pigs veterans. Researcher John Simkin writes:

> The first meeting chaired by [the CIA's Tracy] Barnes took place in his office on 18th January, 1960, and was attended by David Atlee Phillips, E. Howard Hunt, Jack Esterline and Frank Bender. According to Fabian Escalante, a senior officer of the Cuban Department of State Security (G-2), in 1960 Richard Nixon recruited an 'important group of businessmen headed by George Bush (Snr.) and Jack Crichton, both Texas oilmen, to gather the necessary funds for the operation.' This suggests that Operation 40 agents were involved in freelance work. It is known that at this time that George Bush and Jack Crichton were involved in covert right-wing activities. In 1990 The Common Cause magazine argued that: 'The CIA put millionaire and agent George Bush in charge of recruiting exiled Cubans for the CIA's invading army.

Recruits to Operation 40 were hand-picked by José Sanjenis Perdomo, said to be the doorman at the Dakota on December 8, 1980, the day Beatle John Lennon was assassinated.

How many unexplained American murders and acts of terror can be traced to the Nixon/Lindsay reorganization of the CIA? As mentioned, the congressional probes of the '70s had no time for the "assassination stories." Only a select few at the Agency can answer that question today, and asking leads to the suspicion that one is a much-despised "conspiracy theorist," like Sy Hersh...

CHAPTER ONE

HARD RAIN IN THE BALKANS

BLACK CLOUDS OVER WASHINGTON, D.C.:
ILLICIT U.S. ARMS SALES TO EASTERN EUROPE

Small arms sales recently to Albania, Bosnia and FYR of Macedonia could come back to haunt us sooner than we think. Secretary of State Madeleine Albright announced at a September 1998 United Nations meeting that arms exporting states 'bear some responsibility' for a trade which 'fuels conflict, fortifies extremism and destabilizes entire regions' in Africa and worldwide:
– Anna Rich, "U.S. Exports Arms to the World"

Macedonia, Romania, Albania and Bulgaria constitute the "outer ring" of East European black market smuggling routes (and therefore have been beset by the sale of arms from former Yugoslavia): and the governments of these countries act as mediators in major transnational trade, a violation of sanctions imposed by international agreement.

Convicted Macedonian arms smuggler Yuri Malinkovski received a stern slap on the wrist – three years probation in 1999 for lethal violations of the International Emergency Economic Powers and Export Administration Act, and was prohibited from exporting anything for a period of ten years.

At the receiving end, the Macedonian government denied involvement in black trades, but the evidence indicated that a company called Micei-Forten resold them to Serbia.[1] *Aim Sko-*

---

1. CSD Report, "The Outer Ring: The Role of Macedonia, Albania, Romania and

pje commented after the 1996 arrest of Malinkovski: "This is perhaps the greatest scandal the regime has been involved in."

The Macedonian government "has been shaken by all kinds of scandals in the course of this year involving the very top of the administration." One such scandal involved an assassination plot hatched to take out Vanco Cifliganecto, a deputy of the ruling Social Democratic Alliance (SDSM, the former communist party). It was summarily aborted and exposed. "Just after dust had settled [from a] typical mafia-like showdown and the cruel murder which took place close to the Macedonian assembly, a deputy ... nervously asked from the platform of that same assembly: 'Is it true that somebody is trying to *liquidate me*? And is my LIQUIDATION supposed to CONCEAL SOMEBODY'S SINS?'"

Whatever the result, *Aim Skopje* editorialized, "the question of the deputy from Radovis will be remembered as perhaps the unique parliamentary question in the world because a deputy of the ruling party *asked his own government* 'WHY' it wanted him killed."

This question "exploded like a bomb" as a chorus of voices from the press inquired about Macedonian arms smuggling "at the height of the war in Bosnia and blockade of Serbia. Discontent of the public is increasing as the veil is rising," a veil that "carefully concealed the truth that in the 'oasis of peace' ... certain influential politicians and personages [at the highest rungs of authority] made enormous wealth as true war profiteers and black marketeers."[2]

Mr. Cifliganec, the wealthy manager of the Bucim copper mine, confirmed speculation from the Macedonian tabloids that he was threatened "with assassination by [a] certain Zoran Saklev, officer of the Army of the Republic of Macedonia (ARM) at the time. Allegedly, as an experienced intelligence officer trained in the former Yugoslav army and its intelligence service, Saklev was supposed to kill the manager

Bulgaria," http://www.csd.bg/publications/book10/1.3.pdf
2. "Scandal with Weapons," *AIM Skopje*, December 16, 1997. http://www.aimpress.ch/dyn/trae/archive/data/199712/71226-018-trae-sko.htm

of Bucim and the respectable member of the leadership of the ruling party SDSM for 20 thousand German marks."

But the most "interesting" player in the scandal was "public prosecutor Stevan Pavlevski. He confirmed that last year he had looked into data on Zoran Saklev and established that the material gathered by the intelligence service of the Army was thin."

Pavlevski announced that he did not have sufficient evidence to press for criminal charges, but rumors continued to "spread and acquire interesting proportions." The pro-regime press claimed that the rumors were "propaganda with a specific goal and function." The goal, suggested the *Nova Makedonija* daily, served ambitions of the Macedonian intelligence service. "Why? This newspaper does not have an answer for that, [but] believes that it is clear to internal and external enemies."[3]

Christopher Deliso reported on February 26, 2004:

Macedonian President Killed in Bosnia Plane Crash

Macedonians are in a state of shock today as the first incomplete reports of the death of their president, Boris Trajkovski, start to filter back from Bosnia, where the president and eight others died early this morning in a plane crash, in mountainous terrain ... near Croatia's southern coast. Everyone aboard – Trajkovski, six advisors, guards, a two-man crew, were presumed dead. The crash was blamed on inclement weather ... at first.

It was a "sad irony" that "Trajkovski was on his way to an investment conference in Mostar, just as Macedonia's EU application was about to be officially presented in Ireland [which presides on an honorary basis over the EU]."

Trajkovski took office in 1999, and "presided over Macedonia's most difficult period: the turbulence brought on by NATO's Kosovo bombardment and the 2001 war, with its uncertain aftermath. Through it all, Trajkovski was *firmly pro-American*."[4]

---

3. Ibid.
4. Christopher Deliso, "Macedonian President Killed in Bosnia Plane Crash," *Balkan Analysis,* balkanalysis.com, February 26, 2004. http://www.antiwar.com/deliso/?articleid=2043

As a matter of fact, Trajkovski's rise to office was, according to Sam Vaknin, a former economic advisor to the government of Macedonia, "attributed by the opposition – and not only by the opposition – to *mass electoral fraud* among Albanian voters. There were hints of *collusion at the highest levels involving a web of business interests and meddling Western diplomats.*"

The West's geopolitical intrigues bred rot:

> There isn't a single country in the Balkan – Serbia included – whose political elite, past and present, is not thoroughly criminalized. Crime, business, and politics are inextricable in this part of the world. ... The early histories of many nations – perhaps all nations – are studded with rogues, terrorists, criminals, slave traders, eccentrics, and worse. Robber barons, gunslingers, outcasts, slavers, and criminals established both in the United States and Australia, for instance.

Macedonians view U.S. operations in the Outer Ring as contrary to its own interests:

> [The] U.S. first said ... it would act in a manner fair to all sides. But the U.S. breached [this position] when it intervened militarily in Kosovo. It did so not only by favoring one side – the Albanian Kosovo Liberation Army – but by arming and training it and supplying it with military intelligence. Macedonians are bitter at NATO for allowing the KLA to operate with impunity both in Kosovo and in Macedonia, even though it had stated that its goal was to disarm the KLA once UN forces were in place. Many Macedonians, therefore, suspect that the U.S. is assisting the terrorists in order to justify stationing significant forces in the country and making Macedonia into a protectorate, as has already happened in Kosovo and Bosnia.... Serbia has sold its soul to the 'liberal-capitalistic' dream of Western-style prosperity and 'civil society' (which is, in reality, uncivil and asocial). It is now a de facto economic protectorate of the United States and its long arms, the

IMF and the World Bank. Militarily, it is completely de-
fanged. And its corrupt politicians and businessmen are
addicted to Western payouts and handouts. The population is fatigued, bombed into submission.

"The Washington Consensus," he said, "has proved
to be an unmitigated failure in dozens of countries
throughout the world."[5]

Croatian President Stipe Mesic predicted that the Macedonian leader's death would have "political consequences" in
the Balkans: "This afternoon I was supposed to meet Boris at
the conference on investment in Bosnia. Together with him
and the presidents of other states, we worked on the program
of stabilization and reconciliation in southeastern Europe."[6]

There was some speculation before he died, Paul Mojzes wrote
in August 2001, that Trajkovski "might be assassinated by those
who consider him too close to the 'international community.'"[7]

The provocations, *News from Russia* claimed, were the
work of the CIA. It "exposed the U.S. government as an impe-
rial state. It could turn out in the long run that another empire
will find its graveyard in the Balkans if interventionist hawks
prevail in Washington."[8]

President Boris Trajkovski claimed his plot in that graveyard. There were many – including other government leaders
in the Balkans – who doubted the official explanation.

Initially, the crash was blamed on "pilot error." But the son
of pilot Marko Markovski, among others, disputed this verdict.
From the Russian language article, with Markivski's comments:

> Experienced Macedonian pilots surveyed by Dnevnik
> newspaper agreed that Markovski Sr. was "one of the best,"
> a flight instructor and pilot with 30 years flying experience

5. Mickey Bozinovich, "Interview with Serbianna," Buzzle.com. http://www.buz-
zle.com/editorials/5-16-2004-54203.asp
6. Paul Moizes, "Into the inferno? – present-day Macedonia," *Christian Century*,
August 29, 2001. http://www.findarticles.com/p/articles/mi_m1058/is_24_118/
ai_78545549/pg_4
7. Ibid.
8. Raymond Kent, "The Balkans, Blowback and Bodybags," *News from Russia*, September 9, 2003. http://newsfromrussia.com/yougoslavia/2001/09/03/14022.html

in both military and civilian aircraft, a man who had wide experience flying intercontinental and European routes.

The expertise of co-pilot Branko Ivanovski, an experienced officer in the Macedonian air force, is supported by a leaked U.S. Air Force document that I have seen. Dated April 7, 2000, the document records Ivanovski's attendance at a 5-week squadron officer course at Maxwell Air Force Base in Alabama. Signed by a USAF colonel, the document commends Ivanovski's abilities, stating that he displayed "top analytical and decision-making skills," and also "excelled in extremely challenging, dynamic leadership situations.... Bosnian media who spoke with investigators claim that audio tapes record 25 minutes of recorded ground-pilot conversation – followed by a *seven-minute silence* preceding the crash.

The Balkan press brazenly accused NATO of sabotaging the flight.

On February 27, the day after the crash, a Bosnian interior minister explained that when the crash occurred, the plane "was only 15 air kilometers away from the airport in Mostar. That radius vector is under direct control of SFOR's navigation team.... SFOR will be asked to provide more information."

He stated that SFOR (NATO's "Stabilization Force") air traffic controllers were responsible for either ignoring the Macedonian flight or permitting it to approach the landing strip too low. Bosnian officials, crash investigators and the press were all in agreement that SFOR caused the crash, and that it was deliberate.

Deliso:

> The principal evidence against SFOR, for Macedonian and Bosnian critics, is the fact that it took over 24 hours for the wreckage of the plane to be found. The plane disappeared at 8:20 AM on the 26th, and for an entire day, SFOR, citing dangerous weather conditions, didn't allow air searches.... This explanation was attacked at once. Given that the air traffic controllers knew the plane's last coordinates, and that it should have automatically emitted

an emergency radio signal upon crashing, critics argued, why did SFOR fail to locate the wreckage quickly? And why were the Bosnian search teams – the world's best at working in minefields – prevented from searching.

Ivanovski asked why SFOR "didn't announce the exact location of the plane crash and why the search for the missing plane took 24 hours, if they saw on the navigation system where the plane had crashed?"

Zoran Markovski, himself an air traffic controller, agreed: "They [Mostar's SFOR controllers] can register the exact geographic position of the plane, its height and speed. Yet the plane was found 26 hours after the accident and was only 10 kilometers from the airport, and crashed during the landing phase. Why wasn't the Bosnian search team activated – the one which during the war found a crashed plane and saved the pilot in just 17 minutes?"

These suspicions were exacerbated by reports that the flight controllers *fled* after the crash.

Macedonian Prime Minister Branko Crvenkovski: "I don't know whether they are out of Bosnia or not, but wherever they are they cannot avoid being investigated."

Two days later, SFOR spokesman Norbert Hoerpel claimed the French air controllers had already been interrogated by investigators. But Bosnian State Prosecutor Vaso Marinkovic led the investigation, and rebuked him: "No one from our team has talked with them. I do not have information [as to] whom they have … talked [to], but *certainly they have had no talks with us.*"

Hoerpel burbled, "I know that they [the alleged interrogators] were members of the Air Accident Investigation Committee, but I do not know their names." The damage control baton was passed to Bosnia's Europolice spokesperson, Kirsten Haupt, who "denied accusations that Europolice might be responsible for the disinformation [on] the day of the accident."

When all else failed, a new explanation was conceived: The Beechcraft was downed by mechanical failure. Former

Foreign Minister Slobodan Casule suddenly remembered that the plane had almost endangered his life on one occasion. An ex-foreign minister, Slobodan Casule, recalled that the plane's windshield once sailed away during a flight over Romania.

Perhaps a Macedonian president shouldn't have to fly on a rickety 26 year-old deathtrap.

The *Balkan Analysis* article:

> No wonder then that the government has diverted public attention by taking the offensive against SFOR. If it turns out that mechanical and not human error was behind the crash, it will be hard to avoid the embarrassing conclusion that, all heartfelt expressions of sympathy aside, the country actually cares very little for the well-being of its leaders. And this is where we leave the investigation behind and enter into the still more shadowy realm of symbol.

Death Merchants

You play with my world like it's your little toy ...
You put a gun in my hand and you hide from my eyes,
And you turn and run farther when the fast bullets fly.
　　　　　　　　　　– Bob Dylan, "Masters of War"

An underground railroad in the black market arms trade to Macedonia begins in Lexington, Kentucky, with Galls, Inc., a gun dealer and security supply store. A typical Galls proxy statement describes the arms broker as "one of the country's largest suppliers of uniforms and equipment to public safety professionals. This multi-channel business (catalog, telemarketing sales, field sales, the internet and retail) caters to the special needs of people involved in public safety, law enforcement, fire-fighting ... federal government agency ... military and emergency medical services. ..."

"Government agency?" "Military?" "Galls markets public safety equipment and apparel under the Galls, Dynamed and other brand names to over one million individuals, as well as to public safety departments, private security companies and the Military..."

Sally Denton's *The Bluegrass Conspiracy* provides a bit of pre-history. Galls surfaced in her investigation of guns-and-drugs smuggling in Lexington after a cargo plane stuffed full of Uzis, Ingrams, AK-47s, and so on, was discovered by local authorities.

Phillip Galls & Sons was immediately suspected as the source of the illicit weapons transfers, "a wholesale Lexington gun dealer who seemed to have an inordinate supply of weapons warehoused. Licensed to supply the official handguns to all the major police departments in Kentucky, Florida, West Virginia, and Tennessee, the outfit [was] a perfect cover for arms trafficking."[9]

Galls ran a clever scam in the mid-1980s involving firearms and the Kentucky State Police. Denton:

> Every year, [Phillip] Gall ordered a thousand magnum pistols from the Smith & Wesson factory. Since guns could legally be purchased in such massive quantity from a gun manufacturer only if they were to be sold to police departments, Gall made arrangements for the weapons to be sold to the Kentucky State Police. The following year, Gall would order a thousand brand-new guns from Smith & Wesson, claiming they would be provided to the State Police. When the guns arrived, Gall would distribute them to the state troopers free of charge, in exchange for the previous year's weapons.

This exchange "provided the Galls Company with *a surplus of unreported weapons* available for private sale."

And among Galls' leading customers – "government agencies." In the subsequent investigation, it emerged that Galls had a history of "shoddy paperwork and delinquency in filing reports required by the federal government. But, like so many other occurrences in Lexington, the gun dealer had never been the subject of a criminal investigation. To the contrary,

9. Sally Denton, *The Bluegrass Conspiracy*, Author's Guild, 1990, p. 53.

the company's owners enjoyed the social benefits generally bestowed upon reputable, successful businessmen."

Drew Thornton, a former police narcotics detective, Special Forces operative with CIA ties and a cocaine smuggler, purchased his guns from Galls. Twenty years passed after Thornton's body was found plastered to a residential driveway. His parachute gave out in the course of ditching his small, cocaine-bearing plane to evade authorities. The CIA smuggler's packs were so full of coke that the chute couldn't handle the weight. He plummeted to his death.

Years later, Galls is STILL dealing in the black market gun trade, now on an international scale, as *Direct*, an export marketing magazine, reported on September 1, 2004:

> Galls Inc. ... is under investigation for allegedly failing to obtain proper licenses before exporting merchandise overseas, according to federal documents. The firm was contacted in early August by agents of the U.S. Department of Commerce at its Lexington, KY, facility in connection with record-keeping and documentation of certain export sales. The probe involves shipments that had been made over the course of a few years, she said. "We had agents at our headquarters in Lexington and our distribution center in Lexington," said Grow.

This wasn't the first report of criminal activity at Galls: "A Lexington television station had reported that two former Galls employees said they noticed *shipments of military items to Iran* and other countries while they worked for Galls, but were told by managers not to be concerned about it."

Federal agents:

> ... seized bank and credit card records from the house of Yuri Montgomery of Seattle one week before a search warrant was issued at the Galls facilities on July 21. Montgomery was named in an affidavit that agents used to obtain the warrant. The affidavit stated Galls allegedly exported items to an address in Macedonia that were paid

for using Montgomery's personal credit card, according to the AP report. The affidavit also stated Montgomery had his export privileges denied by a federal court.

In 1998, Yuri Montgomery pled guilty "to violating federal export controls by exporting laser rifle sights, ballistic helmets, optical sights, handcuffs and stun guns to Macedonia and Slovenia. He served three years' probation and agreed to leave the export business."[10]

Thornton and Montgomery had one thing in common: Galls, a covert ops arms depot.

Corporate and CIA connections: Galls is owned by Aramark, Inc., a diversified food services company with interests in Saudi Arabia.

Aramark is a division of Pepsico, a multinational that operated a heroin refinery for the CIA in Laos – as we know since Alfred McCoy reported it 40 years ago in the *Politics of Heroin in Southeast Asia* – with impunity during the Vietnam War era. Ray Hunt from the infamous Texas clan sits on the Pepsico board of directors.[11] Thomas Kean, former governor of New Jersey, chairman of the 9/11 Commission, is also a Pepsico director.[12] Kean has had vaguely defined business dealings with Khalid bin Mahfouz of the Saudi-owned National Commercial Bank and BCCI.[13]

Pepsico was a driving force in the overthrow of Salvador Allende and rise of Operation Condor. Journalist Greg Palast wrote in the *Observer* that the coup plot, "using CIA 'sub-machine guns and ammo,' was the direct result of a plea for action a month earlier by Donald Kendall, chairman of PepsiCo, in two telephone calls to the company's former lawyer, President Richard Nixon."

10. Bill Grabarek, "Galls' Export Practices under Investigation," *Direct,* September 1, 2004.
11.   http://www.whitehouseforsale.org/ContributorsAndPaybacks/pioneer_profile.cfm?pioneer_ID=618
12. Matthew Callan, "Meet the New Boss," *Freezerbox,* January 17, 2003.
13. Chris Marsden, "Former US Ambassador to Chile tells Britain's *Observer* newspaper of American plots against Allende," November 13, 1998. http://www.wsws.org/news/1998/nov1998/cia-n13.shtml

It was Kendall who "arranged for the owner of the company's Chilean bottling operation to meet National Security Adviser Henry Kissinger on September 15. Hours later, Nixon called in his CIA chief, Richard Helms, and, according to Helms's handwritten notes, ordered the CIA to prevent Allende's inauguration."[14]

Aramark, Inc. is represented by the Baker Botts law firm (close ties to CIA and GOP).

The Galls Bust

All of this adds up to a reserve of clout. Even after Phillip Galls himself committed serious violations of domestic export law and was caught at it, others took the fall. The full story has never appeared on newsprint.

Phillip Galls & Sons is the proverbial merchant of death.

The Galls illegal arms trade saga was foreshadowed by the arrest and conviction of Yuri Montgomery, a Macedonian immigrant, by a U.S. district court judge in Washington D.C. on January 15, 1999.

Montgomery, according to Department of Commerce records, pled guilty to "exporting various U.S.-origin crime control items from the United States to Macedonia and Slovenia without the required export licenses. The investigation was conducted by the <u>Office of Export Enforcement</u>'s Boston division and the U.S. Customs Service."[15]

The probationary sentence followed *a prior conviction* in 1996. Brian Wood and Johan Peleman, in *The Arms Fixers*, report that Montgomery (also known as Yuri Malinkovsky) had connections to the "former Yugoslavia and ran a company called Fortend USA." Fortend USA sent the equipment sans valid export licenses. "It is believed that some of this may have ended up in Serbian <u>hands since torture</u> with such shock weapons began in Kosovo."[16]

14. Greg Palast, "A Marxist threat to cola sales? Pepsi demands a US coup. Goodbye Allende. Hello Pinochet," November 8, 1998. http://www.gregpalast.com/a-marxist-threat-to-cola-sales-pepsi-demands-a-us-coup-goodbye-allende-hello-pinochet
15. *Bureau of Industry and Security Annual Report – FY 1999*, chapter seven, "Office of Chemical and Biological Controls and Treaty of Compliance," U.S. Department of Commerce. http://www.bis.doc.gov/news/Publications/99AnnReport/Ann99Chap7.html
16. Wood and Peleman, "Back to the High Tech Future," *The Arms Fixers: Controlling the Brokers and Shipping Agents*. http://www.nisat.org/publications/armsfixers/

Montgomery qualified for the three-time loser club when he was caught at it yet again, this time in collaboration with a black market arms dealer in Lexington.

According to a news report on WTVQ-TV in Seattle in June 2004, a local man "whose home was searched last year shortly before the raid of a Lexington military and police equipment supply company has been charged with shipping illegal goods to Macedonia. Yuri Montgomery has been charged with making eleven illegal shipments to that country." Commerce Department authorities said that a twelfth shipment was intercepted at the Cincinnati-Northern Kentucky International Airport.[17]

AP reported that Montgomery's bank and credit cards were seized. His banking records led police to Lexington.

A search warrant was issued at Galls on July 21.

The arrest affidavit stated that Galls exported military and security hardware to an address in Macedonia, paid for with Montgomery's personal credit card, according to the AP report. The affidavit also stated Montgomery had export privileges denied by a federal court.

Galls was charged with exporting the sanctioned items to Macedonia.[18] Wood and Peleman observe that U.S. arms export laws are "sometimes a paradox." Loose regulation of gun sales have meant

> ... a steady flow of small weapons smuggled across the borders, particularly into Mexico. However, a relatively tough U.S. law on international arms brokering was introduced in March 1998. It requires any U.S. citizen, wherever located, and any foreign person located in the USA or subject to U.S. jurisdiction, engaged in the brokering of arms, to first register and to obtain prior written approval for each proposed transaction. Registration and license approval must be obtained from the Office of Defense Trade Controls of the U.S. Department of State. These requirements are set out in the Arms Export Con-

---

17. http://www.wtvq.com/servlet/
18. Grabarek. http://directmag.com/mag/marketing_galls_export_practices/

trol Act and related regulations, the International Traffic in Arms Regulation and the Munitions List. The latter defines what are termed "defense articles."

The Montgomery-Galls bust barely rated a ripple of scandal stateside, but in Macedonia the arrest of Yuri Montgomery did not pass unnoticed. The commotion was on a par with the Iran-contra affair in this country. It was reported in *Aim Skopje* that the "most bizarre" protagonist of the scandal was "deputy Vanco Cifliganec. With his public appearance in the Assembly, he hinted that there are other participants [in the weapons transfers] and that they are very powerful."

At the "tip of this newest profit-making pyramid" was "the leadership of the state."

There were the usual scripted cover stories, but "defense minister Lazar Kitanovski was not convincing either while he was fruitlessly explaining that Macedonia had not violated the embargo and bought American weapons without a permit."

Cifliganec announced "that the persons in charge would investigate who was responsible," and this "just added fuel to the fire."

It all began when a short piece of news of Associated Press from America exploded like a bomb in Macedonian media. Quoting the register of court proceedings in the USA, the respectable AP published that criminal proceedings had been instigated against the enterprise called Fortend-USA for illegal sale of weapons to Macedonia and Slovenia. Macedonian media immediately linked Fortend-USA with a Macedonian firm called MIKEI-Fortend. Macedonian Fortend is one of the suppliers of military and other equipment for the Macedonian government from the time of the embargo on arms and selling of weapons in the Balkans.

It was immediately made public that the owner of the American Fortend was a certain Jurij Montgomery, alias Uros Malinkovski. He turned out to be the brother of Pance Malinkovski, the owner of Macedonian Fortend. The coincidence was too self-evident. The link is quite logical for the domestic public: if the American court has raised charges against Fortend-USA, the Macedonian MIKEI-Fortend must have something to do with it, the name cannot be the only connection between the two.

Once such a connection was established, an avalanche of revelations started in public.

The father of assassin Zoran Saklev, Kamce Saklev, boasted that his son "had revealed in America the dirty business of the brothers Malinkovski, who jointly supplied Macedonia with weapons during the embargo." They may have even armed the army. Then again, "father and son Saklev have themselves registered an enterprise for import and sale of weapons called Mak-Bereta, which did not succeed to become the supplier of Macedonian ministries of defense and interior affairs."

The Macedonia government chose Mikei-Fortend.[19]

Seismic upheavals in politics have hinged on a minor slip-up. If not for a piece of tape, whither Richard Nixon? If Eugene Hassenfuss hadn't crashed a plane, those Tow missile sales to Iran might have been an obscure footnote in a Latin American political journal. The "piece of tape" that brought down this scandal was a box of police uniforms purchased by Montgomery-Malinkovski from Galls & Sons, carelessly shipped to Syria, among other countries on the federal export-denied list.

This illicit shipment was one of a dozen such exports tracked by the Department of Commerce. *Direct*, a marketing journal, reported that Galls was contacted by agents of the U.S. Department of Commerce "in connection with record-keeping and documentation of certain export sales. Galls is cooperating with the investigation" of "certain" exports by shredding documents, according to employees.

The investigation involved mostly undefined "shipments that had been made over the course of a few years" – until 2001, in fact, a long time to hang back – an arms transfer flow

19. "Scandal with Weapons: Politicians, Smugglers, Professional Murderers in the Game," *AIM Skopje*, December 16, 1997. http://www.aimpress.ch/dyn/trae/archive/data/199712/71226-018-trae-sko.htm

that continued unabated by the feds. "Despite the investigation, the company is in full operation and is fulfilling and shipping orders…. Galls is a subsidiary of Aramark Corp., Philadelphia."

Another corporation, among the first tainted by the scandal, was FedEx, based in Memphis, Tennessee.

FedEx agreed to a $40,000 civil penalty "to settle charges pertaining to a total of five violations of the EAR in connection with exporting on the behalf of [Yuri Montgomery], *transporting WITH KNOWLEDGE of a violation of the regulations …* to SYRIA without the required license, and misrepresentations of license code on automated export system records."[20]

FedEx *continued* to ship military goods to "terrorist" countries for Malinkovski as late as 2001 – two years after his conviction and placement on the export denial list.

Who at FedEx *"with knowledge"* considered it imperative to ship banned items to Syria and elsewhere – for years – all the while shrugging off proper licensing regulations and falsifying documents to place torture weapons in the hands of the "enemy," seeing as how they could easily be turned on Americans, as Madeleine Albright observed, an act of sedition that the Chamber of Commerce frowns upon.

The destabilization of Macedonia – resulting in massive public demonstrations, Mafia-like shoot-outs, ubiquitous "conspiracy theories" – that we have witnessed up close came about after FedEx shipments to that country were exposed.

FedEx is part and parcel of the military-postal-industrial complex. The *Wall Street Journal* reports that *the* private mail service has signed on "for a frontline role in the war on terror." The Bush administration claimed that, "the struggle against terrorism is an unorthodox fight where information and intelligence is as important as guns and bullets. Information is what FedEx has in spades."[21]

20. Wood and Peleman, *The Arms Fixers*. http://www.nisat.org/publications/arms-fixers/Chapter8.html
21. Robert Block, "In Terrorism Fight, Government Finds a Surprising Ally: FedEx," *Wall Street Journal*, May 26, 2005. The company has "opened the international portion of its databases, including credit-card details, to government officials."

Some FedEx officers have interesting histories, including:

- **Frederick W. Smith** – a Bonesman (Yale class of 1966) – founder of FedEx and CEO. Smith served four years as an active duty pilot and platoon leader in the US Marine Corps (1966-70). He flew in the Vietnam War, went on to buy a controlling interest in Ark Aviation Sales, an aircraft maintenance service. On June 18, 1971, Smith incorporated Federal Express with $91 million in investment capital and his $4 million inheritance.[22]
- **Juan Cento** – Cuban-born president of the FedEx Express Division in Miami. Cento previously worked with Flying Tigers Airline – one of the better-known CIA dummy fronts. Flying Tigers was operated during WW II by Claire Chennault of the OSS, later a heroin-transport proprietary of the CIA grafted to FedEx in 1989 by corporate merger. Cento is a member of the Beacon Council and The World Trade Center in Miami.[23]
- **Michael L. Ducker** – executive VP, International Express Freight Services, appointed by President Bush as one of three U.S. representatives on the Asia Business Advisory Council, an adjunct to the Asia-Pacific Economic Cooperation Council (APEC).[24]

Incidentally, it was a FedEx plane that crashed in Winnipeg on October 6, 2005 with six vials of deadly research viruses aboard. Canadians took to calling it the "Plague Plane." This crash followed an incident in which a FedEx courier

And FedEx has mustered a police force "recognized by the state of Tennessee that works alongside the Federal Bureau of Investigation. Moreover, the company is encouraging its 250,000 employees to be spotters of would-be terrorists. It is setting up a system designed to send reports of suspicious activities directly to the Department of Homeland Security via a special computer link." On the FedEx board of directors sits Charles Manatt, chairman of the Democratic National Committee, 1981-1985. He was co-chair of the 1992 Clinton/Gore campaign; also, Steven R. Loranger, chairman, president & CEO of ITT Corp.

22. "List of Skull & Bones Members," Wikipedia entry. http://en.wikipedia.org/wiki/List_of_Skull_and_Bones_Members
23. Flying Tigers web site: "China Tiger: Claire Lee Chennault, 1893-1958 (part 2)." "The CIA loaned money to keep the airline in business, and eventually it bought out Chennault's company..." http://www.warbirdforum.com/clc2.htm Director bios: FedEx web site. http://www.fedex.com/us/about/today/bios.html#1
24. Ibid.

truck, involved in a collision in Winnipeg, was found to be transporting ebola, tuberculosis and hepatitis bacilli.[25]

There is a distinct possibility that the Galls deliveries to Macedonia were calculated on high and enjoyed covert sanction. But they were mere drops of the hard rain that has fallen across Macedonia and the Outer Ring since the fall of the Iron Curtain. The weapons were shipped to enemies of the United States: Syria, Iran, terrorists in the Balkans. And they were *shipped in direct violation of U.S. export law by FedEx* (a company founded by a Marine that did, in fact, merge with a CIA proprietary, Flying Tigers, and is on close terms with both the military and the Agency).

And none of this has appeared in the domestic public print. The pieces lay scattered about the sinking American Empire for any reporter to reconstruct.

The death of Boris Trajkovsky has been widely blamed on his successor, Branko Crvenkovski, a former communist. Todor Petrov, leader of the World Macedonian Congress, has gone so far as to make the charge publicly, exactly as "reporters" on Richard Mellon Scaife's payroll blamed Clinton for Ron Brown's 1996 plane crash, also in Croatia.[26]

But Branko Crvenkovski does not control the area where the plane was disabled and crashed, and the obvious delay in "finding" the downed plane was an integral part of the death plot. Elements of SFOR, on the other hand, were practiced at this sort of thing and furtively in league with extremists in Macedonia.

The plane "exploded" seven minutes before it crashed into a mountainous Croatian terrain – in airspace controlled by Croatian SFOR.[27] The commander of SFOR when the plane

25 See, "Plague Plane Down? FedEx Cargo Included Lab Viruses," *Peace, Earth & Justice News*, October 6, 2005. http://www.pej.org/html/modules.php?op=modload&name=News&file=article&sid=3418&mode=thread&order=0&thold=0
26. See, "Branko Crvenkovski secrets will be ever discovered?" August 17, 2004. http://www.macedoniainfo.com/branko_crvenkovski.htm
27. For reference, cf. SFOR web page: http://www.nato.int/sfor/docu/d981116a.htm "On 14 December 1995 the General Framework Agreement for Peace (GFAP) was signed in Paris, after it had been negotiated in Dayton, Ohio. On 16 December the Alliance's North Atlantic Council launched the largest military operation ever undertaken by the Alliance, Operation Joint Endeavour. Based on UN Security Council Resolution 1031, NATO was given the mandate to implement the military aspects of the Peace Agreement. A NATO-led multinational force, called the

crashed was Lt. Gen. William E. "Kip" Ward, a hardened American combat veteran.[28]

From the NATO web site: "*SFOR Command Structure –* The Stabilization Force has a unified command and is NA-TO-led under the political direction and control of the Alliance's North Atlantic Council." Military authority is "in the hands of NATO's Supreme Allied Commander Europe (SACEUR). As from 19 February 2001, Allied Forces Southern Europe (AF South) has become Joint Force Commander (JFC) for SFOR, as it has been for KFOR since 18 January 2001."[29]

Lt. Gen. Ward was the Commander of SFOR (COMSFOR). Jared Israel and Rick Rozoff have written a series of bombshell articles exposing SFOR as back-stabbers and *collaborators with Balkan terrorists*. The strategy: "KFOR (that is, NATO) bombs Yugoslavia," "KFOR occupies Kosovo," and "KFOR trains 'terrorists' who attack the rest of Serbia." Then "KFOR detains some of those terrorists," and "out of the kindness of its military heart, KFOR declares an amnesty and forgives – whom? Whom does KFOR forgive? The *terrorists* it has trained."[30]

NATO has trained these forces since the initial assault on southern Serbia. The region hasn't forgotten NATO's "humanitarian bombing" campaigns.

Washington controlled SFOR when Boris Trajkovsky's plane went down – to be specific, the Bush administration. It's extremely doubtful that anyone but SFOR could have downed the plane, given its military "stabilization" mission in the region it controlled. And it was SFOR issuing the lame excuses that angered Macedonians.

The cover-up proves the crime.

Implementation Force (IFOR), started its mission on 20 December 1995. IFOR was given a one-year mandate. Its primary mission was to implement Annex 1A (Military Aspects) of the Peace Agreement…"
28. SFOR Informer's bio page for William Ward: http://152.152.96.1/sfor/index-inf/149/p10a/t02p10a.htm
29. http://www.nato.int/sfor/docu/d981116a.htm
30. Jared Israel and Rick Rozoff, "TERRORISM AGAINST SERBIA IS NO CRIME," *Global Resistance, 25 May* 2001.http://globalresistance.com/articles/jared/nocrime.htm; Jared Israel, "Gentle Reign: Washington Makes It Perfectly Clear in Kosovo & Macedonia," March 17, 2001: http://emperors-clothes.com/articles/jared/gentle.htm

Transcript:
Alone in the tower cab, the controller verified that the assigned runway, 22, was clear, but didn't notice that the Comair jet was in the wrong place.

CHAPTER TWO

THE LEXINGTON COMAIR CRASH

THE HAND ON THE DATA STREAM –
THE TETERBORO INCIDENT –
DARWIN'S DEVOLUTION, CIA TERRORISM –
FLIGHT LESSON – TETERBORO & THE CIA

Monday morning, weekend already fading into memory. An ache impales the axis of your brain. You push through the doors at the corner coffee shop, order a large.

A layer of innocence is about to be stripped away from you like a coal deposit in a Pennsylvania butte, but you have no idea and pick out a muffin.

A ruffled newspaper waits at a table. You sit down to the front-page story about a plane crash near Lexington, Kentucky. All passengers dead. *What?*

There is a book about Lexington, Sally Denton's *The Bluegrass Conspiracy*. Never received much press. You recall a scattering of details … CIA-trained police, cocaine smuggling, multiple murders. Who'd think to find so much political intrigue in stove-pipe country? The very idea.

The governor was involved in the Bluegrass scandal, and The Company, a criminal network with ties to Oliver North and Adnan Khashoggi.

But this downed commuter jet in horse country had noth-ing to do with all that ancient history, you tell yourself, stirring in a little raw sugar. The plane taxied on the wrong runway … heart-breaking. You imagine the plane grinding through the night … the moment when the headlights beamed the fence ahead, the trees, the furious attempt to rise clear of them be-fore the quake of rent metal from below, the bellow of fuel combustion behind…

"The lone dispatcher was distracted by 'paper work.'" A lit-any of ludicrous errors. Pointless deaths. The authorities ruled out foul play…

You take the paper cup and newspaper, push through the doors into the autumn sunlight, content that life – now sea-soned by a warm neurotoxic glow – is merely meaningless and bleak, tainted not by foul play but common human failings.

Two days pass. You watch the news. Back to the murky run-way, the 40-degree error in take-off heading, the burning plane. That flight number 5191.

You pick a name from the Flight 5191 passenger list, Fen-ton Dawson, and do a Google search…

Fenton Dawson is survived by his wife and had two chil-dren. He had a steady job…

Dawson, who worked for Affiliated Computer Services in the government solutions department, was on his way to a business conference in Washington, D.C., when Flight 5191 crashed…[1] Affiliated Computer Services … ACS … a com-pany then under investigation by the Justice Department for backdating stock options. Fenton Dawson, the government liaison at ACS, was on his way to Washington to attend a con-ference – other sources said seminar, minor difference – and the pilots tried to take off on the wrong runway. One mean-ingless death among many.

The founder and chairman of the ACS board is Mr. Dar-win Deason, a generous contributor to the Republican Party.

1.http://www.kentucky.com/mld/kentucky/news/15385951.htmsource=rss&chan-nel=kentucky_news

Deason's "partner in crime" at ACS, and a ranking company director, is J. Livingston Kosberg – a former S&L thief.

Pete Brewton, in *The Mafia, CIA and George Bush*, wrote about "Gibraltar Savings, whose chairman, J. Livingston Kosberg, was a prominent fundraiser in Texas for the Democratic Party."[2]

Patriots. "Prominent," too. Their company lost a government solutions man on August 27, 2006 – no one will ask him what he knows about backdating stock options or anything else. A flush of suspicion freezes your gaze ... Back to the Internet, take another look at that S&L, get to know the pre-history of Fenton Dawson's employer.

At Gibraltar Savings down in Dallas, there was this nasty business...

"Robert Strauss, Dallas attorney; U.S. Ambassador to Moscow and former chairman of the Democratic National Committee; friend of George [HW] Bush and former business partner with James A. Baker III; he and his son, Richard, were involved in a number of failed Texas S&Ls, including Lamar and Gibraltar."

Gibraltar, like the other S&L heists of the '80s, was a CIA/Mafia operation. The CIA/Mafia combination, like ACS, has "prominent" friends at the pinnacles of both political parties.

The late Mr. Dawson must have known about many of them.

A quick search turns up another interesting connection to ACS – the destruction of the World Trade Center.

ACS approved the change in Mohammed Atta's visa status in the U.S. from tourist to student, according to the testimony of Huffman Aviation CEO Rudy Dekkers, and Tom Blodgett, a managing director at ACS, before the Kean Commission.[3]

How far, exactly, was ACS involved in CIA business? The *GovExec* website reports, "in November 2003, Bethesda, Md.-based Lockheed Martin Corp. acquired a government con-

---

2. Brewton, P., *The Mafia, CIA and George Bush*, 1992, p. 241.
3. Library of Congress: "TESTIMONY OF TOM BLODGETT, MANAGING DIRECTOR, BUSINESS PROCESS SOLUTIONS, AFFILIATED COMPUTER SERVICES, INC.," and "TESTIMONY OF RUDI DEKKERS, CEO, HUFFMAN AVIATION INTERNATIONAL, INC." http://www.globalsecurity.org/

tracts division of Affiliated Computer Services Inc., a smaller firm, headquartered in Dallas, with *deep connections to the intelligence agencies.*"[4] Oh, the very idea.

The ACS division purchased by Lockheed was responsible for torture at Guantanamo Bay.

What a busy little computer company.

One week before the Comair crash in Lexington, on August 20, 2006, the Associated Press reported on the "ACS Bribery and Federal Contract Fixing" scandal: "Affiliated Computer Services, Inc., one of the companies negotiating with the Family and Social Services Administration for a state welfare eligibility contract worth an estimated $1 billion over 10 years, formerly employed FSSA Secretary Mitch Roob." But most significantly, ES&S and Sequoia voting machine concerns are effectively controlled by the same company, Affiliated Computer Services (ACS) of Dallas, Texas.

Voting machines. And it was an election year...

While digging for information, you will find an anonymous blogger who observes that ACS and ES&S are "a major player in providing technology services to the U.S. court system, USPS, DOT, FCC, the US Senate, the White House, and several other government agencies.... It's an interesting concentration of power. If one controls the datastream of an organization, one has a great deal of knowledge of what it's really doing. Actually, in this case, it would be interesting to know the relationship between ACS and the GOP and the Bush family."[5]

Fenton Dawson was just the man to know all about that relationship. But he's dead.

The Teterboro Incident

Had he lived, it's certain that Fenton Dawson, a government liaison at ACS, would have been called as a witness

4. Shane Harris, "Intelligence Inc.," May 15, 2005. http://www.govexec.com/features/0505-15/0505-15s1.htm.
5. Anon., "A Parable of the U.S. 2000 Election," http://www.ecis.com/~alizard/vote2000.html

in any federal probe into the litany of illegalities that the company had racked up, including stock fraud, domestic spying, torture at Gitmo, vote–rigging, even a possible role in 9/11, any or all of these excesses ... assuming, of course, investigation and possibly even renovation of Bush's congressional Mustang Ranch by an incoming Democratic majority.

My God, you think ... *48 unsuspecting passengers on that flight may have been murdered to silence a witness to a multitude of crimes.*

The motive was transparent: If anyone knew where the bloody ACS/CIA bones were buried, it was a government point man.

But shallow media reports weren't much help ... "Dawson graduated from Trigg County High School in 1978 and worked in Lexington for Affiliated Computer Services ... the 46-year old was headed to Washington on business ..." You consider that the business that ACS does is grounds for a lengthy prison sentence in most civilized countries. Why precisely did Dawson leave home in the middle of the night to board Flight 5191? Didn't other press reports state that he was headed for an unspecified "conference," or "seminar," in DC? The questions left begging to be asked trail off into a media babblesphere. So do the newspaper reports, the fake caring. "ACS is a tightly-knit organization, and we are deeply saddened by the loss of one of our employees..." ACS is a backdating, torturing, techno-fascist business empire with ties to the pyramidal eyes of both parties, a CIA creation run by a pair of former Dallas S&L thieves with Total Information Awareness Disorder.

And ruptures of scandal at ACS were sinking the ship:

Fraud: North Carolina Terminates $171 Million Medicaid Contract with ACS – The state alleges breach of contract by ACS; ACS responds with legal action ... said Kevin Lightfoot, vice president of corporate communications at ACS...

ID theft: Another week, another identity theft scandal: ... computers from the offices of Motorola's human resources services provider, Affiliated Computer Services.

Bribery: Canada: "ACS, Cops Charged in Camera Bribery Scandal" … "Wednesday formally charged photo enforcement vendor Affiliated Computer Services (ACS) with bribing…"

Illegal lobbying, contract fixing: "…ACS has donated $12,500 to Republican Gov. Mitch Daniels' campaign committee over the past three years, including the maximum $5,000 each of the past two years…" (Daniels subsequently reviewed a billion–dollar ACS contract, a possible conflict of interest.[6])

ACSgate is a multi-faceted beast. It embraces the Republican Party: "Subj: NewsFlash: Affiliated Computer Services (ACS) contributed $258,275 to repubs., $0 to dems, 1995-2000 …"[7]

Break time.

You stop to watch the morning news: "President and first lady help 'Make a Difference.'" A presidential plug. That's all you need at the break of dawn. "*Today* host Matt Lauer talks to George and Laura Bush about the rebuilding efforts and their help delivering a Habitat for Humanity house…"

Well, at least Bush isn't a full-time pariah – there's still time for charitable pursuits, you tell yourself.

Break over, back to work. Bush's supposed altruism and Lauer's nasal voice fade to background noise.

ACS data-mining on the Internet proves to be a highly constructive process. There's more information regarding the failed savings-and-loan controlled by Deason and J. Livingston Kosberg: "The two also were involved in an ACS spin-off that filed for bankruptcy in Dallas federal court in 2001 and a lawsuit over its demise, which resulted in a cash settlement – with Deason himself paying out $3 million." The reprobate's crimes followed him to the computer business, and so: "ACS Adds SEC Investigation to Bribery Charges, Other Woes."[8]

This thriving computer company and criminalized sectors of government are symbiotic. Do they still do background checks in the District of Columbia? "Lawrence C. Hale is the

6. AP, "Company vying for $1 billion state contract had problems elsewhere," August 20, 2006.
7. http://www.dnovus.com/companynews.asp.
8.http://www.informationweek.com/news/showArticle.jhtml?articleID=181501504.

Chief Information Security Officer for ACS. He joined the Company in January 2005 from the U.S. Department of Homeland Security (DHS), where he served as deputy director of the National Cyber Security Division's Computer Emergency Readiness Team.... While at the Pentagon, he was a member of the Joint Staff Information Operations Response Cell during a number of cyber events and exercises that helped shape the U.S. government's computer security policy."[9]

The ACS crime data mining goes on, a surfeit of ill-gotten profits – but you're looking for specific answers to the death of Fenton Dawson and 48 others.

Then you find this – A PRIOR PLANE CRASH: "... ACS recently said it plans to sell a corporate jet it originally purchased from a firm owned by ACS founder and chairman Darwin Deason. The firm, DDH Aviation, has fallen under the scrutiny of the Federal Aviation Administration as part of an investigation into a February 2005 crash at New Jersey's Teterboro Airport that injured 20 people. The jet is owned by DDH..."[10]

The downed flight was a "bootleg," a violation of aviation law. The *Dallas Business Journal* reported in July 2005 that it's "not uncommon for owners of expensive business jets to put their planes to work earning revenue – without benefit of obtaining a Part 135 certificate – by flying others in what the industry calls 'bootleg' charter flights." There are "numerous other variations on that theme that are equally illegal, according to industry sources..." Another splintered law to throw on the ACS burnpile.

DDH "declined to comment." Curiously enough, the Federal Aviation Administration, in a July 8th letter to Platinum Jet Management, proposed a fine of $1.86 million, "which in the industry is considered unusually large." But the plane's owner was not touched by the FAA: "Deason's company that

9. Paul McDougall, "ACS Adds SEC Investigation to Bribery Charges, Other Woes," *Information Week*, Mar 7, 2006, http://66.102.7.104/search?q=cachc:oEVms9sgYM-wJ:www.acs-inc.com/about/bios/larry.html+%22Lynn+Blodgett%22+and+HOME-LAND&hl=en&gl=us&ct=clnk&cd=6
10. Ibid.

owned the aircraft – DDH Operating Ltd. – has not been cited by the FAA for any violations."[11]

> The Teterboro crash was similar to the Lexington disaster: A CL-600 Bombadier (the Comair plane was also a Bombadier) corporate jet bound for Chicago with 12 people on board shot off runway six during take-off early in the morning, about 7:23 am, colliding with two automobiles on Route 46, leaving two people with serious head trauma, and plowing through a wall at the Strawberry Clothing Warehouse across the highway. The jet skidded across Route 46. Further casualties were prevented only by the red light at Huyler Street, where 20 to 30 westbound vehicles waited for the light to change. The passengers were injured and doused with jet fuel but managed to walk away, despite the fires that erupted at the clothing store.[12]

The Teterboro Airport would be in the news again on October 11, 2006 when Yankee pitcher Cory Lidle and Tyler Stanger, his flight instructor, would commence flight there in a Cirrus SR20 en route to Tennessee, only to collide fatally 13 minutes later with the Belaire condominium at 524 East 72nd Street.

Many in the "mainstream" media jumped to the conclusion, because the temperature was 20 degrees that morning, that the cause of the crash was "ice." But according to NTSB staff and wire reports, "investigators said Thursday [February 3] they have found *no evidence of ice* on the wings of a corporate jet that skidded off a runway, crossed a busy highway and slammed into a warehouse.... None saw any evidence of ice on the wings or other surfaces of the plane, the National Transportation Safety Board said."[13]

The pilot, John Kimberling of Fort Lauderdale, Fla., the pilot, told investigators that the plane's controls malfunc-

---

11. Ibid.
12. The National Center for Crisis and Continuity Coordination, "NC4 INCIDENT MONITORING CENTER FEATURED INCIDENT: Teterboro, NJ Plane Crash," http://www.nc4.us/nc4/NJPlaneCrash.php.
13. Anon., "Pilot in Teterboro crash goes home," PhillyBurbs.com. February18, 2005. http://www.phillyburbs.com/pb-dyn/articlePrint.cfm?id=452359

tioned, forcing him to abort takeoff.[14] Now we are looking at the possibility of sabotage.

"Five of the passengers aboard the runaway CL-600 were employees of Kelso & Co., a private-equity investment firm with offices at 320 Park Ave. in Manhattan, and three were business associates, company officials said."

AP reported the day after the accident, "Kelso & Co. declined to identify the five employees and three guests on board."[15] Why?

Kelso & Co. is another firm with considerable political influence. In 1999, K&C donated $7,000 to the short-lived Dan Quayle presidential campaign. "Quayle surprised everybody in the most positive way with his insights, judgments and ability to net out the issues," Joseph S. Schuchert Jr., chairman of Kelso & Co., explained to *Business Week* in October 2005.[16]

Once again, you think, contemporary physicists must be correct in assuming the existence of a quantum dimension parallel to our own. And it was right there on newspaper pages all along....

Darwin's Devolution and CIA-Republican Terrorism 101

Hard questions come begging again with a tin cup. Did executives of ACS orchestrate the Teterboro crash? (Only a select few knew about the bootleg charter: Deason, his fellow DDH officers, the nameless Kelso employees on the plane, their three guests. It was a hushed-up flight. This narrows the list of possible suspects, if indeed the plane was sabotaged.) Complicity might be easier to establish if the identities of the Kelso & Co. officers on that illegal DDH charter were known. Spokespeople for Kelso and Deason's DDH stonewalled reporters. So you begin with secrecy, and that speaks, maybe volumes.

---

14. AP, "Authorities Probe N.J. Plane Crash," cf. FoxNews.com, February 3, 2005. http://www.foxnews.com/story/0,2933,146275,00.html

15. Center for Responsive Politics press release, "BUNDLES PROLIFERATE IN LATEST PRESIDENTIAL FILINGS," July 22, 1999.

16. Anon., "They're Not Telling Quayle Jokes At Cerberus," *Business Week*, October 3, 2005. http://www.businessweek.com/magazine/content/05_40/b3953117.htm

Deason knows a thing or two about corporate turpitude, but is he capable of murder?

A profile of the ACS founder, published in *D* [for Dallas] *Magazine* in 2003, is revealing … it wasn't illustrated by Goya, but could have been:

> Accounts differ as to what exactly happened aboard the Cartoush II during its pleasure cruise in the Bahamas in September 2001. Darwin Deason denies that he threatened to kill the chef. Others claim he did. "There certainly was a threat of getting a gun and doing something," says one person intimately acquainted with the details of the incident. As for the chef, he isn't saying much.

Deason's guests on this cruise included ex-Cowboy punter Mike Saxon, Carter Abercrombie of Dallas, and their wives.

The yacht sluiced along the Exuma island chain, the sun was high "when the trouble started." Deason "flew into a rage. 'The guy was definitely having a psychotic episode,' says a source. He began yelling at the chef, Vinny Feola, who locked himself in his quarters. As the standoff dragged on for hours, the ship's captain, Don Hopkins, worked the satellite phone, frantically trying to reach someone back in Dallas who could mollify Deason. Another source says that Deason pulled Saxon and Abercrombie aside and asked them, 'Would you guys be willing to beat the shit out of the chef for me if I asked you to?'"[17] Later, Deason couldn't recall exactly what had incited him, burbled that the chef had been "insubordinate."

Deason's tirades shrink in comparison to the violence he commits as a CIA contractor. Lest we forget the torture charges, *People's Weekly World* reported in 2004 that the CIA torture scandal was in fact the ACS torture scandal: "According to the Springfield, Va.-based *Federal Times*, ACS in 2002 …" – a year before Lockheed bought out ACS Government Services – "provided 30 intelligence analysts and 15 to 20 *interrogators* for the U.S. Navy's prison at Guantanamo Bay, Cuba."[18]

---

17. Tim Rogers, "Lifestyles of the Rich and Shameless," *D Magazine*, June 1, 2003. http://www.findarticles.com/p/articles/mi_qa3862/is_200306/ai_n9293138
18. Jeremy Ryan, "Contractor Probed on Guantanamo Deal," *People's Weekly*

The Feds and Lockheed/ACS execs attempted to keep a lid on the deal for obvious reasons. At the time, violations of the Geneva Convention didn't have the blessing of congress. They conspired to bury it in secrecy, "because the $13.3 million contract states that ACS was to provide technology services to the government, not interrogators and intelligence analysts. According to the *Federal Times,* the U.S. Southern Command contacted the GSA in October 2002 for help in hiring interrogators for the prison at Guantanamo Bay. The GSA put the contract up for bid, but not as an intelligence-gathering contract." There was a cover story. "Instead, the contract stated that that GSA was seeking information technology workers to assist with a project that the U.S. Department of Interior was overseeing at Fort Huachuca, Ariz."

It can safely be said that Deason, founder of ACS, a "tightly-knit organization" of spooks and "interrogators," is capable of extreme, second-hand violence. When the CIA needed competent torturers, to whom did it turn? The Special Forces? Sandanista death squads? The School of the Americas? No.

The Agency turned to a scandal-ridden computer company in Dallas.

This isn't to say that Deason was responsible for Teterboro or the Lexington crash, but he was capable of it.

Hold that thought.

Hypothetical problem, you are a CIA-Republican terrorist and your well-financed cell intends to bring down a domestic flight to kill off troublesome witnesses. You might hire a "mechanic" to sabotage the fuel line, short-circuit the flight controls, plant a radio-bomb in the cargo hold – but these forms of subterfuge might be detected in the post-crash forensic investigation. You might call a favor from Pakistan's ISI, arrange to have a suicide-bomber on board. But suicide-bombers are mentally unstable and explosive residue is traceable. A reporter might connect the dots, and you've been wary of the press since the S&L debacle, not to mention the stock manipulation and torture charges hanging over your head.

What to do? Destroy the plane without messy explosives and addled suicide-bombers. Clue: It only takes a "MOMENT." (Any trained pilot will know the answer immediately.)

Flight Lesson

In our hypothetical example – CIA-Republican terrorist facing criminal charges plots to crash plane, silence witnesses – it's assumed that this practice is fairly common. Is it?

Families of the victims in this instance have their own perspective: "Havana, Oct 3 (*Prensa Latina*) Cuba investigators held Tuesday the Central Intelligence Agency responsible for the explosion in mid-air of a Cuban airplane with 73 people aboard in 1976..."[19]

Pan Am 103 was destroyed by terrorists facing criminal charges. Look not to Libya, but to "Coreans": "...It was the McKee team that reportedly uncovered evidence that a 'rogue' CIA unit, COREA, based in Wiesbaden, was doing business with Monzar Al-Kassar [of Iran-contra infamy]."

A Syrian arms broker and narco-terrorist "Al-Kassar was part of the secret network run by US Lt. Colonel Oliver North." Outraged that COREA was doing business with a Syrian "who made money from drugs/arms/terrorism," the McKee team "decided to fly to CIA HQ in Virginia to expose COREA. They flew on Pan Am flight 103..."[20]

Then there was Dorothy Hunt. Carmel, CA political researcher Mae Brussell found that the Plumber's wife was carrying a fat bundle of cash with consecutive serial numbers when the plane crashed.... "Dorothy Hunt, the wife of convicted White House 'plumber' E. Howard Hunt, was killed, along with 41 other people, when United Airlines Flight 553 crashed near Chicago's Midway Airport on Dec. 8, 1972." Mrs. Hunt was a CIA employee, reportedly carrying $100,000 in "hush" money "so her husband would not implicate White House officials in Watergate. The day after the crash, White

19. Anon., "Cuba: CIA Sabotaged Cuban Plane – Terrorist act of 1976 was at agency's behest," Prensa Latina, 03 October 2006. http://www.cuba-solidarity.org.uk/news.asp?ItemID=872
20. http://spookterror.blogspot.com/2005/08/lockerbie-bomb-london-bombs.html

House aide Egil (Bud) Krogh was appointed Undersecretary of Transportation, supervising the National Transportation Safety Board and the Federal Aviation Association – the two agencies charged with investigating the airline crash. A week later, Nixon's deputy assistant Alexander Butterfield was made the new head of the FAA, and five weeks later Dwight Chapin, the president's appointment secretary, was dispatched to Chicago to become a top executive with United Airlines. The airplane crash was blamed on equipment malfunctions."[22]

Langley patriots consider aviation a well-stone of assassination politics.

Ron Brown might look into it if he was alive. And if the wife or children are on board –who's to know? A CIA-Republican terrorist has no regard for human life (he is a totalitarian gestalt of armed "conservative principles.").

This is a fine science. It doesn't necessarily stoop to wild-eyed Arabs with box-cutters or radio bombs planted in the cargo hold – that's for show. There are more subtle means. As in the martial arts, the CIA-Republican terrorist looks for a weakness to exploit: "Weight Is Focus of Plane Safety" – *New York Times.*[21]

The distribution of weight is a critical factor in any airplane flight. A miscalculation can be fatal, and there are standard formulae used before every takeoff to determine if the plane is balanced properly. The *NewsReleaseWire* published a story the day after the Comair crash that comes to the same conclusion:

Passenger Obesity as a Contributing Factor in Commuter Airplane Crashes

In January 2003 an Air Midwest Beech 1900 with 19 passengers aboard failed to gain altitude quickly enough and crashed into an airport hanger during takeoff in Charlotte, North Carolina. All passengers and crew died in the incident. The National Transportation Safety Board determined that Air Midwest used "substantially inaccurate weight and balance calculations for company airplanes," which were based on incorrect "average passenger and baggage weights ..."[22]

21. Mae Brussell, "30 Watergate Witnesses Have Met Violent Deaths," *Midnight,* July 12, 1976. http://www.maebrussell.com/Mae%20Brussell%20Articles/Watergate%20Deaths.html
22. Mark Schrimsher (president, CalorieLab, Inc.), "Passenger obesity as a contributing factor in commuter airplane crashes (backgrounder),"

Aviation News has also reported on a plane brought down by a balance miscalculation: "MAY 2006: Weight distribution factor in West Caribbean MD-82 accident French newspaper *Le Figaro*, quoting an anonymous source, reported that the West Caribbean MD-82 that crashed in Venezuela, August 2005, was overloaded. It reportedly had a takeoff weight of 70,300 kilos, where mow is 67,600 kilos. The cargo was badly distributed as well..."[23] An airplane has a center of gravity and it must be respected or...

There's this:

> "A weighty issue. And a balancing act too" – [A] commuter airliner has all chairs occupied as the Captain rotates. After a brief normal flight profile the nose of the airplane pitches up to the extreme. After a breathtaking stall the airplane plunges back onto the airport surface killing all on board. What happened here?... Because the flight was full, and standard passenger and baggage weights were used, there is a possibility that the aircraft was severely overweight and out of CG. The second possibility is that the baggage in the aft cargo bay shifted after rotation creating an extreme aft CG. Lastly, there is a potential mechanical problem in the elevator mechanism itself.[24]

Back to Teterboro:

First Findings See No Brakes Used in Most of Jet's Path

> The National Transportation Safety Board, which is investigating the crash of a corporate jet at Teterboro Airport in New Jersey on Wednesday, said yesterday that its findings indicated no braking system was in effect until the plane was 5,000 feet along the 6,013-foot runway. Normally, a liftoff take place around 3,000 feet...

Hold that thought.

The cause of the Teterboro crash was reported by the *New York Times* on March 24, 2005: "The corporate jet that crashed into a warehouse in Teterboro, N.J., last month with

August 28, 2006. http://www.expertclick.com/NewsReleaseWire/default.cfm?Action=ReleaseDetail&ID=1362
23. http://aviation-safety.net/news/news.php?field=datumcode&var=200605%25
24. http://stoenworks.com/A%20Weighty%20Issue.html

11 people on board was *carrying too much of its weight in front*, federal investigators said in a preliminary report released yesterday..."[25]

Excess baggage loaded toward the front of the plane pushed down the nose. The jet was unable to take flight, unknown to the pilot who initially thought that the problem was a malfunction. The failure to lift off the tarmac was caused by baggage load distribution. The plane accelerated 3,000 down the runway, but gravity held the nose down and the jet would not rise from the tarmac. The pilots attempted take-off for another 2,000 feet ... it stubbornly refused to fly. At 5,000 feet they applied the brakes and aborted the flight.

Too late. The plane shot off the end of the runway, across the street and into the warehouse.

The baggage was loaded on the illegal charter flight by Darwin Deason's tiny DDH, Inc. He owned the jet and the charter company. Was the flight deliberately sabotaged by the CIA's ranking rendition airline? You come to realize that this may be the only possible explanation by considering that before *any* flight – a trained pilot calculates the weight of passengers and luggage to determine if it is safe to fly. There are standard calculations for baggage distribution. The pilot does not want to die. He knows that if the weight and balance of the plane are off, he and his passengers could crash.

The pilots at Teterboro did their calculations. They assumed the cargo was loaded properly. Satisfied that it was safe to fly, the plane headed out, unaware that the plane was off-trim.

There was sufficient appearance of wrong doing here to blind a saint. The cargo loaders knew their jobs, and the balance of the plane is always a critical issue before take-off. Did DDH employees – a sample of which we've already visited at Guantanamo Bay – deliberately pile cargo toward the front of the plane and feed false data to the pilots?

25. Patrick McGeehan, "Plane in Crash Was Imbalanced, Investigators Say," *New York Times*, March 24, 2005. http://topics.nytimes.com/top/reference/timestopics/organizations/n/national_transportation_safety_board/index.html?s=closest&query=TETERBORO%20(NJ)&field=geo&match=exact

Teterboro & the CIA

Before returning to Lexington, we must look at the airport in Teterboro – whispers overheard at the airport coffee shop, insinuations, rumors, gaps in the record, men in uniform, obscure movements in the middle of the night.

Teterboro is the home of Bendix Corp., a company that demonstrated during the German-American industrial-based WWII that Nazi total-war profiteering is a multinational capitalist's wet dream, and an arm of the notorious Stuttgart-based Bosch patent pool that sent American military data to Germany as late as May, 1940 – today, a division of AlliedSignal.[26]

Teterboro has a busy airport. Some very well-known aviators have called it home and made their mark in history, you would recognize their names in an instant:

April-July 2001: Hani Hanjour Receives More Flight Training; Rents Small Aircraft – According to the 9/11 Commission, soon after settling in the area, hijacker Hani Hanjour starts receiving "ground instruction" at AIR FLEET TRAINING SYSTEMS, a flight school in Teterboro, New Jersey. While there, he flies the Hudson Corridor: "a low-altitude 'hallway' along the Hudson River that passes New York landmarks like the World Trade Center." His instructor refuses a second request to fly the Corridor, "because of what he considered Hanjour's poor piloting skills."[27]

Shortly, another aviator connected to 9/11 will surface in Teterboro.

From the Air Fleet website, we learn that the facility is "the only Part 141 school within easy public transportation reach of New York City." The school is run by the Bopps. There is a comet named after them. "The Bopps, who own and operate Air Fleet, have a much longer family history of involvement in aviation. Beginning in the 1950s, Paul Arnold (Susan Bopp's father) was the Chief Pilot for Bendix Corporation, now better known as AlliedSignal, for more than twenty years. During

26. Mae Brussell notes, Michael Sayers & Albert E. Kahn, "Sabotage! The Secret War Against America," *Harpers*, 1942. http://www.maebrussell.com/Sabotage/Sabotage%20outline.html
27. http://www.cooperativeresearch.org/context.jsp?item=a0301paterson

that time, he also assisted with the development of some of the equipment now used in aircraft. He was also responsible for instilling a love of aviation in his daughter, Susan..."[28]

There is some tension in Teterboro among the locals concerning obscure, "immoral" political activities (apart from Nazi collaboration, death squad training, human experimentation, drug trafficking...)

Troubling uses for Teterboro –
Moral issues raised over flight bookings
MIKE KELLY
Bergen Record, April 10, 2005

... One of the most disturbing revelations about recent Teterboro jet traffic almost slipped under the public's radar screen. It seems that Teterboro was the launching pad for a secret flight in which U.S. agents sent a suspected al-Qaida operative to Syria, where he says he was tortured.

The story of Maher Arar has emerged as a focal point in congressional debates over the secret Bush administration policy of "rendition" – or sending suspected terrorists to nations where they can be tortured. But almost lost in the story is this footnote: After American agents apprehended Arar in late September 2002 and held him for two weeks, they secretly took him to Teterboro and hopped aboard a chartered private jet that eventually made its way to Syria.

Arar, a Syrian-born Canadian citizen who denies he is a terrorist, was released 10 months later. He is now suing the United States, claiming he was brutally tortured in Syria.

Teterboro Airport was used in the early 1990s by federal agents to fly mob boss John Gotti on a small chartered plane to a federal prison in Illinois. The airport was also linked in the 1980s to a Virginia firm that chartered private jets through a Teterboro-based carrier to fly CIA agents and U.S. military commando units on covert missions.

But the secret trip by U.S. agents with Maher Arar raises an additional concern. Obviously, the agents wanted to keep a low profile. But it's one thing to use Teterboro's privacy to transport a convicted mob boss or CIA agents. It's something else when the airport is used to maintain the secrecy of a controversial program that involves torturing suspected terrorists.

28. http://www.airfleettraining.com/

Is this why North Jersey residents should endure the hassles of Teterboro? That question is important, not just for the moral debate over torture of suspected terrorists, but because of the thousands of northern New Jersey residents whose lives are affected by Teterboro's low-flying jets.

With so many ordinary citizens in the flight path of these jets, it's important to question the safety and noise of the airport. But once safety or noise is debated, then authorities should discuss what kinds of flights come in and out of Teterboro. Are we interrupting the lives of thousands of area residents for the convenience of guests at Trump's wedding, professional basketball stars and now possible torture victims? And if U.S. authorities plan to use Teterboro for more rendition flights, will the airport and surrounding community need additional security?

All sides agree that the neighborhoods around Teterboro Airport are too congested. After a jet rolled off a Teterboro runway in February and smashed into a warehouse, even airport supporters conceded they wished there was more room at the end of runways for crash barriers. But the far-more-basic question about Teterboro is this: Who uses this airport anyway?

The story of Maher Arar and his possible torture adds a moral component to that question about Teterboro's future and the federal grants to soundproof schools. It's about time. Ultimately, the dangers of Teterboro's jets are really a moral issue.[29]

Some of the CIA rendition flights from Teterboro, complete with tail numbers:[30]

N829MG – N259SK
Teterboro (USA) Hahn (Germany) 07/06/2003

N1HC
Teterboro (USA) Northolt (UK) 16/12/2003
Budapest (Hungary) Teterboro (USA) 09/09/2005

N50BH
Teterboro (USA) Coventry (UK) 02/04/2005

29. http://www.house.gov/rothman/SRR%20Clips/04%20April/041005_Teterboro_Bergen%20Record.htm
30. "RESEARCH ON THE PLANES USED BY THE CIA." http://www.statewatch.org/news/2006/jun/ep-cia-inq-research-report-Rapporteur.pdf

Then there was N829MG-N259SK – a peek at the plane's registration files is revealing.[31]

A Gulfstream III (Grumman G-1159A), this plane carried Canadian national Maher Arar from the US to Jordan, where he was transferred overland to Syria. He was tortured during 13 months of detention without charge, and was released in October 2003. The plane has also made over 100 trips to Guantanamo Bay. There are 380 relevant FAA recorded landings or take-offs between March 2001 and May 2005. Registered by MJG Aviation in October 2000 in Florida; the company dissolved July 2004. MJG's owner also owned Presidential Aviation, a company first registered in Florida in 1998 and dissolved November 2004. The aircraft was re-registered as 259SK in March 2004 by S&K Aviation LLC. S&K Aviation was first registered in Florida in December 2003 and is an active company with a registered agent. Range and capacity: average range of 3,715 nautical miles. The aircraft can transport up to 22 passengers, but it is usually configured for 10/12 people.

Destinations: Recorded movements of N829MG-N259SK include landings and take offs from the following airports:

> Belgium Antwerp 1/Canada Gander, Newfoundland 10/France Le Bourget 2/Germany Frankfurt 1/Germany, Frankfurt-Hahn 1/Germany Nurnberg 1/Ireland Shannon 2/Italy Rome … United States of America Guantánamo Bay US Naval Air Station, Cuba 2/United States of America Teterboro 3/United States of America Washington, DC-2…

One of the key companies involved in the rendition flights was Aero Contractors. Pacifica Radio's Amy Goodman has discussed Aero's renditions…

> **AMY GOODMAN**: And where did they fly Maher Arar out of from the New York area?

---

31. Amy Goodman interview, *Democracy Now!* "Ghost Plane: The True Story of the CIA Torture Program," Pacifica radio network, October 19th, 2006. http://www.democracynow.org/article.pl?sid=06/10/19/1347246

STEPHEN GREY: He was flown out of the local airport here in New Jersey, Teterboro, picked up there. There was an FBI involvement in that particular operation, because it came out of New York, the U.S. airspace. So it wasn't a sort of typical rendition. He was flown from Teterboro to Dulles Airport, where a new team took over. And then he was flown from there to – via Athens – sorry, via Rome in Italy, and then the plane then landed in Jordan. At that point, I think, the CIA took over.

He was then taken – he was beaten in Jordan, and then he was driven over the border into Syria to this place. You've mentioned the Palestine Branch. It's one of the worst interrogation centers in the world. And what I found [is] that he wasn't the only person that had been sent there by the United States. Up to seven other prisoners were sitting in these same cells about the size of graves, three-foot wide, six-foot wide. And up to seven other prisoners there at the time had all been sent there by the United States.

AMY GOODMAN: Are they still there?

STEPHEN GREY: Well, some of them are. I mean, the whole story of this rendition program is that there are only a few people who have emerged to tell their stories, and so many others have DISAPPEARED completely. We don't know where they are. There's no accountability as to what's happened to them.

Residents of Teterboro might also have a few questions to ask the CIA about the mentor of Mohammed Atta:

Rudi Dekkers – CIA Plane Repeatedly Taking Off and Landing at Teterboro owned by Wally Hilliard

According to European sources who were instrumental in assisting the Council of Europe in its investigation of CIA rendition flights and secret prisons in Eastern Europe, the CIA's Learjet 35A, owned by Aircraft Guaranty Corporation, a brass plate located at 515 N. Sam Houston Parkway East, Suite 305, Houston, Texas, and flying with tail number N35NK, has used Billund, Denmark as a base of operations.

Until June 2004, the plane was owned by Wally Hilliard's Plane 1 Leasing Co. of Naples, Florida. Plane 1 Leasing is owned by WALLY HILLIARD, the business partner of Rudi Dekkers, whose Venice, Florida-based Huffmann Aviation flight school helped train Mohammed Atta to prepare for the 9-11 attack. N35NK made a flight to Guantanamo in April 2004.

9/24/2003 KTEB USA Teterboro, NJ KLBB USA Lubbock, TX N35NK Learjet 35A, Aircraft Guaranty

N35NK has also been leased to Nordic Aviation Contractor at St. Petersburg-Clearwater airport in Florida. The home headquarters of Nordic Aviation in Billund, Denmark. In 2005, N35NK was re-leased to JetSmart of Connecticut and is now on sale for $2,395,000.[32]

Concerned residents of Teterboro may also want to write their elected representatives about the extent of black operations launched at the airport, particularly those involving guns-'n'-drugs:

US: Secret Task Led to Web Of Firms;
Virginian Ran Covert Missions
Washington Post, March 22, 1987

...ANMC provided consulting services for Southern Air Transport of Miami. A Southern Air spokesman said last week that a Gadd company acted as a broker and occasionally was paid a commission for finding charter business for Southern. Southern Air officials have said that the company performed some maintenance work on the aircraft that was shot down Oct. 5 in Nicaragua, which led to public disclosure of the contra resupply operation.

According to a former official of Executive AIR FLEET [where Hanjour took his training?] at New Jersey's Teterboro Airport, Gadd's companies contracted for 100 to 150 hours of domestic air charter service a year, at a rate of $3,400 an hour for such small, fast, long-range passenger planes as Gulfstreams II.

By 1985, ANMC assets had increased to $ 680,466, up 10-fold from the previous year, and Gadd's EAST had assets of $ 386,308, according to Delaware franchise tax records.

---

32. Wayne Madsen. http://www.waynemadsenreport.com/2006_06040610.php

Employees of ANMC were mostly former military men with security clearances, trained not to ask too many questions, according to some of those employees. But by early 1986, it was evident even to them that Gadd was involved in some highly sensitive projects.

According to a report in Knight-Ridder newspapers, persons responding to an ANMC recruiting ad in the Dec. 2, 1985 Air Force Times were told by Gadd that they would be given a stateside job with the company only after working for six months in Honduras.[33]

CHAPTER THREE

PROJECT ANTHRAX

Part I

SAIC, Stephen Hatfill, et al. & Bio-Economic State Terrorism

"It was his own fault, I thought," said Tom Ivins. "What he did, he screwed himself up. He got involved with the wrong people..."

The West Nile Virus outbreak of 1999 made 67 people in New York City sick, and brought with it endemic anxiety. But the anthrax mailings two years later brought death. Emergency measures in a jingoistic package, under consideration in the House of Representatives, arrived at the same time as the Ames strain and the emergency measures floated through Congress on a cloud of lethal white powder.

Right-wing propagandists stepped up to finger the "obvious" culprit. Laurie Mylroie explained to CNN, "it takes a highly sophisticated agency to produce anthrax in the lethal form. Not many parties can do that." Saddam Hussein "continues his part of the war in the form of terrorism. It is unlikely that anthrax will remain in letters. It is likely that it will be used in the subway of a city, or in the ventilation system of a U.S. building. Saddam wants revenge against us. He wants to do to the U.S. what we've done to Iraq."

This cover story didn't survive close scrutiny, however. The true culprit – it emerged after Dr. Barbara Rosenberg of the Federation of American Scientists pestered the Bureau with facts and public exposure – was an obscure, right-wing biochemical warfare "counterterrorist." One of the perpetrators took his training at the NIH in Bethesda, Maryland and other federal facilities, also a two-year fellowship from the National Research Council, the country's leading CBW defense lab. He moved on to the U.S. Army Medical Research Institute of Infectious Diseases – USAMRIID – at Fort Detrick. He experimented with biological responses to filoviridae, the family of viruses that transmit Ebola. In September 1999 – as the Jerry Hauer-SAIC-Fort Detrick-USAMRIID West Nile Virus was taking hold in New York – the terrorist began working at the very same lab.

By March of 2002, it was clear that the FBI was protecting him. Spokesmen for the Bureau were evasive about the source of the anthrax but it gradually emerged, by process of elimination and genetic analysis, that the culprit, Steven Hatfill, worked at the same classified USAMRIID facility in Maryland that employed Jerry Hauer, New York Mayor Rudy Giuliani's right-hand man.

Project Coast

CounterPunch commented a month later on geographic connections that bore directly on the case: "The South African media [have] been abuzz with details of that nation's former biological warfare program and its links to the CIA." The program was code-named Project Coast, based at the Roodeplat Research Laboratories. It maintained ties to the U.S. bio-warfare laboratories at Fort Detrick and the UK's Porton Down.

The head of the South African program, Dr. Wouter Basson, was reportedly offered a job with the CIA in the United States after the fall of the apartheid regime. According to former South African National Intelligence Agency deputy director Michael Kennedy, when Basson refused the offer, the CIA threatened to kill him.

The U.S. pressured President Mandela to relinquish Basson's research files, and *they were transported to Fort Detrick.*[1]

1. Wayne Madsen, "Anthrax and The Agency – Thinking The Unthinkable," Coun-

The FBI pushed on with the investigation but withheld from public disclosure that the terrorist had worked with Wouter Basson in South Africa, and that he'd been a member of the South African Nazi Party.

But some of Hatfill's closest friends maintained his innocence. Stan Bedlington, a veteran CIA agent, told the *Washington Post* that he'd known Hatfill for several years: "They were drinking buddies who'd both been involved in anti-terrorism efforts long before the World Trade Center crumbled. Now, suddenly, people were saying that Hatfill could be responsible for the country's first case of domestic bioterrorism, a release of lethal anthrax through the mail that had left five people dead and seventeen others infected in the fall of 2001."

Bedlington had fond memories of Hatfill, though he hadn't seen him for some time. They'd met at a Baltimore symposium on bioterrorism. Bedlington had spent six years bent over a senior analyst desk at the CIA's Counter-terrorism Center. Hatfill was a virologist at the U.S. Army-SAIC Medical Research Institute of Infectious Diseases, "where he'd begun making a name for himself preaching the dangers of a bioterror attack. Soon they ran into each other again at Charley's Place in McLean, then a favorite hangout for the U.S. intelligence community."

Hatfill arrived with "men whom Bedlington recognized as bodyguards for Saudi Arabian Prince Bandar bin Sultan."[2]

To respond to intrusive media, Hatfill's cohort Pat Clawson served as spokesman. Clawson was a radio executive who worked with Iran-contra's Oliver North.

Clawson, reports the *Baltimore Sun*, was a "former CNN reporter who has known Hatfill socially for six years. [He] said he and Hatfill are part of a group of friends who visited a house in the Virginia mountains near Shenandoah National Park in October for a weekend of skeet-shooting and socializing." The visit "came at the peak of anthrax hysteria, Clawson said. He

terPunch.org, April 8, 2002.
2. David Tell, "The Hunting of Steven J. Hatfill: Why are so many people eager to believe that this man is the anthrax killer?" *Evening Standard*, vol. 8, no. 1, September 16, 2002.

told Hatfill that a few weeks earlier he had opened a vitriolic letter addressed to Oliver North, whose radio program is produced by Clawson's employer, Radio America. White powder had spilled from the envelope, which Clawson discarded"[3]

After Steven J. Hatfill was named as the FBI's lead suspect, the same ultra-conservative media opinion-shapers who had immediately blamed Saddam Hussein now hustled to Hatfill's defense. Rupert Murdoch's *Evening Standard* opined that his status as "interesting" to federal investigators "inspired a mini-industry of speculation that he may somehow be implicated in last fall's deadly anthrax attacks. [But] much of that speculation pretends to be something more: certainty of his guilt, and certainty that in every nook and cranny of his life must be found some blot or scar or mark of the devil that proves his guilt"[4]

The evidence of of Hatfill's guilt is compelling:

- Bloodhounds found him of some interest after snuffling a letter inside of an envelope put there by Hatfill, preserved in a hermetically-sealed bag. The hounds responded to him alone.

- A return address on one of the anthrax-bearing envelopes was Greendale, Rhodesia. Hatfill lived in Greendale.

- The neo-fascist Selous Scouts in Rhodesia spread anthrax. Hatfill was a member of the Scouts at the time of the contagion's spread.

- Hatfill had no fit alibi for the days of the anthrax mailings.

- Hatfill's PhD was forged. He was caught lying on his resumé.

- He failed a CIA lie-detector test regarding his activities in Rhodesia before the anthrax attacks. He failed a lie detector test afterward concerning his involvement in them.

---

3. Scott Shane, "FBI defends anthrax inquiry," *Baltimore Sun*, August 13, 2002. http://www.baltimoresun.com/bal-te.hatfill13aug13.story
4. Marilyn W. Thompson, "The Pursuit of Steven Hatfill," *Washington Post*, September 14, 2003, p. W-6 http://www.washingtonpost.com/ac2/wp-dyn/A49717-2003Sep9?language=printer

Some of the most damaging evidence was discovered in ponds dredged near his home. Objects pulled from the silt included a clear box with insert holes for rubber gloves to protect lab techs working with toxic materials. Also recovered were glass vials in plastic wrap and a pair of gloves.[5]

One wonders about the expletive David Kay, the SAIC vice president and Hatfill's boss, whispered to himself the moment he heard that these items had been found, not to mention a positive lab test for traces of anthrax FBI technicians found on these objects, later changed to "inconclusive."[6] ... But then, Kay was out of the country at the time, conducting a WMD "search" of his own.

Part II

SAIC, Protected Conspirator Stephen Hatfill & Bio-Economic State Terrorism

Introduction to BioPort

"As it happens, one of the Scouts' favored tactics was the mailing of anthrax spores, embedded in the glue on envelope flaps..."

The epidemic swept through Zimbabwe (the former British colony of Southern Rhodesia) in the late 1970s. It killed 180 people, infected over 10,000, devastated livestock, brought with it economic disaster and widespread hunger ... but not throughout Zimbabwe indiscriminately, as one might expect; only in *black* neighborhoods. This epidemic was respectful of gated white communities and politely kept out.[7]

Stephen Hatfill signed on with the Rhodesian Special Air Service (SAS) and the Selous Scouts, a counter-insurgency death squad that enforced apartheid rule, before arriving at the Godfrey Huggins School of Medicine.

---

5. See The Biovangelist web site. http://jdo.org/hatfill.htm
6. Ibid.
7. Meryl Nass, M.D., "Zimbabwe's Anthrax Epizoodic," *Bioterror: Manufacturing Wars the American Way*, edited by Ellen Ray and William H. Schaap, New York: Ocean Press, 2003, p. 29.

Some of the faculty was curious why the Yank would stoop to study at a backwater academy like Huggins.

His admission to the school was arranged by Robert Burns Symington, an anatomy professor and devoted neo-Nazi. "Symington is strongly believed to have worked with the Ian Smith-led white supremacist regime on its biological warfare project," Africa's *Sunday Mirror* reported in 2002:

> The Zimbabwe authorities have since established that [Smith's] security forces, particularly the much feared Selous Scouts, stealthily distributed the deadly anthrax spore among the hungry cattle of the Rhodesian Tribal Trust Lands, where most Africans lived, and seeded cholera into the rivers.

Sturm und Drang (und Jurms)

After the war, a former senior officer of the Rhodesian security force admitted, "it is true that anthrax was used in an experimental role and the idea came from the Army Psychological Operations." Guerillas were scapegoated for the outbreak.[8]

Among the Scout's favored tactics was the mailing of anthrax spores embedded in the glue on *envelope* flaps.[9]

Hatfill ... you may know the type. A student at the medical school's radiation oncology department recalls that he sported a 9mm pistol and boasted of past paramilitary glories in Vietnam and Zimbabwe.[10]

8. "Zimbabwean authorities have made several reports that indicate that Rhodesians were using biological warfare against guerillas during the liberation war, but these have not received international coverage." – Innocent Chofamba-Sithole and Norman Mlambo, "Ex-Rhodesian under probe for US anthrax attacks," *Sunday Mirror*, July 9, 2002. http://www.africaonline.co.zw/mirror/stage/archive/020709/national8599.html

9. Wayne Madsen, "Anthrax and the Agency," CounterPunch.org, April 8, 2002.

10. See, "The Anthrax Letters," http://www.monitor.net/monitor/0208a/0208a-404.html. This site features a description of the paramilitary tactics of the Selous Scouts wolf pack. A handful of fighters would drop into the back country disguised as rebels. Living off the land for weeks, "they would relentlessly track down their opponents and kill them, even if it meant crossing into neighboring countries in violation of international law. Their training taught them to live off the barren land during their long pursuit on foot, drinking fetid water and eating carrion scraps.

In 1984, Hatfill moved on to study at South African medical schools and joined the military. While in the area, he befriended Eugene Terre Blanche, leader of the Afrikaner Resistance Movement, the South African Nazi Party.[11]

After a year-long tour in Antarctica, he pressed on to the States and found employment at the National Institutes of Health. "The PhD certificate he submitted to NIH could have easily been tracked back by authorities and exposed as a forgery," Marilyn Thompson, author of *The Killer Strain: Anthrax and a Government Exposed*, explained in a blogged Q&A hosted by UCLA's School of Public Health in 2003, "but it was overlooked and Hatfill's credentials helped him gain access to sensitive government agencies. USAMRIID allowed him in as a contract researcher."[12]

The first casualty of the anthrax mailings was Bob Stevens, a photo editor at a tabloid that had run an article blasting the Saudi royals – Hatfill's friend Prince Bandar, a Fox News director, for instance.

From the CDC report: "On October 4, 2001, we confirmed the first bio-terrorism-related anthrax case identified in the United States is a resident of Palm Beach County, Florida. Epidemiologic investigation indicated that exposure occurred at the workplace through intentionally contaminated mail."[13]

It is within the realm of possibility that 9/11 hijackers Mohammed Atta and Ahmed Alhanzawi were among the first to come into contact with the spores, despite FBI denials. These have not held up well against a fusillade of questions from the press.

In March 2002, the *New York Times* reported that Atta and his entourage "identified themselves as pilots when they came

Some articles claim that they were responsible for two out of every three enemy fatalities in the civil war. Admirers and vets boast that the Selous Scouts were the most skilled and ruthless guerrilla warfare fighters in history."

11. "The Biovangelist" web site. http://jdo.org/hatfill.htm

12. UClA Department of Epidemiology, School of Public Health, "Reporter Interview on Steven Hatfill Article," September 15, 2003. http://www.ph.ucla.edu/epi/bioter/reporterinterview.html,

13. Centers for Disease Control, "Bioterrorism-Related Anthrax: First Case of Bioterrorism-Related Inhalational Anthrax in the United States, Palm Beach County, Florida, 2001." http://www.cdc.gov/ncidod/EID/vol8no10/02-0354.htm

to the emergency room of Holy Cross Hospital in Fort Lauderdale, Fla., last June. One had an ugly, dark lesion on his leg," and "in October, a pharmacist in Delray Beach, Fla., said he had told the F.B.I. that two of the hijackers, Mohamad Atta and Marwan al-Shehhi, came into the pharmacy looking for something to treat irritations on Mr. Atta's hands."

Dr. Christos Tsonas thought Alhanzawi's wound curious, but cleaned it and prescribed medication. "After Sept. 11, when federal investigators found the medicine among the possessions of one of the hijackers, Ahmed Alhaznawi, Dr. Tsonas reviewed the case and arrived at a new diagnosis." The lesion was "consistent with cutaneous anthrax." Dr. Thomas Inglesby of John Hopkins, and Dr. Tara O'Toole, assistant secretary for health and safety at the Energy Department, sided with Dr. Tsonas.

Thompson followed every step in the Bureau's investigation, and she finds it probable that Atta and Alhaznawi had some contact with anthrax spores:

> The FBI contends that it pursued a hijacker connection in the early days and became convinced that they were not involved in these mailings – mainly because the anthrax strain used was a military research strain. Many people in Florida, however, who know about the hijackers' movements in that part of the country in the months before 9/11, do not believe the FBI pursued this with enough vigor...

The *Times*: "In an interview, Dr. O'Toole said that after consulting with additional medical experts on the Alhaznawi case, she was 'more persuaded than ever' that the diagnosis of cutaneous anthrax was correct..."

Mohammed Atta's terror cell took flight school training in Boca Raton, not far from American Media, Inc. where victim Bob Stevens worked. Atta rented apartments from the wife of an editor of *The Sun*, published by AMI.[14]

---

14. William J. Broad and David Johnston, "Report Linking Anthrax and Hijackers Is Investigated," *New York Times*, March 23, 2002.

The mailings continued after the collapse of the towers. The *Times*: "They would probably have needed an accomplice to mail the tainted letters…. The four recovered anthrax letters were postmarked on Sept. 18 and Oct. 9 in Trenton."[15]

But the mailings weren't constrained by domestic borders. In November 2001, the CDC's web site in Atlanta confirmed that a tainted letter had been sent from Switzerland to Chile. Dr. Antonio Banfi, a pediatrician at a children's hospital in Santiago, received the letter. He suspected that something was amiss because it was postmarked Zurich, but had a Florida return address.[16]

In 2003, the *South Florida Sun-Sentinel* reports, Maureen Stevens, the widow of the first victim, filed a wrongful-death suit that "could embarrass the U.S. government and provide insight into the ongoing investigation of the fall 2001 bioterrorism attacks."

The "embarrassing" lawsuit held that anthrax spores "were known to be missing from an Army laboratory at Fort Detrick, Md., as early as 1992," and that the litigants "accuse the government of failing to adequately secure them. 'The bottom line is that a lot of our [FOIA] requests were not acknowledged or were not answered.'"[17]

Maureen Stevens' lawsuit was filed in Palm Beach County Circuit Court. It named Ft. Detrick-USAMRIID, Battelle Memorial Institute, other possible sources of the anthrax, and BioPort Corp. of Lansing, Michigan, a vaccine manufacturer.

The name BioPort is synonymous with mismanagement and contaminated product.

The company was founded on June 22, 1995 by Yoav Stern, a former avionics systems officer specializing in F-15, A-4, Mirage and Kfir fighter jets for the Israeli Air Force. He was also commander of a flight-training unit, and a deputy squadron commander. The BioPort web site reports that one Zive R. Nedivi has been the CEO, president and a director of

15. Ibid.
16. AP report, "Anthrax Case in Chile Confirmed," November 23, 2001. http://www.usenet.com/newsgroups/talk.environment/msg06625.html
17. Kathy Bushouse, "Security at Issue in Widow's Case," *South Florida Sun-Sentinel,* September 28, 2003.

the company since June 1995. Mr. Nedivi also served in the Israeli Air Force and was the founder of "the predecessor of the company, an indirectly wholly-owned subsidiary of Rada Electronic Industries Ltd."[18]

Also on Bioport's board of directors:

> Niv Harizman: A company director since December 1997. From January 1998 on, Harizman was a principal with BT Alex. Brown Incorporated, the investment banking subsidiary of Bankers Trust New York Corporation. From June 1996 until January 1998, Mr. Harizman was a VP with Alex. Brown. He started there in 1995.

> General William Lyon: Retired Air Force general, currently serves as a director of the board at Fidelity National Financial, Inc. Chairman of the Research and Development Institute at the Air Force Academy.

Yet another Iran-contra connection to 9/11 sat on the Bio-Port board:

> Admiral William J. Crowe, Jr.: Named a director in March 1999. From 1985-89, the Admiral held the position of chairman of the Joint Chiefs under President Reagan. After retirement from the military in 1989, Admiral Crowe was a counselor at the Center for Strategic and International Studies in Washington. He has also served as chairman of the notorious President's Foreign Intelligence Advisory Board, 1993-94, and served as U.S. ambassador to the UK and Northern Ireland, 1994-97. Admiral Crowe has been a director of Merrill Lynch, Texaco and General Dynamics. He is currently a director of Bioport and Intervac, an investment firm. He is a part-time senior advisor to Global Options LLC. Admiral Crowe commanded U.S. forces in the Middle East, was the commander-in-chief of NATO forces in Southern Europe, and headed up the nation's largest geographical military operation, the U.S. Pacific Command.[19]

---

18. Alex Constantine, "Adm. Crowe, Bioport and the Put Option Activity," December 5, 2001. http://groups.google.com/ groups?hl=en&lr=&frame=right&th=88439d-0c0d6bf5d2&seekm=alexx1265A234.12015319122000%40nntp.we.mediaone.net
19. CSIS web site: http://www.csis.org/html/alumni/crowew.html14) E-mail exchange with author, December 5, 2001.

Military, industrial; but the Project Anthrax complex reaches deeply into the financial sector. It's in BioPort's own records. Compare them with the well-known put option activity preceding 9/11, find jostling for position in financial circles that suggests premeditation in the anthrax attacks, according to a Napa Valley, California investment consultant asked to respond to this report:

> Niv Harizman was with Alex. Brown (BT for Bankers Trust). This is the firm that executed the 'puts' prior to September 11, plunging the stocks of American Airlines, United Airlines, Boeing, some brokerage houses, and several reinsurance companies (some inter-locked) including AXA Assurance, Swiss Re and Munich Re. These trades hubbed from Alex. Brown, which was acquired with Deutsche Bank's acquisition of Bankers Trust. The gent heading Alex. Brown unit, Deutsche's trading-brokerage arm, was terminated rather suddenly. Former director of enforcement for SEC, Richard Walker, took a position as staff counsel for Deutsche.
>
> Niv Harizman represents the dark side of the Chicago Board of Options Exchange (put into play by First Chicago Group's Robert Angelo Podesta) when Peter G. Peterson (schooled by MI-6) was Secretary of Commerce in 1972-73 under Richard Nixon. And Robert Podesta was UnderSecretary of Commerce – both Chicago – pushed through legislation to approve creation of Chicago Board of Options Exchange. (Can't have options trading as it exists in its current form without options on equities to pair, i.e., can't have a bubble economy without a bubble machine). Peterson, currently chairman of the New York Fed, moved up the ranks along notorious Chicago bank lines – 1985 sets up the Blackstone Group and [Iran-contra's] Frank Carlucci sets up the Carlyle Group the same year. Admiral Crowe, following retirement in 1989, held board positions at Merrill Lynch, General Dynamics and Texaco, all very 'Republican' companies at the time ... [20]

---

20. Ibid.

Intermission: Press Gallery

Blackstone Group, Larry Silverstein, Kroll Associates, Eliot Spitzer

http://www.nymegaphone.com/node/24

New York real estate baron Larry Silverstein became primary lease-holder on the World Trade Center a mere six weeks
before 9/11. It had never changed hands before. For a down
payment, Silverstein put up only $14 million of his own mon-
ey, and his friends at the powerful investment bank Blackstone
Group kicked in another $111 million. After 9/11, Silverstein
demanded a whopping $7 billion insurance payout, in the form
of two $3.5 billion payments. He argued the two different plane
crashes were two separate "occurrences" of two separate attacks.

The Megaphone has now learned that as attorney general,
Spitzer got involved behind the scenes, and in the courts, filing a amicus curiae ("friend of the court") brief on Silverstein's
behalf on Jan. 15, 2003. For years, this brief languished in the
files of the public records room on the 17th floor of the Second Circuit Court in Manhattan, until it was discovered and
brought to The New York Megaphone by NYC attorney and
author Carl Person. The court ended up agreeing with Spitzer
and Silverstein, over-turning the decision of a lower court.
Spitzer helped mid-wife a fat compromise and an eventual
$4.5 billion payout for Silverstein. The Megaphone's multiple
requests for comment from Governor Spitzer were ignored.

Attorney Carl Person told The Megaphone, "I was sur-
prised to see that Spitzer had used his position as attorney
general to support one private litigant over another. Normally, this is not done..."

Silverstein's World Trade Center Building 7 collapsed at
5:20 p.m. on 9/11. It wasn't hit by an airplane. Thirty seven
eyewitnesses working on the ground as firefighters, EMTs
and reporters recalled being warned in advance the tower was
coming down. The official story however, claims a fire ignited
a fuel tank in the building, hastening its sudden collapse.

WTC 7 was the NY headquarters of CIA and the SEC
office investigating Enron. 9/11 skeptics believe the building
was taken down by controlled demolition.

The Kroll Connection

This past August, another scandal radiated from the Spitzer
circle. This time it was Nixon's arch-strategist Roger Stone

leaving a threatening voice mail for Spitzer's dad, Bernard. Stone allegedly claimed he would subpoena the elder Spitzer for the $5 million in illegal loans. Spitzer senior made to his son during his 1998 Attorney General campaign. Stone denied he had made the call. To prove he did, the Spitzer family hired Kroll Associates to trace the call. Why Kroll? Spitzer has a long relationship with this powerful, cryptic security company.

Kroll's CEO on 9/11 was one of Spitzer's old mentors from the Manhattan DA's office, Michael Cherkasky. Cherkasky investigated bank BCCI (which had links to both Islamic terror and the CIA), and the mysterious 1993 World Trade Center (WTC) bombing. Cherkasky's 2002 book Forewarned: Why the Government is Failing to Protect Us, and What We Must Do to Protect Ourselves is a confused mix of fear-mongering and insider's analysis. He sheepishly admits that the CIA was in part culpable for the 1993 WTC bombing, since they helped pull known terrorist "Blind Sheikh" Abdel bin-Rahman into the country. Cherkasky admits the FBI had a mole inside Rahman's 1993 WTC bombing cell, and lays blame for the bombing on the FBI.

After observing the 1993 WTC bombing as an operation penetrated by CIA and FBI, Cherkasky he became head of Kroll, the "the CIA of Wall Street." Kroll took on the management of WTC after the 1993 bombing. Blackstone Group, the same financiers who backed the Larry Silverstein, have also been involved with Kroll, owning big chunks of Kroll stock on occasion, according to SEC reports.

Cherkasky has donated $14,500 to Eliot Spitzer's political campaigns.

The Anthrax Connection

Eliot Spitzer's connection to key 9/11 players extends to a fellow life-long Democrat, Jerome Hauer, managing director of Kroll on 9/11. Jerome Hauer and Rudolph Giuliani were indicted by the San Diego Citizens Grand Jury.

According to Bay Area News, Hauer warned the Bush White House to go on Cipro, the anti-anthrax drug, on 9/11/01. Hauer denied this allegation to The Megaphone. The White House did go on Cipro. Six days later, the anthrax attacks began and sent the country into further paroxysms of terror.

Government watchdog group Judicial Watch demanded to know who warned the Bush White House, but not the public, about anthrax. The White House stonewalled on JW's Freedom of Information Act requests.

"I read that the White House did know, and they went on the antibiotics," says Judicial Watch founder Larry Klayman. He was involved because, "African American employees at Brentwood [US Postal Facility] were basically left out there to twist in the wind when the white guys up on Capitol Hill got immediate treatment."

Post-9/11, Jerome Hauer went on to be coordinator of the National Institute of Health investigation of the anthrax murders. His report blamed Osama bin Laden and al Qaeda. That assertion has been widely discredited, since the five deaths in 2001 were from a fine, "weaponized" form of anthrax, the "Ames Strain" that only the U.S. military and U.S. federal government possessed.

On 9/11, Jerome Hauer appeared on television with Dan Rather. Rather posited that the 9/11 attacks must have had state sponsorship. Hauer urged Rather to blame Bin Laden. When Rather voiced suspicions about the way the buildings fell, Hauer offered that they simply came down because they were hit by a plane. Without an investigation, Hauer somehow knew two major parts of 9/11's official story before it emerged.

Hauer is biological terrorism expert whose resume includes time at Science Applications International Corp. (SAIC), a military contractor doing work in nuclear issues and psyops, also Bioport, manufacturer of the controversial anthrax vaccine.

and anthrax go way Jerry Hauer back. In May of 1998, he spoke at the Council on Foreign Relations on the topic of "Building a 'Biobomb': Terrorist Challenge."

That evening Hauer co-presented with Steven Hatfill on the topic.

A year after their CFR presentations, Hatfill and Hauer would become coworkers at SAIC's Center for Counterterrorism Technology and Analysis.

Hatfill worked at Ft. Detrick, the U.S. Army's bio-weapons lab in Maryland. He was never convicted or even prosecuted. A judge ruled that five top national reporters would have to reveal the confidential government sources who fingered Hatfill.

In his interview with The Megaphone, Hauer repeatedly referred to the Grand Jury as "a bunch of nutjobs" and he defended Steven Hatfill. But when asked directly if Hatfill was innocent, Hauer was less than clear:"I think that the FBI should not have said anything about Hatfill until they knew more. I do not believe Hatfill is a murderer. And I think Steve

Hatfill is very passionate, but I don't think he's a murderer, and I don't believe he did it."

Hauer was not willing to conclusively say that Hatfill was uninvolved in the anthrax attacks, stating, "I'm not going to get into those details."

Of the five people who died from anthrax exposure, one was a New Yorker. Kathy Nguyen, a hospital worker in the Bronx, was a victim of inhalation anthrax. She died alone in a hospital on October 31, 2001.

A 2004 petition gathered 100,000 signatures begging then-Attorney General Eliot Spitzer to investigate the true source of the 2001 anthrax mailings. A Zogby poll that year likewise found that 66 per cent of voters wanted Eliot Spitzer to tackle these tough questions. What those poll respondents didn't know is that Spitzer can't investigate 9/11 or anthrax. He would have to indict his friends from Kroll, Jerry Hauer and Michael Cherkasky. That's the real scandal.

Scam: Bear Stearns – Timothy Geithner & the Blackstone-BCCI Set-Up

Summary

The Blackstone Group (a major private equity firm tied to foreign policy influence lobbying groups such as Kissinger Associates, Scowcroft Advisors, and the Madeline Albright Group) had an affiliate, BlackRock, evaluate the "fairness" to shareholders of the JP Morgan acquisition of Bear Stearns. The deal involved a bailout of Bear Stearns creditors through cash infusions via the Fed's open window of lending, including the lending of billions to Citibank in exchange for mortgage collateral. The lead negotiator of the deal, the President of the NY Fed, Tim Geithner, is a former employee of Kissinger Associates, a Saudi-China lobbying firm, and was appointed to the Fed by Peter Peterson at Blackstone. He also worked for Secretary Rubin at the Clinton Treasury Department. Secretary Rubin went on to be an executive at Citibank, a major beneficiary of the bailout. Citibank has major Saudi shareholders and as such is not really an American bank. Citibank has been investigated for illegal terrorist money laundering activities in the Middle East, and Geithner was an employee at Kissinger Associates when it was engaged in merger discussions with BCCI, later indicted for drug money laundering.

Chronology

1986: East Asian International economic specialist Timothy Geithner joins Kissinger and Associates, a major Chinese Financial lobbying firm with ties to the Kingdom of Saudi Arabia. At the time, both Kissinger and Brent Scowcroft are partners, and so is international economist Alan Stoga. It is not clear whether Geitner worked with Stoga at this time, but his expertise in China would be welcome in its China Joint Venture.

1988: Blackstone forms BlackRock as a mortgage investment subsidiary. Its CEO is Peter Peterson, also CEO of the Council on Foreign Relations. Henry Kissinger, Brent Scowcroft, and Robert Rubin are officers.

1986-89: Kissinger Associates, Stoga and consultant/ambassador Sergio Correa discuss a merger between BCCI and Kissinger Associates. Correa acts as a front man for BCCI in acquisition explorations as a paid retained consultant to both BCCI, and separately to Kissinger Associates. Stoga arranges contacts between BCCI Saudi-linked executives Gaith Pharaon and Abol Helmy. It is not known whether Geithner worked on these transactions.

c. 1989: BCCI is indicted, Kissinger Associates ends discussions. Geithner leaves Kissinger Associates and begins work as a civil servant in the Treasury Department. He is confirmed as Asst. Secretary for International Affairs in Treasury working for Secretary Rubin of the Clinton Administration.

1992: BlackRock is a spinoff of Blackstone and becomes independent.

2002: Geithner joins International Monetary Fund.

2003: Blackstone CEO Peter Peterson names Geithner as President of the New York Federal Reserve Bank.

2007: Peterson's Blackstone sells 3-billion dollar stake in Blackstone to the People's Republic of China. Rubin 's Citibank receives billions in bailout loans in exchange for mortgage collateral.

March 2008: Blackrock creates a firm to buy distressed mortgage securities

April 3, 2008: Blackstone mentioned as advisor to Bear Stearns valuation, later amended to be Blackrock, founded by Blackstone.[21]

21. "Bernanke Defends Fed's Role in Bear Stearns Deal." http://www.pbs.org/news-

BlackRock?

NewYork Fed Names Timothy F. Geithner President

BlackRock is set to profit from Mortgage Distress Bailout. The new company has been formed by BlackRock, High-fields, and a management team of mortgage industry led by Stanford Kurland, Private National Mortgage Acceptance Company's (PennyMac) chairman and CEO. PennyMac will raise capital from private investors, acquire loans from financial institutions seeking to reduce its mortgage exposures, and seek to create value for both borrowers and investors through distinctive loan servicing.[22]

Part III

Bruce "Lone Gunman" Ivins, Bioport, Booz-Allen Hamilton, the CIA & the Bush Administration

... Bruce Ivins ... played a lead role in helping a private company, BIOPORT, win regulatory approval to continue making the vaccine required for U.S. service personnel deployed to Iraq, Afghanistan and other regions. From 2000 to early 2002, Ivins and two colleagues from USAMRIID helped BioPort resolve problems related to the potency of the vaccine. Because of those and other manufacturing difficulties, production had been suspended. The efforts of Ivins and his colleagues helped BioPort win FDA approval to resume production....
http://rinf.com/alt-news/war-terrorism/anthrax-scientist-bruce-ivins-stood-to-benefit-from-a-panic/4228/

Bioport

The stock market symbol for BioPort, Inc. needs to be pi – its corruption goes on indefinitely, or so it seems when you begin to sift through the records. ...

hour/updates/business/jan-june08/fed_04-03.html; "BCCI AND KISSINGER ASSOCIATES," Congressional Report, 1992. http://www.fas.org/irp/congress/1992_rpt/bcci/20kiss.htmBlackstone?" http://www.corpwatch.org/article.php?id=14995
22. http://www.banking-business-review.com/article_news.asp?guid=17D0DB88-3917-44F6-AFF3-1D1AECC10E77

Fuad El-Hibri

The company's founder and CEO is Mr. Fuad El-Hibri, a German of Lebanese extraction and a naturalized American citizen. In 1998, El-Hibri entered into a leveraged buyout of theState of Michigan-owned Biological Products Institute (MBPI). This company held the exclusive contract on the U.S. supply of anthrax vaccine ... and it wasn't all that effective against the disease from the start. The *Wall Street Journal* discovered: "While its vaccine worked well against the Vollum strain of anthrax (used by Russia), it was more problematic against the Ames strain." So the company "conducted tests with the virulent Ames strain on guinea pigs, mice and monkeys with mixed results. BioPort's spokesperson confirmed that it had access to the virulent Ames strain for testing on animals."

For the sole purpose of acquiring MBPI, El-Hibri became an American citizen. He gave retired Admiral William J. Crowe Jr. a large chunk of Intervac, "one of the corporations involved in the maneuver. The controlling shareholder was the same I&F Holdings used to take control of the British biotech lab, CAMR." The company was rebranded BioPort, and it "controlled America's anthrax vaccine, was apparently of some interest to scientists in Afghanistan since an environmental assessment report of its planned laboratory renovations turned up in the house of a Pakistani scientist in Kabul."[23]

Crowe made no investment in either company, but owns 22.5 percent of all Intervac shares. Another 30 percent went to El-Hibri's wife. In 1999, ABC reported that the remainder of the Intervac shares were "in the hands of I&F Holdings, a company directed by Nancy El-Hibri's father-in-law, Ibrahim El-Hibri, a Venezuelan citizen, and her husband, Fuad El-Hibri, a German citizen of Lebanese descent.... Crowe's ownership of Intervac stock gives him a 13 percent share of Bioport."

The company's web site lists El-Hibri's bona fides: "... helped establish regional offices in Singapore and Sydney for Booz-Allen & Hamilton..."

23. Edward Jay Epstein, "FBI Overlooks Foreign Sources of Anthrax," *Wall Street Journal*, December 24, 2001. http://edwardjayepstein.com/archived/anthrax.htm 2) *ABC News, 20/20* (March 12, 1999).

In 1990, El-Hibri also arranged the purchase of anthrax vaccine for Saudi Arabia. Did he perform this service for Booz-Allen or the CIA? The well-connected security firm had extensive ties to the intelligence sector – and silky Fahd palaces, as well.

Students of the CIA know Booz-Allen as a privatized branch of the Agency with Saudi defense contracts worth billions. The company trained the Saudi marine corps and operates the country's Armed Forces Staff College.[24] On 14 June 2000, the Pentagon's Defense Security Cooperation Agency announced that the Royal Saudi Naval Forces had begun a ten year development program that drew on the services of two American contractors – SAIC and Booz-Allen Hamilton.[25]

The FBI's Dale Watson was a leading "investigator" of the 1993 WTC bombing, the Oklahoma City bombing, the East Africa Embassy bombings, Khobar Towers, USS Cole, the September 11 attacks and the anthrax mailings before he "retired" to work for Booz-Allen Hamilton. Former CIA director James Woolsey is a VP there.

> As a Senior Associate and resident project manager, Mr. El-Hibri led consulting projects in Jakarta, Kuala Lumpur, Singapore, Sydney, and Wellington. Before joining Booz-Allen, he was a manager of Citicorp in New York (Mergers and Acquisitions) and in Jeddah, Saudi Arabia.

All of this is more than grounds for investigation. In January 2003, the *Free Press* web site opined:

> Let's recall Bush's strange relationship with that bizarre little company in Lansing, Michigan, known as Bioport. The company, despite failing various FDA inspections and being accused of bad record-keeping, holds the only federal contract for producing the anthrax vaccine. Bush has rewarded Bioport with favors such as ongoing mili-

24. Ken Silverstein, "Privatizing War: How affairs of state are outsourced to corporations beyond public control," *The Nation*, July 28, 1997. http://www.mtholyoke.edu/acad/intrel/silver.htm
25. GlobalSecurity.org, "Royal Saudi Naval Forces (RSNF)": http://www.globalsecurity.org/military/world/gulf/rsnf.htm

tary protection, and within weeks of 9/11 granted them a contract that tripled the price per vaccine.

Now, add into the mix that the Strangelovian CIA-connected Battelle and Britain's top secret Porton Down labs are partners with Bioport.... Public records and foreign press reports have linked El-Hibri to the selling of anthrax to Saudi Arabia after the Pentagon refused to. He's also a business associate of the bin Laden family. A real Congressional investigation of Bush's relationships with the bin Laden family, El-Hibri and the related drug bank BCCI would easily lead to the President's impeachment.[26]

The ABC report was a horror show of rampant side-effects produced by BioPort. The bottom line was human agony:

Widespread Mistrust Among The Ranks
20/20 REPORT

PFC Matthew Baker who was stationed at Fort Stewart, Ga. went AWOL after his first sergeant threatened to have him strapped to a gurney and forcibly injected with the anthrax vaccine.

MAJ Sonnie Bates, USAF, one of many pilots at Dover, AFB Del. was headed for a court martial and up to five years in prison until he went on 60 Minutes and told what was going on. Soon the Air Force scrapped their hard-line tactics and Bates was allowed to leave the service.

More than a dozen members of Bates' squadron came down sick with a variety of illnesses. Thyroid and liver damage, memory loss, bone and joint pain, fevers, dizziness, infected cysts and lesions. The only common thread was these maladies immediately followed anthrax injections.

In a letter to the Air Force, Bates stated his position was a matter of principle.

I'm doing what I've always been trained and taught to do. If you know it's right, you stand up for it. And likewise, if you know it's wrong, you have to challenge it, no matter what the consequences.

26. Bob Fitrakis, "Impeach Bush," *Free Press* Site. http://www.freepress.org/columns/display/3/2003/22

After 13 years of exemplary service to my country, I am willing to give up my job, my rank, and everything I have worked for to avoid taking an unsafe drug.

Army SPC Kevin Edwards started to feel sick a few weeks after his third anthrax shot. He nearly died. Bleeding sores covered the soldier's entire body. Rep. Walter Jones of North Carolina said he could barely keep his composure after seeing pictures taken of Edwards at an Army hospital. Jones is one of three dozen congressmen calling for a halt to the forced anthrax immunization program.

Texas Army National Guard CPT Jody Grenga, a medical operations officer with nearly 18 years service, was kicked out of the Army for refusing the anthrax shots on religious grounds. The highly respected officer said she also refused the immunizations because of her medical history of adverse reactions to medications.

PFC Jemekia Barber, an African-American Army soldier who was forced out of the service with a less-than-honorable discharge after she refused the shots, has filed suit in U.S. District Court in Colorado. Her lawyers contend the mandatory shot order violated Barber's Constitutional rights. Herbert Fenster argued that because his client is of child-bearing age, ordering her to take the anthrax vaccine injections could subject her to risk of bearing a child with birth defects.

Two former Connecticut Air National Guard pilots, MAJ Russell Dingle and MAJ Thomas "Buzz" Rempfer said they concluded the Pentagon's use of the vaccine was illegal because of serious questions about its safety and effectiveness. They said they refused an order to not to talk to the press, and with seven other pilots in their unit, the 103rd Fighter Wing, resigned.

More than thirty pilots and 17 KC-10 tanker crew-members at Travis AFB in California quit rather than take the shots. So did pilots in the Wisconsin Air National Guard. And Air Force Capt. Clifton Volpe, assigned to a VIP transport squadron at Andrews AFB Maryland, is getting the boot for refusing to take the controversial injections.

Perhaps the most eloquent of the military opponents of the mandatory anthrax inoculation program is retired Air Force Lt. Col. Redmond Handy. Named the "most outstanding officer" in 1996 by the Reserve Officers Association, Handy was a full colonel on "the fast track to stars" when he quit his Pentagon job and decided to speak out. He didn't have the minimum time in grade requirement as a full colonel, but Handy put principle ahead of pay and left the Air Force as a light colonel.

> It is appalling that Admiral Crowe, who was a key player in the effort to let all U.S. citizens sleep better at night by leading our defenders of freedom to defeat communism, now keeps these same defenders and their families awake at night wondering if their health will be defeated by his company's product.

Intermission II: Bruce Ivins and BioPort

From "The Anthrax Attacks: Sunlight Is the Best Disinfectant," by Bill Simpich, *IndyMedia*, August 4, 2008:

> Ivins' work is the focus of a 2004 book by Gary Matsumoto, *Vaccine A: The Covert Government Experiment That's Killing Our Soldiers*. Matsumoto is not shy about making controversial statements, which only adds to the aura of intrigue around both Ivins and himself.
> The premise of Vaccine A is that since the 1991 Gulf War US soldiers have been unwittingly exposed to a "second-generation" experimental anthrax vaccine designed by Ivins and his colleagues, which improperly contained an oil-based substance known as squalene. Matsumoto and others claim squalene is the main cause of the auto-immune disorder known as "Gulf War Syndrome." From 1991 to the present day, many soldiers have refused to submit to military vaccinations for anthrax for fear of contracting Gulf War Syndrome. There are strong arguments on both sides of the squalene dispute, and this is an ongoing controversy.
> The work of Bruce Ivins is known to many of these vets – especially those who suffered Gulf War Syndrome,

or those who were court-martialed for refusing to use the vaccine in fear it was tainted. It is intriguing that Matsumoto paid special attention to Ivins, claiming that Ivins knew that the experimental oil-boosted vaccine "can provoke toxic, allergic, ulcerative, or lethal reactions."

Matsumuto's 2004 book focuses on Ivins as the man with the motive to be pushing to get approval for the new second-generation vaccine.

Only one paper at the workshop reported near perfect results – 100 percent protection from the Ames strain with just one or two shots ... As an old Marine Corps expression goes, this particular paper shined "like a diamond inside a goat's ass."

USAMRIID's Bruce Ivins had reported at this very same workshop that his "one-shot wonder" – protective antigen or mere fragments of it combined with oil additives – protected every animal challenged with Ames with a single injection." Matsumoto, Vaccine A, page 87.

The BioThrax vaccine was approved by Homeland Security in 2006. It is currently the only anthrax vaccine approved for use. Made by the BioPort Corporation, the new vaccine is derived from Ivins' experimental second-generation vaccine – however, BioPort maintains that no squalene is involved in its manufacture. The controversy continues – and Matsumoto's role in controversy will return later on.

A little background on the origins of the anthrax vaccine dispute is helpful here. On December 15, 1997, Secretary of Defense William S. Cohen announced that all US military personnel would be vaccinated in order to guard against the biological warfare agent anthrax, which was allegedly proliferating as a bioweapon in other nations. Rep. Christopher Shays, at the beginning of a 1999 hearing on oversight of the anthrax vaccine inoculation program, asked: "Why would active duty, Reserve and National Guard personnel jeopardize their military careers, and even their liberty, rather than take the vaccine? ... The missing element of the mandatory anthrax vaccine program is trust. Radiation testing, Agent Orange, the reckless use of experimental drugs and mysterious Gulf War illness have made military men and women understandably distrustful of the Pentagon on medical matters."

The controversy over the anthrax vaccine among US military troops has been constant from the first Gulf War to the present. In a 2003 decision, US District Court Judge Emmet Sullivan ruled in favor of six anonymous military litigants, holding that the military's mandatory administration of the vaccine was illegal because the Food and Drug Administration had not approved its use for inhalation anthrax, only for anthrax contracted through the skin.

Judge Sullivan's ruling forced the Pentagon to suspend its involuntary program almost continually between December 2003 and February 2007, until the FDA ruled the vaccine was safe and efficient for all forms of anthrax and permitted the Pentagon to reorder. Based on this decision, another federal judge admonished the Air Force Board in April 2008, for refusing to compensate military personnel for refusing the vaccine between 1999 and 2004. ...[27]

Part IV

The BioPort Loop, Hatfill & Special Forces, Introduction to Vaxgen, Ivins Redux & Rumsfeld

The media concentration on the anthrax mailings took the heat off of BioPort and DoD for the highly toxic vaccine – which, by some measures, produced a medical situation far more dire than that brought about by the 2001 mailings blamed on Bruce Ivins:

"Our family has been through a living hell, to almost see your 23-year-old son die..." exclaims Cheryl. "The government is wrong, and they need to take care of all these people that they've hurt." The Department of Defense says they continue to believe that the vaccine is "safe" – Firstcoastnews.com

27. http://www.indybay.org/newsitems/2008/08/04/18522953.php

Fuad El-Hibri arranged investments for well-heeled Saudi clients as a broker at Citibank's Jeddah office. Tom Suber, a contributor to the Rouge Forum, a grassroots Internet think-tank, reports that the broker handled "the individual financial holdings of the bin Laden family group and the larger $18 billion Carlyle Group."

The bin Ladens and Carlyle are "reputed to have had *partnership* interests with Fuad El-Hibri's Porton International and Bioport investments. These embarrassing partnerships are the result of complex web of interlocking private corporate holdings and are publicly denied by the El-Hibri family."[28]

Carlyle Management Group, of course, is America's eleventh leading defense contractor, founded by Iran-contra's Frank Carlucci, James Baker III and George H.W. Bush.

Ties to the bin Ladens and Carlyle constituted one "embarrassing" pact with the devil.

Another was El-Hibri's acquisition of the Center for Applied Microbiology and Research (CAMR) at Porton Down in the UK, a government-held toxic stockpile-research laboratory privatized by Margaret Thatcher. CAMR was launched under private ownership – El-Hibri's – as Porton International in 1993.

Porton Down was the English mirror-image of Ft. Detrick. Both military laboratories conducted Auschwitz-style experiments on human subjects during the Cold War. In 2002, *Express* reported that scientists of the Ministry of Defense faced prosecution "over *horrifying experiments on service men and women* during chemical and biological weapons tests."

Subjects were duped into volunteering, led to believe that the military doctors were searching for an innocuous "cold cure." The guinea-pigs said they were "impregnated with deadly chemical agents such as sarin and mustard gas." Ronald Maddison, a volunteer airman, died after a cloth treated with sarin was wrapped round his arm. Another subject said he was coerced to participate "under threat of court martial. During three nightmare weeks at the center, he said he was stripped

28. Tom Suber, "3500 Martin Luther King Jr. Blvd," Rouge Forum, February 2003. http://www.pipeline.com/~rgibson/rouge_forum/newspaper/winter2003/Suber-Anthrax.htm

to his underpants and marched repeatedly into gas chambers where he was impregnated with sarin, tabin and mustard gas."[29]

El-Hibri inherited a horror factory, and this it remained.

By 1996, Suber says, "the rape of the public resources of Great Britain was virtually complete," speaking of the conservative agenda behind privatization. The profit-lusting "interests of the Saudis and the Carlyle Group began to look to the United States for more promising plunder."

Michigan Governor John Engler was urged by fellow Republicans to privatize the state-owned vaccination lab – exactly as Thatcher had done with CAMR. It was renamed the Michigan Biologics Products Institute.

> Governor Engler gave the most respectable and profitable agency in Michigan government to Fuad El-Hibri without any individual investment whatsoever," Suber writes. The new owners "incurred no individual expense, made no investments, and did not owe any individual promissory notes or obligations of any kind for their new lab purchase." Receipt of a $180 million business for absolutely nothing. The next hand-out the company received was an unsecured, interest-free loan of $18.7 million as an advance payment from the Defense Department.[30]

All this fuss over a vaccine that didn't even work against *inhalation* anthrax ... it made those already-afflicted *worse*.

But homeland defense was never the idea, as Houston attorney Linda Minor noted after scanning BioPort's directors' page: "This group is obviously an investment syndicate composed of numerous intelligence agency members representing assorted countries..."[31]

Bio-economic terrorism is the CIA's kind of low-intensity conflict. Dr. Edgar J. DaSilva, director of the Division

---

29. Alun Reesand Cyril Dixon, "Scandal of the British soldiers 'poisoned in MoD tests,'" Express, November 7 , 2000. http://www.mindcontrolforums.com/profreedom.co.uk/n1020-d.html
30. Suber. Also see: Subcommittee on National Security, Veterans Affairs, and International Relations of the House Committee on Government Reform, June 30, 1999.
31. Linda Minor, e-mail exchange with author, November 8, 2004.

of Life Sciences of the UN, says the approach is predicated on "the undermining and destruction of economic progress and stability" by "the development and use of biological agents against economic targets such as crops, livestock and ecosystems."

Germs, bacilli and viruses have certain advantages over conventional armaments – explosives and noxious gases have to be explained, but viral agents are plausibly deniable: "Such warfare can always be carried out under the pretexts that such traumatic occurrences are the result of natural circumstances that lead to outbreaks of diseases and disasters of either endemic or epidemic proportions."[32]

The Zimbabwe anthrax outbreak, and the West Nile Virus, were conceived at SAIC-USAMRIID, for instance. Add a trained provocateur – a biochemical warfare specialist hailing from a Rhodesian death squad with a parafascist history will do – a little media manipulation, and the result is anthrax psychosis.

That's exactly what the collective response was called in Argentina when a false alarm was tripped by a suspect piece of mail. "Anthrax psychosis," an Argentine newspaper reported, spread in October 2001, "when a travel brochure mailed from Miami to a Buenos Aires family initially tested positive." The spores tested inactive the second time, but "within hours, frantic citizens swamped police stations, hospitals and all kinds of government offices throughout the country with about 1,000 pieces of suspicious mail, most of them posted from the United States or Pakistan."[33]

The Ames strain did get around. The lethal dust was found in mail rooms … in a Princeton borough … in the Senate … in Dan Rather's CBS office … in a Kabul factory … in New York City Hall … in a diplomatic pouch to the US Consulate General in Yekaterinburg, Russia … in the Supreme Court's base-

32. Wayne Madsen, "Combining biological and economic warfare," Online Journal, May 3, 2003. http://www.911review.org/Wget/www.onlinejournal.com/Special_Reports/050303Ma dsen/050303madsen.html
33. Juan Pérez Cabral, "Anthrax, Anti-Semitism and Anguish In Argentina," November 9, 2001. http://www.thegully.com/essays/argentina/011109_debt_default_wtc.html

ment mailroom ... in a letter mailed to Kenya ... at the Bureau of Prisons headquarters in Washington ... at the broadcaster's headquarters ... 30 Rockefeller Plaza ... and on and on.

And the FBI, by focusing on Hatfill alone, gave the impression that the perpetrator was a lone nut. But he had accomplices, and apparently ran with a death squad in the United States as he did in Rhodesia.

The West Nile and anthrax plots – as reconstructed by Leonard Horowitz, Robert Lederman and other independent researchers – began with the meeting at the White House regarding the fate of OraVax, attended by representatives of the company, the administration, and DoD officials. It was agreed that the company, facing bankruptcy, would receive a pass to inventory vaccines.

But some of those attending this meeting were active in this American Pinay Circle. One of them was William Patrick III, President and CEO of Advanced Biosystems Inc. (ABS). Patrick ran the anthrax "weaponization" program at the Ft. Detrick-SAIC lab where Hatfill worked. In 1999, Patrick wrote a study, according to the *Baltimore Sun*, that discussed "the danger of anthrax spores spreading through the air and the requirements for decontamination after various kinds of attacks. The author, William C. Patrick III, describes placing 2.5 grams of Bacillus globigii, an anthrax simulant, in a standard business envelope – slightly more than the estimated amount of anthrax in each of the letters that killed five people last fall..."

Stephen Hatfill, come to find out, "is a friend and protegé of Patrick, 75, a bio-weapons legend who has himself experienced the dual status of expert and possible suspect..."[34]

"Protegé?"

In 2002, the *Washington Post* reported allegations that Partick had produced a blueprint for the anthrax mailings:

Hatfill commissioned William Patrick III, a biological weapons expert, to write a report on how to deal with

34. Scott Shane, "Scientist theorized anthrax mail attack – FBI searched apartment of expert linked to study," *Baltimore Sun*, June 27, 2002. http://www.baltimoresun.com/bal-te.anthrax27jun27,0,3331733.story

anthrax sent through the mail. "It was a public service," Glasberg said, and Patrick was paid only $500. Hatfill and a colleague took Patrick's report to the Centers for Disease Control and Prevention in Atlanta and submitted it to its bioterrorism preparation center. The CDC was working on the same project, Glasberg said, and produced the same findings and recommendations as Patrick...

The concept of a report on anthrax mail attacks – two years before last October's mailings – intrigued the FBI. In particular, Patrick's report discussed mailing 2.5 grams of anthrax powder, about the same amount contained in the deadly anthrax letters.

Glasberg said Patrick used 2.5 grams because that was the amount of talc he poured into an envelope, as a test, to see how much could pass unobtrusively through the mails. Some media reports have called Patrick's report a "blueprint" for the fatal mailings...

Boris Lederer, who worked with Hatfill at Science Applications International, recalled his colleague's reaction when the anthrax mailings occurred. "It was just shock and complete disbelief that this was happening," Lederer said.[35]

Disbelief at a lethal domestic covert operation? The most relevant clues went unreported by the "mainstream" media, for instance, per the *Washington Post:*

> Hatfill's résumé detailing those periods has created another storm. Hatfill claimed on a 1997 résumé that he served in the Army Special Forces. Army records show that he enlisted in the Reserve in 1975, served a year of active duty and attended — but dropped out of – Special Forces training. Glasberg declined to comment on Hatfill's military record... [36]

The relevant corporate connections, ala BioPort, were played down. One of them was especially interesting in light of the deep history of the AIDS virus. McClatchy:

35. Tom Jackman, "Ex-Army Scientist Denies Role in Anthrax Attacks," *Washington Post*, August 11, 2002.
36. Ibid.

Before the Sept. 11 attacks, Ivins had worked on and held a share of two anthrax vaccine patents, at least one of which was licensed to VaxGen, Inc., a California firm that later won an $877 million contract to make the vaccine for the U.S. Department of Health and Human Services' Bioshield program. But when VaxGen failed to meet deadlines, the government scrapped the contract...[37]

Background details of the VaxGen contract reveal a motive for one of the mailings. The motive for the overall plot centers on this pharmaceutical house – VaxGen and BioPort together had the most to gain from the patent on the anthrax vaccine, though this charge has since been widely leveled at the late Bruce Ivins:

A few months before he was targeted in the deadly 2001 anthrax attacks, then-Senate Majority Leader Tom Daschle sent a letter to Defense Secretary Donald Rumsfeld questioning whether the anthrax vaccine the military was giving soldiers was unsafe and should be discontinued. The letter, obtained by The Courant, was written with the help of a number of Connecticut officials. They were concerned about complaints from local National Guard members who refused to take the vaccine because they feared it would make them ill.

Apart from raising the issue of the vaccine's safety, the criticism may have had an unintended effect. NBC News reported Tuesday that federal authorities today will reveal that those same complaints could be among the motives in the anthrax attacks that left an Oxford woman and four others dead.

The suspected killer, Bruce Ivins, was one of the Army's lead scientists on the anthrax vaccine and was angered by suggestions that it made recipients ill, NBC reported...

Ivins ... was a member of a panel that the government convened to study the vaccine's effectiveness... The committee was formed by the Department of Defense before the anthrax mailings and was still meeting at the time the letters were mailed, according to Chairman Jack Melling. He is the former head of Porton Down.[38]

37. http://www.mcclatchydc.com/251/story/46642.html
38. Marisa Taylor and Greg Gordo, "After suicide, prosecutors reveal circumstan-

Now the anatomy of an inside job becomes apparent to anyone – even Americans reporters – there was no "lone gunman." Donald Rumsfeld was in the loop:

> In the letter to Rumsfeld, Daschle raised concerns that the vaccine didn't work and may have made soldiers sick. He noted that the U.S. Food and Drug Administration approves drugs only after they are proven safe and effective.
>
> "A growing number of people believe that the use of the anthrax vaccine as currently formulated to protect humans against inhalation of anthrax spores fails to meet this test," wrote Daschle, a South Dakota Democrat. "We all acknowledge that the threat posed by biological weapons, including anthrax, is a real one that the Administration and the Congress have a responsibility to address."
>
> The letter, also signed by then House Minority Leader Richard Gephardt, was sent to Rumsfeld on June 21, 2001. The first anthrax letters were postmarked Sept. 18, 2001. The anthrax-laced letters sent to the offices of Daschle and Vermont Sen. Patrick Leahy were postmarked Oct. 9, 2001.
>
> Ottilie Lundgren, 94, of Oxford, was killed in November 2001 when she opened an anthrax-laced letter that passed through the same sorting machine in a New Jersey postal facility as the letter to Daschle. Daschle could not be reached for comment Tuesday night.
>
> He has criticized the FBI investigation of the anthrax letters and the agency's refusal to update him and other victims on their progress. The FBI is expected to meet with the victims and their families today and might release documents that authorities say link Ivins to the crime. Daschle got involved in the anthrax vaccine issue through U.S. Sen. Christopher Dodd of Connecticut and state Attorney General Richard Blumenthal, whose office represented Connecticut National Guard members who refused to take the anthrax vaccine.
>
> Blumenthal said Tuesday that attorneys in his office worked closely with Dodd and Daschle to craft the letter to Rumsfeld...[39]

tial anthrax case." McClatchy Newspapers. http://www.mcclatchydc.com/251/story/46642.html
39. Dave Alatimari, "Anthrax Vaccine Safety Complaints Part Of Ivins Case," Hart-

Part V

Operation Jefferson

You simply don't develop a new hyper-weaponized strain of anthrax powder for military defense, and then commission the top U.S. anthrax expert to report on this new weapon's capability and lethality from mailed delivery, unless that's how you foresee it being used.
– Ingri Cassel, director, National Vaccination Liberation Association

Officials in the post-9/11 war profiteering loop derive a childlike thrill from their weaponized anthrax stockpiles. A "new and highly lethal strain" was produced in advance of 9/11, a nameless Pentagon general told the *New York Times* in September 2001.

He mentioned something called Operation Jefferson.[40]

What was "Operation Jefferson?"

Before the anthrax mailings, William Patrick III went to work at the Battelle Memorial Institute (BMI) in West Jefferson, Ohio. Patrick holds five classified patents in the manufacture of weapons-grade anthrax.

BMI – a contractual partner of BioPort – hired him to conduct a risk-assessment study involving the dissemination of anthrax powder through the mail system.[41] The work was done at the BL-3 Anthrax Lab.[42]

Battelle had exclusive control of the Ames strain, a fact the press has not made clear. It's true that Dugway Proving Ground had an anthrax program of its own, as reported, but Battelle directed that program as well. This narrows it down quite a bit...

ford Courant, August 6, 2008. http://www.courant.com/news/nationworld/hc-anthrax0806.artaug06,0,5888202.story
40. Nick Papadimitriou, "Anthrax Attacks Linked to CIA and Drug Industry?" Institute of Science in Society (UK), February 14, 2002. http://www.i-sis.org.uk/isisnews/i-sisnews13-12.php
41. Ibid.
42. Bob Fitrakis, "Battelle Exposed In Anthrax Biochemical Conspiracy," FreePress.org, January 14, 2002.

The FBI was drawn straight to William Patrick III, Stephen Hatfill's "mentor" at Ft. Detrick, and Ken Alibeck, a BMI consultant with a background in CBW research for the Soviets.[43]

One independent Internet news site reports that the FBI investigated "the possibility that financial gain was the motive behind the anthrax mailings."

Two federal laboratories were searched, BMI and Dugway, but "a contradictory announcement was relayed the same day [December 21, 2001] by Ohio Senator Mike DeWine. Based on an ABC News report concerning a BMI employee who had been under FBI investigation for an anthrax threat, FBI Director Robert Mueller had, according to *The Dispatch*, assured Senator DeWine that the bureau was not investigating, nor intending to investigate, anyone with, or formerly with, BMI."[44]

Case closed.

Nevertheless, the FBI's stalling perplexed reporters assigned to the story. George Monbiot wrote in the *Guardian* in May 2002: "Last week, I phoned the FBI. Why, I asked, when the evidence was so abundant, did the trail appear to have gone cold? 'The investigation is continuing,' the spokesman replied. 'Has it gone cold because it has led you to a government office?' I asked. He put down the phone." Had the FBI spokesman remained on the line, there were a number of related outrages he might have explained:

> The Army's development of weaponized anthrax [the processed Ames strain], for example, directly contravenes both the biological weapons convention and domestic law. So does its plan to test live microbes in `aerosol chambers' at the Edgewood Chemical Biological Center, also in Maryland. So does its development of a genetically modified fungus for attacking coca crops in Colombia, and GM bacteria for destroying materials belonging to enemy forces. These, as the research group Project Sunshine has discovered, appear to be just a tiny sample of the illegal

43. Ibid.
44. Anon., "FBI Implicated in Anthrax Mailings Cover-up." http://www.world-newsstand.net/news/anthrax.htm

99

JACKALS - THE STENCH OF FASCISM

offensive biological research programmes which the US government has secretly funded...[45]

Some of the government's anthrax has been weaponized and kills effectively but is otherwise useless. It is also illegal. Ingri Cassel, director of the National Vaccination Liberation Association, points out that vaccines "are developed to help guard against pre-existing threats." Ames was processed *illegally*, "apparently for offensive military uses, sabotage, and even terrorism. You simply don't develop a new hyper-weaponized strain of anthrax powder for military defense … and then commission the top U.S. anthrax expert [William C. Patrick, III] to report on this new weapon's capability and lethality from mailed delivery, unless that's how you foresee it being used."[46]

Once the anthrax was weaponized and milled, capable of airborne transmission, BMI ran a classified test in the Nevada desert in early September 2001.

It was reported that Patrick's study on the mailing of milled anthrax spores was instrumental to the test.

Was Stephen Hatfill recruited for the next phase of "testing?"

This appears to be the case, and explains the FBI's capricious explanations to the press. "Operation Jefferson" was a federally-sanctioned covert operation that would have never come to light had it not been for the doggedness of independent journalists and the scientific community.

Wayne Madsen also points to past bio-warfare studies:

> In 1957, at the Dugway Proving Grounds in Utah, the Q-Fever toxin was discharged by an airborne F-100A plane. If a more potent dose had been used, the Army concluded 99 per cent of the humans in the area would have been infected. In the 1960s, conscientious objecting Seventh Day Adventists, serving in non-combat positions in the Army, were exposed to airborne tularemia...[47]

---

45. George Monbiot, "Riddle of the spores: Why has the FBI investigation into the anthrax attacks stalled?" *Guardian*, May 21, 2002.
46. Ingri Cassel, "Public Health Expert Says Solving the Anthrax Mailing Mystery May Be Easy: FBI Doesn't Seem Interested," NVLA press release, Nov. 12, 2001. http://www.tetrahedron.org/news/NR011112.html
47. Wayne Madsen, "Thinking the Unthinkable," CounterPunch.org, April 8, 2002.

The West Nile outbreak and the anthrax mailings began with a 1998 BioVax meeting held in the Truman Room of the White House, attended by SAIC's Jerry Hauer and William Patrick.

Another participant at the meeting was William Cohen, who, as a Republican Senator, signed off on the biased Cheney-Hamilton Iran-contra report. In 2004, he was elected to the American International Group's (AIG) Board of Directors.

AIG is a part-owner of Kroll Associates, the famous private security firm. Kroll – run by former CIA, FBI, British secret service, Scotland Yard and British Special Air Service agents – was once known as the CIA of Wall Street because the firm did everything from corporate espionage to the training of foreign armies. A Kroll partner offers counter-terrorism instruction in Saudi Arabia.

Cohen is also a member of the Center for Strategic and International Studies (CSIS), the Cold War propaganda brokerage and ultraconservative academic base of the late Ray Cline, John Hamre, Admiral Crowe, Zbigniew Brzezinski, former GE CEO Kenneth Langone, Henry Kissinger and other post-9/11 war profiteers.

Another attendee "of interest" at the 1998 Truman Room conference was Thomas Monath, former chief of the virology division at the SAIC-USAMIID facility at Ft. Detrick, VP/chief scientific officer at BioVax, since renamed Acimbis.

Monath was another friend of Stephen Hatfill's. He was introduced to Rudolph Giuliani by Jerry Hauer, SAIC scientist and president of Rockefeller University – the fruits of this relationship were the aerial spraying of malathion, resmethrin or sumithrin in the New York City area to ward off West Nile.48 Nevertheless, the mosquito-borne disease has spread rapidly across the country.

The anthrax scourge recurs from time to time. An increasingly feasible theory for the origin of Gulf War Syndrome is military experimentation with anthrax vaccines. Were the following incidents further "tests" of anthrax delivery systems by the "counter-terrorists" at SAIC-Ft. Detrick?

Then there was exposure at this children's hospital, blamed on "accidental" shipment of live spores from the Southern

48. See   http://www.democraticunderground.com/cgi-bin/duforum/duboard.cgi?az=printer_format&om=5074&forum=DCForumID43

Research Institute in Frederick, Maryland. (BioPort director David Franz hails from SRI, a leading producer of depleted uranium. Franz worked closely with Bruce Ivins, and would later opine to the press that he found it difficult to believe that his colleague was guilty as charged.):

Researchers Exposed To Anthrax
Health Highlights
June 7-13, 2004

A possible shipping mistake in late May resulted in at least half a dozen researchers at Children's Hospital Oakland Research Institute being exposed to live anthrax.

Some of the researchers, working on an anthrax vaccine, handled the live anthrax bacterium and others were present at the time. So far, none have shown any signs of illness. Seven of the workers are taking the antibiotic Cipro as a precautionary measure, the Oakland Tribune reported.

State health officials said there is no risk to other staff or residents living in the area.

The researchers believed they were handling a dead sample of the anthrax bacterium. However, according to hospital officials, the researchers were mistakenly sent live anthrax by the supplier, Southern Research Institute of Frederick, Md.

The U.S. Centers for Disease Control and Prevention is investigating the incident.

Part VI

Vaxgen's Donald Frances & AIDS; The Thai Experiments; The Mailings as Nazi-Style "Clinical Trials"

The anthrax mailings and the development of vaccines were inseparable – both involved animal and human experimentation. On August 3, 2008, *USA Today* explained the work that Dr. Ivins did at Ft. Detrick, specifically – *terminal animal experiments*: "Ivins performed research that required exposing research animals to airborne anthrax, according to a 1998 report in the journal *Vaccine*. The goal was to test whether a new vaccine could guard against anthrax inhaled in a bioterrorist attack."

The strain of anthrax employed "in Ivins' vaccine experiments was a wet form sprayed into the faces of macaque monkeys through a mask."

In the FBI cover story, crazed, conveniently-suicidal Dr. Ivins was the "lone assassin." Clouds of confusion gather around the sacrificial goat and entire covert op (the famed "hall of mirrors" effect) when everyone involved points the finger elsewhere. Dr. Franz steered attention away from the lab:

Q: Did Ivins and other researchers for the U.S. Army Medical Research Institute of Infectious Diseases at Fort Detrick, Md., work with dried anthrax spores?

A: No, says Col. David Franz, the institute's commander until 1998 and now with the Midwest Research Institute.

Q: Would Ivins have had the opportunity to make dried anthrax?

A: Not in the lab, Franz says.

Q: Did the lab have equipment to produce dried anthrax?

A: No, Franz says, adding that it would be difficult for Ivins or others to carry out the work without detection.

Colonel David Franz, Ivins' colleague and another Special Forces vet, was a cheerful "counter-terrorist." Franz served in the U.S. Army Medical Research and Materiel Command for 23 of 27 years on active duty. He served as commander of the U.S. Army Medical Research Institute of Infectious Diseases and as deputy commander of the Medical Research and Materiel Command. Prior to joining the Command, he served as group veterinarian for the 10th Special Forces Group, Airborne. Franz was the chief inspector on three United Nations Special Commission biological warfare inspection missions to Iraq and served as technical advisor on long-term monitoring.

He told ABC News on April 4, 2002 that a "lot of good" had come of the anthrax attacks. Sad Sacks and Dreary Donnas may tremble because "five people have died, but we've put about $6 billion in our budget."

Thumbs up.

> Dr. Charles E. McQueary, per his DoD bio, "former President of General Dynamics Advanced Technology Systems in Greensboro, N.C. He has also been President and Vice President of business units for AT&T, Lucent Technologies, and a Director for AT&T Bell Laboratories. Early in his career at Bell Laboratories, Dr. McQueary served as head of the Missile Operations Department for the SAFEGUARD Antiballistic Missile Test Program. ... Dr. McQueary is a former executive board member of the National Security Industrial Association and the American Defense Preparedness Association (ADPA: Combined to form the National Defense Industrial Association.)"[49]

A sunny disposition can carry one far in the military hierarchy. Dr. Franz was appointed to the Homeland Security Science and Technology Committee in February 2004 by Dr. McQueary, undersecretary for science and technology at the Department of Homeland Security.

Biological threats loomed on the horizon, the Pentagon's viral visionaries assured with psychic certainty. Peculiar, though ... read the small print on the packaging and it's clear that the newly emerging diseases and vaccines created to repel them hung in clusters. Ingri Cassel comments, "Cipro and smallpox vaccine have much in common besides capturing America's urgent attention." Unfortunately, the corporate parents of the companies that produce the "favored elixirs for anthrax and smallpox bioterrorism are linked, strangely enough, to an infamous history involving contaminated blood, the Central Intelligence Agency (CIA), and even the Nazi [ties] that the FBI doesn't seem anxious to explore."

Cipro is manufactured by Germany's Bayer AG (formerly I.G. Farben, and the smallpox vaccine's newly-incorporated producer is Acambis – formerly OraVax, the West Nile peo-

49. http://www.defenselink.mil/bios/biographydetail.aspx?biographyid=119

ple. "All have jaded histories. The 'Big Three' – Bayer, Baxter, and Rhone-Poulenc – are [infamous] for having infected more than 7,000 American hemophiliacs with the AIDS virus during the early 1980s. They admitted foreknowledge in selling HIV-tainted blood clotting products and settled the class action case for $100,000 per claimant."[50]

Two shrouded power bases of the Third Reich, Bayer and Hoechst, were spun from IG Farben following World War Two. Hermann Schmitz, president of Farben during the war (with its partial control of the Deutsche Bank) "held as much stock in Standard Oil of New Jersey as did the Rockefellers," according to author Paul Manning. He wrote that on August 10, 1944, the Rockefeller-Farben group filtered flight capital through "affiliated German/French, American, British and Swiss banks 'for the new Germany.'" These reserves secured "the sophisticated distribution of national and corporate assets to safe havens" across the globe, ensuring the continuation of the "Neuordnung (New Order)" for the petrochemical, drug and banking cartels[51]

An upcoming distiller of the "elixirs," joining BioPort and Bayer, is VaxGen (owned by Genentech (55.6%-owned by Hoffmann-La Roche – owned by Roche AG of Switzerland, an ally of IG Farben and the Reich).

In November 2004, the company publicized a contract under the auspices of Project BioShield worth $877 million over five years, with the government paying VaxGen to produce 75 million doses of anthrax vaccine. In addition, the company was to receive $123 million in further payments from the government in late 2007.[52]

And it was just one more hyper-boondoggle, if the history of AidsVax, the company's HIV drug failure, is any indication.

50. Ingri Cassel, "Public Health Expert Says Solving the Anthrax Mailing Mystery May Be Easy: FBI Doesn't Seem Interested," press release, Tetrahedron LLC, Nov. 12, 2001.
51. Paul Manning, Martin Bormann: Nazi in Exile, Secaucus. Lyle Stuart, 1981.
52. Adam Feuerstein, "VaxGen Hits Anthrax Jackpot," TheStreet.com, November 5, 2004. http://www.thestreet.com/_googlen/comment/adamfeuerstein/10193015.html?cm_ven=GOOGLEN&cm_cat=FREE&cm_ite=NA

On October 3, 1999, the *Times* of London reported that before VaxGen went public, "the most important government cheerleader for AidsVax," Dr. William Heyward, head of HIV vaccine research at the CDC, "had a secret deal to join the company."

From the CDC, Dr. Heyward "lobbied policymakers and approved $8 million in grants for VaxGen. But the company had already drawn this chart on his future duties, and in January 2000, he joined ex-CDC staffer Dr. Donald Francis, VaxGen president, who also hired former CDC deputy director Dr. Walter Dowdle to head its influential data monitoring board."

In US v William L. Heyward, prosecutors charged him with violation of anti-graft laws. Dr. Heyward skipped up the corporate ladder to a VP's desk at VaxGen, but eventually confessed to the flagrant conflict of interest, paid a $32,500 fine, "and escaped a high-profile criminal trial that might have proved devastating to the AidsVax project," the *Times* reported.

On March 17 2003, a class action suit was filed against VaxGen. The lawsuit claimed securities fraud after Dr. Heyward wrote a series of glowing reports on the potential of AidsVax that inflated the stock price, but proved baseless when the drug failed in clinical trials.

A word about those "trials": There was little that was "clinical" about them. Testing of the vaccine was sponsored by the NIH, FDA, World Bank, UN agencies and the International Aids Vaccine Initiative.[53]

The tests were overseen by Dr. Donald Pinkston Francis, president of VaxGen, who, along with molecular biologist Dr. Philip Berman, founded the company in 1995. Dr. Francis, 62, was bestowed with an honorary Doctor of Science degree from Harvard in 1979. Since 1978, he has been chief of the epidemiology division at the Hepatitis Labs Division of the CDC. Under the auspices of the Agency for International Development (AID), he served as an epidemiologist in Rivers State, Nigeria (1971). He was American "epidemiological intelligence service officer" at the CDC (1971-73). In *And the Band Played On*, Ran-

---

53. Brian Deer, "AidsVax: The VaxGen Experiment," *Sunday Times Magazine* (UK), October 3 1999.

dy Shilts's 1987 Aids book, Dr. Francis is found on no less than 76 pages – a driven, scolding, at times hysterical presence. In the movie, he's played by *Full Metal Jacket*'s Matthew Modine."[54]

The *Times* of London detailed the "clinical trials" conducted by Dr. Francis's team in Thailand. As Dr. Heyward sees it, "only through such trials will further knowledge be gained." Thumbs up...

The "trials" followed the Farben model:

AIDSVAX: THE VAXGEN EXPERIMENT
By Brian Deer

Sunday Times Magazine (UK), October 3, 1999

... At first glance, Thailand is a strange location to carry out medical trials.... Corruption is de rigueur, while police are accused by Amnesty International of "extra-judicial killings." Much of its profile relies on sex: first with young women and later with children.

Since the coup, however, quick cheap, experiments on the Thai population have been added to the country's attractions. Dozens of projects are currently in progress, run by foreign pharmaceutical companies and sponsored by the CDC and WHO. With an estimated 800,000 Thais infected with HIV, Aids is the big one, with tests of drugs, immune-system stimulants, and top of the list Francis's AidsVax trial.

It makes sense to test products where the risk of Aids is greatest, but my attention was drawn to potential problems during a conference in a Bangkok hotel. The topic was Aids vaccines. Francis spoke. And a doctor pointed out that some volunteers in an AZT trial were mothers from remote hill tribes. "They come across the border from Burma," he said.

"They don't speak Thai, so there is the question of whether they can understand enough to give informed consent."

The question was brushed aside ("They keep coming back.") and might not have meant much if I hadn't also met an activist from the northern town of Chiang Mai. Despite grilling 11 people who swallowed tablets daily, he complained that he couldn't discover even the name of the product or the pharmaceutical company involved. This man was a former heroin user, so I asked him where VaxGen was recruiting. "Go to Khlong Toei," he said, "by Port Authority Building. That's where they'll get people for the trial."

---

54. Ibid.

Khlong Toei is a slum; a sewage-stinking wasteland; a cauldron of disease and drug use. The better-off live in concrete hutches, with wire-fenced windows and balconies. Next down in the social scale are wooden-shack coops on plots of flood-prone ground. Then there are kennels: festering shantytown alleys of plank, sheet-iron and debris sheds. The "streets" are dim corridors, with boardwalk floors, cluttered with children and dogs. At night frail figures shuffle around, suffering from Aids, tuberculosis or both.

Thailand was once praised for anti-HIV efforts in disease hot zones such as this. But evidence suggests that since the 1992 coup priorities have changed. In 1992, a health minister complained that talk about the virus had "seriously affected tourism." And now, official figures show that Aids prevention has been slashed by one third against comparable public health programmes.

The biggest cuts have been in initiatives aimed specifically at drug misusers. "There used to be a project for clean needles in the early 90s, but now it's gone," a spokeswoman for a Khlong Toei charity, the Duang Prateep Foundation, told me...

Nobody could explain the thinking, but the effect on the junkies can be measured. Blood tests reveal that HIV prevalence peaked among female prostitutes in 1993 – when 30% were positive – and has since fallen back to 21%. Among rent boys, prevalence peaked in the following year at 18%, and is now half that figure. But prevalence among heroin-injectors has leapt from 31% in 1994 to a staggering 47% now.

Were these changes evidence that the government were allowing the junkies to be put at greater risk to make them useful for experiments? (Health department officials told me that if AidsVax is marketed, they expect a billion-dollar manufacturing plant.) I couldn't find out. People wouldn't talk when I raised such contentious concerns. Even Bangkok's Medicines Sans Frontieres staff went silent when asked about the trial.

Francis is convinced that nothing is amiss, and his collaborators voice no worries. "All have assured me that this has been done ethically," he told me, when eventually we met. "We are going out of our way not to increase the vulnerability of an already vulnerable population." The trial was conducted in Thailand, he said, for scientific reasons. Different parts of the world are linked with different HIV subtypes, with their myriad subsidiary strains. B subtype strains, for instance, are most common in North America, Europe and Australasia; A, C and D in Africa. In Thailand, there's a mix of B and E strains and, for technical reasons to do with E strains, the company argues that success is more likely there "than anywhere else in the world."

But there are aspects of the project which suggest that the junkies may be involved in an unusual way. A parallel trial among gay men at American clinics is having problems finding and keeping volunteers, due to scepticism towards the venture. But at Kachit's clinics the programme has features which may help to avoid these snags. The junkies get methadone, an oral heroin substitute, plus $10 expenses for each of up to 17 visits. The risk is the appearance of offering drugs and money as inducements to this desperate group.

There's also a feature of the experiment's design that seems self-contradictory. If the methadone liquid got people off injecting heroin, the volunteers' risk of infection would slump and they would be of little use to the vaccine trial. In fact, documents drawn up with the CDC and WHO show that that 7% of clinic users are expected to become HIV-infected each year. So, despite the oral methadone, they keep injecting heroin. They may even buy it with VaxGen's money and have an increased risk of getting Aids.

The logic of the trial creates a dilemma for Francis. The moral uncertainties about using junkies as GUINEA PIGS might be offset by humanity's greater needs. But there would need to be plausible scientific grounds to think that AidsVax might work. And on that the VaxGen experiment is open to even greater doubts...

AidsVax cannot give volunteers Aids, but there may be something even more terrifying than the anxiety that it might accelerate their disease if they are later infected with HIV. Some scientists think that, if it works at all, the product may have a dangerous effect on the evolution of HIV. Five years ago, Los Alamos scientists declared that there was "no simple answer" as to whether Aids could become contagious through coughs and sneezes – and other researchers argue that, in much the same way as a partial course of antibiotics can promote resistant bacteria, so a poorly-effective vaccine may promote more deadly and infectious strains.

This may sound like journalistic scare, but HIV's best-understood RNA cousin is influenza virus, which produces devastating mutations every 20 or 30 years. Hepatitis B virus, meanwhile, has already produced mutant strains accepted as being vaccine-induced. "When you use a vaccine, you are introducing another selective pressure," Dr. Paul

Ewald, professor of biology at Amherst College, Massachusetts, explained. "It could make the problem more damaging, or less damaging, depending on the antigen you use."

Researchers told me that, compared with the potential
risks to volunteers, this doomsday scenario was "unlikely."
But with agencies standing by to jab hundreds of millions of
people, some wondered if, for our species' safety, "unlikely"
was reassuring enough. "My personal view," Dr. Art Am-
mann, president of the San Francisco-based Global Strategy
for HIV Prevention, and a former AidsVax researcher, said,
"is that we could face a global nightmare."

In September 2008, Senate Judiciary Chairman Patrick
Leahy, the recipient of a letter contaminated with anthrax,
stated in an open hearing that he did not believe Bruce Ivins
acted alone.

"I believe there are others involved, either as accessories
before or accessories after the fact," the Vermont Democrat
said. "I believe that there are others out there. I believe there
are others who could be charged with murder."

Leahy's statement was a response to Mueller's testimony that
the FBI director was convinced Ivins was the sole perpetrator.

"We have looked at every lead and followed every lead to
determine whether anybody else was involved, and we will
continue to do so," Mueller told Leahy. He insisted that the
FBI's case against Ivins was irreproachable.

Leahy asked whether the anthrax came from labs other
than Battelle and Dugway Proving Ground. Mueller offered
that there were fifteen labs in the United States and three overseas that could have produced the Ames strain.

"It should be a concern of all Americans that biological
weapons were used on the Congress and the American people," Leahy said.

Senator Chuck Grassley, a Republican from Iowa, also
pressured the FBI to release more information on the mailings: "Given all the time and money sunk into this investigation, I believe the American people deserve more than just a
press conference and a few briefings," he said.

CHAPTER FOUR

GOP TIES TO THREE OF THE 9/11 HIJACKERS

S aleh Ibn Abdul Rahman al-Hussayen was lodged in the thick of terror. On September 10, 2001, three of the 9/11 hijackers stayed in same hotel as the Saudi "Minister for the Holy Places," England's *Telegraph* reported three years after the event:

> A senior Saudi Arabian official stayed at the same hotel as three September 11 hijackers the night before the suicide attacks. American investigators are trying to make sense of the disclosure that Saleh Ibn Abdul Rahman al-Hussayen, who returned to Saudi Arabia shortly after the attacks, stayed at the Marriott Residence Inn in Herndon, Virginia.

Hussayen, president of affairs at the Holy Mosque in Mecca, was "a prominent figure in the world of Saudi-funded charities." David Nevin, his nephew's American attorney, denied "any sinister aspects to the older man's travels."

Hussayen was questioned by the FBI after the air commando ops that demolished the World Trade Center – and he "feigned a seizure," quaking and choking and "prompting the agents to take him to a hospital, where the attending physicians found nothing wrong with him..."[1]

The agents suggested that the Saudi "epileptic" should be detained and questioned, but "as soon as flights resumed on Sept. 19, Mr. Hussayen and his wife flew home."

1. cf. *The Telegraph*, October 3, 2003. http://www.unknownnews.net/031003911.html

111

The FBI later learned that while touring in the States, Sheikh Hussayen "visited or contacted several Saudi-sponsored charities now accused of links to terrorist groups."

Prosecutors later maintained that Hussayen financed the Islamic Assembly of North America (IANA), accused of distributing "the teachings of two Saudi clerics who advocate violence against the United States."

Sami Omar Hussayen, his nephew, is in federal detention "on charges of visa fraud," accused of failing to disclose his role as an internet webmaster for IANA. Federal court filings alleged that the son "administered an internet site for IANA that expressly advocated suicide attacks and using airliners as weapons. IANA received about £2 million from abroad since 1995, court papers allege, including £60,000 from Saleh al-Hussayen."

Kim Lindquist, an assistant federal attorney assigned to the investigation of Hussayen in Boise, Idaho, said: "We're investigating the IANA. We have the money flowing to the IANA through the nephew from the uncle. We have the uncle visiting the United States just prior to September 11, and upon his return to the East Coast he's in the same hotel as the hijackers. According to FBI agents he feigns a seizure. It is something that we cannot ignore."

Lindquist wanted to "take the extra step" of connecting Saudi rulers to the events of September 11 because the Sheik's travels and "contacts are seen as a 'road map' of how Saudi money has poured into the United States in support of Wahhabism, the puritanical and intolerant form of Islam backed by the Saudi royal family."[2]

Two weeks after the belated story on Hussayen appeared, the wire services reported that recently unsealed court documents exposed "a secretive group of Muslim charities and businesses in Northern Virginia [that] funneled millions of dollars to foreign terrorists – and the network was set up with donations from a wealthy (unnamed) Saudi family."

An affidavit from Homeland Security's David Kane charged that the Safa Group in Herndon had pipelined "more

2. Ibid.

than $26 million in untraceable money overseas and that leaders of the organization have committed and conspired to … provide material support to foreign terrorist organizations. The probe of the Herndon groups is the largest federal investigation of terrorism financing in the world."

There was *no innocent explanation* "for the use of layers and layers of transactions between Safa Group companies and charities other than to throw law enforcement authorities off the trail," Kane said.

The express purpose of the Safa Group was to "set up primarily with donations from a wealthy Saudi family, was to fund terrorism and hide millions of dollars."

Kane insisted that the dizzying nature of "the myriad financial transactions and the fact that much of the money was sent to tax havens with bank secrecy laws make it impossible to trace the final destination of much of the money."[3]

But, once again, the trail going the opposite direction leads back to the true source of terrorist funding: the District of Columbia.

From *The Atlanta Journal-Constitution*:

- GOP heavyweight Grover Norquist, a former board member of the foundation, was "a Safa apologist." Norquist "said the group is not political; rather it is focused on educational issues."

- "The men have given more than $84,000 since 1990 to a variety of federal candidates and political groups, including $5,500 to Energy Secretary Spencer Abraham, a Michigan Republican, and $4,000 to former Rep. Lee Hamilton, an Indiana Democrat, according to the Center for Responsive Politics, a political watchdog group."

- "The main leaders of the Safa Group of companies include … Taha Alalwani, a naturalized American citizen who runs an Islamic graduate school where nine of the 12 Muslim chaplains in the U.S. military have been trained."

3. "Terror Probe Points to Va. Muslims," October 17, 2003. http://www.littlegreen-footballs.com/weblog/?entry=8593

- "Khaled Saffuri, chairman of the Washington-based Islamic Free Market Institute Foundation, was at the April
4 luncheon with the former treasury secretary.... Saffuri,
who has met with many top-level administration officials in recent years, including Secretary of State Colin
Powell and FBI Director Robert Mueller, is also listed
in Federal Election Committee reports as the treasurer
of National Muslims for a Greater America, a defunct
political action committee that received $5,200 from
people connected to the Safa Group investigation..."

- The affidavit linked Safa to Abdurahman Alamoudi,
"a politically connected Muslim activist, who was wel-
comed at the White House by former President Bill Clinton and President Bush for his work on behalf of Muslim causes." Alamoudi had recently pled not guilty to "an
18-count federal indictment alleging that he laundered
money and violated immigration and customs laws by
accepting $340,000 from the Libyan government, which
the government considers a state sponsor of terrorism.
The $84,000 in contributions came from several of the
alleged principals of the Safa Group and Alamoudi."[4]

On March 25, 2002, the Guardian offered up details of
more "embarrassing" domestic political connections, including this insight into the "epileptic" Saleh Ibn Abdul Rahman
al-Hussayen, the Safra Trust, and 9/11":

FBI raids pro-Republicans
By Duncan Campbell
The Guardian, March 25, 2002

The target of an anti-terrorist raid in the United States last
week provided funds for an Islamic group with close ties to
the Republican Party and the White House. The Safa trust,
a Saudi-backed charity, has provided funds for a political
group called the Islamic Institute, which was set up to mobilize support for the Republican party. It shares an office in
Washington with the Republican activist Grover Norquist.

The institute, founded in 1999 to win influence in the
Republican Party, has helped to arrange meetings between

---

4. Eunice Moscoso and Rebecca Carr, "Targets of terror financing probe had political clout," *Atlanta Journal-Constitution*, January 2, 2003.

senior Bush officials and Islamic leaders, according to the report in Newsweek magazine. Its chairman, Khaled Saffuri, and Mr. Norquist cooperated to arrange the meetings.

The trust gave $20,000 (£14,000) to the institute, which also received $20,000 from a board member of the Success Foundation, according to the report. The institute has also received money from abroad, including$200,000 from Qatar and $55,000 from Kuwait. The institute says that none of the money came with strings attached.

Mr. Norquist, who is a member of the institute's board, said that it existed "to promote democracy and free markets. Any effort to imply guilt by association is incompetent McCarthyism."

All of this leads back to mysterious Sheik al-Hussayen, the "epileptic" holy man and his room at the Marriott Residence Inn in Herndon, Virginia on December 10, 2001 ... and those three hijackers down the hall. Some neo-conservative thought programmers would find this certain evidence of Saudi "sponsorship" of 9/11 ... and have done precisely that (namely the *National Review* and David Horowitz).

But not so fast...

A capsule history of these Middle Eastern connections is enlightening enough. *The* (pre-Murdoch) *Wall Street Journal*:

Mr. Norquist started the nonprofit Islamic Free Market Institute. In collaboration with Mr. [Karl] Rove, now Mr. Bush's chief political adviser, he and other institute leaders courted Muslim voters for the Bush 2000 presidential campaign. Mr. Norquist even credits gains among Muslims with putting Mr. Bush in a position to win the critical Florida contest ... To run the nonprofit's day-to-day operations, Mr. Norquist turned to Khalid Saffuri, a Palestinian-American raised in Kuwait who had been an official of the American Muslim Council, a political group in Washington. The institute's founding chairman was a Palestinian American, Talat Othman, who had served with Mr. Bush on the board of Harken Energy Corp. and later visited the president in the White House, according to records obtained by the National Security News Service.[5]

5. Tom Hamburger and Glenn R. Simpson, "In Difficult Times, Muslims Count

Othman had long been a booster of the Bush family. He delivered the benediction at the August 2000 GOP national convention in Philadelphia.

And, with Barzinji, he was seated on the board of Amana Mutual Funds Trust. The Trust's founder was M. Yacub Mirza of Virginia. It was Mirza's records the Treasury Department seized in the raid. "Two nonprofits affiliated with Mr. Mirza and named in the search warrant, the SAAR Foundation Inc. [another title for Safa] and the Heritage Education Trust Inc., held large blocks of shares in Amana's mutual funds in 1997, according to SEC records. ... Othman also is on the board of Mr. Saffuri's [and Norquist's] Islamic Institute, the GOP-leaning group that received $20,000.00 from the Safa Trust, one of the raid's targets. The president of the Safa Trust, Jamal Barzinji, is a former business associate of Switzerland based investor Youssef Nada, whose assets were frozen last fall after the Treasury designated him a person suspected of giving aid to terrorists."

A few words on these financial ties: Youssef Nada, journalist Richard Lebeviere informs us, was a Nazi collaborator during WW II. "He was known to the Egyptian intelligence services, who have evidence of his membership in the armed branch of the fraternity of the Muslim Brothers in the 1940s ... [when] he was working for the Abwehr under Admiral Canaris and took part in a plot against King Farouk."[6]

Othman had a history of mingling with GOP cronies, as reported by the *Chicago Tribune* on August 10, 2003: "In 1990, media reports implied that Othman was a front man for [Abdullah Taha] Bakhsh, who had acquired a 17.6 percent stake in Harken Energy Corp. in the 1980s. Serving alongside Othman was a Harken corporate officer: then-presidential son George W. Bush."[7]

on Unlikely Advocate," *Wall Street Journal*, June 11, 2003. http://www.spitfirelist.com/f415.html

6. Richard Labeviere, *Dollars for Terror: The United States and Islam*, Algora Books, 2000, pp. 140-141.

7. Brian Grow, "Muslim financier pushes peace effort," *Chicago Tribune*, August 10, 2003, p. 1.

This, then, is the "shadowy network" behind the 9/11 hijackers and the "mysterious" Sheik at the Marriott Hotel in Herndon, VA., from one end of the terror loop to the other.

Speaking of where the hijackers spent the night on September 10, 2001, five others deserve mention: "One of the most bizarre ironies of all this is that five of the hijackers lived in a motel right outside the gates of the NSA." – *BBC News*, June 8, 2002.

As for the dangling ties to BCCI: In December 1992, Senator John Kerry published a report – a primal scream if read between the lines – in the form of an interim statement on BCCI submitted to the Senate Committee on Foreign Relations. In it, Kerry groused that the CIA had stubbornly refused to cooperate with his investigation. Former CIA officials, including Richard Helms, and foreign intelligence officials, including Kamal Adham and Abdul Raouf Khalil, dragged their feet. Prime foreign agents "such as Adnan Khashoggi and Manucher Ghorbanifar, float in and out of BCCI at critical times in its history, and participate simultaneously in the making of key episodes in U.S. foreign policy, ranging from the Camp David peace talks to the arming of Iran as part of the Iran contra affair."

Agency officials claimed they had "no information on file" regarding contact with the above, "raising questions about ... its candor with the Subcommittee." CIA protestations of ignorance concerning their involvement in BCCI were out of sync with the Agency's early knowledge of numerous aspects of the bank's operations, structure, personnel, and history.

Some of the documents handed over to Kerry's subcommittee early on, he complained, were "untrue." Subsequent CIA files were "incomplete." The Agency "resisted providing a full account about its knowledge of BCCI until almost a year after the initial requests for the information." The live circuit among former CIA operatives and "BCCI front men and nominees, including [Khashoggi partner] Kamal Adham, Abdul Khalil, and Mohammed Irvani, require further investigation."

CHAPTER FIVE

HOLOCAUST PROFITEERING,
STARVING CONGOLESE CHILDREN & FIXING ELECTIONS:
THE MANHATTAN INSTITUTE'S PAUL E. SINGER

With Western-style journalistic aplomb, Romania's *Business Review* reported in June 2012 that the East European state's Property Fund (*Fondul Proprietatea*) boosted its net income by 20 percent year-to-year to EUR 128 million in 2011, and sought a second listing on the Warsaw Stock Exchange. "The heirs of Nicolae Malaxa, the Romanian industrialist, whose stake in the fund is close to 7 percent, have already expressed their agreement with the move."

The article glossed over the bloody history of military-industrialist Nicolae Malaxa, the pre-WWII chairman of the Ford Motor Company's Romania division.

Time reports that in the 1930s, Malaxa, the "Krupp of Romania," parlayed modest investments into a combine of arms factories, and forged a partnership with the country's largest iron works. The Malaxa industrial plants ranked among the largest in Eastern Europe, key suppliers to the Romanian railways. They built, among other things, state-of-the-art steam and diesel locomotives, and made Malaxa one of the wealthiest men in Romania.

His Wikipedia entry is a descent into Holocaust Hell:

Unlike most other large industries in the country, Malaxa's was not tied to British, French or Czechoslovak interests. Instead, Nicolae Malaxa maintained business links with Nazi Germany as early as 1935. At a time when

119

Nazi Germany was gaining more influence in Romania, Nicolae Malaxa collaborated with Hermann Goering in confiscating the assets of the Jewish Auschnitt (who had been arrested and prosecuted on false charges in September 1939), and subsequently placed his industrial empire in the service of the Reichswerke during World War II. ... Nicolae Malaxa, of course, is reasonably well-known for his sponsorship of the Romanian Iron Guard death squad ... and postwar ties to America's Republican Party.

Probably sympathizing with Nazi ideology, he had financed the activities of the Romanian far-right Iron Guard organization as early as the mid-1930s, and especially throughout the National Legionary State the latter established. During the Rebellion and Pogrom it provoked in January 1941, the Guard made use of arms manufactured by Malaxa, as well of his house (turned into a citadel and attacked by the Romanian Army).... Alongside accusations involving his endorsement of the Iron Guard, it was alleged that he had been collaborating with the Romanian Communist Party during his last years in Romania. In 1955, while Malaxa was visiting Argentina, the Immigration and Naturalization Service briefly revoked his reentry permit. Both charges were again voiced by Democratic Party politicians during Richard Nixon's 1962 electoral campaign for Governor in California, after focus was placed on the friendship and business connections between Nixon and Malaxa. A government investigation dismissed the accusations, but in 1979 his pro-Nazi past was again investigated by The Washington Post (which claimed that high-ranking American officials close to Malaxa had been involved in a cover-up)...

After Hitler's forces were defeated militarily, the SS collaborator fled to the U.S. where he was protected by Richard Nixon and the Republican Party. The family fortune was confiscated by the Communist Party, and Malaxa sentenced to death *in absentia* for war crimes.

The military-industrialist's daughter, Irina Malaxa, married George Emil Palade, a scientist, in 1946. Palade was a recipient of the Nobel prize in 1974. Their children, Georgia Palade Van Düsen, Philip Palade, and Loreen Ellen Malaxa, sought the return of some USD 310 million from the Property Fund, a financial pool established to compensate victims of Communist nationalization. The three Malaxa heirs, who reside in the U.S., own a seven percent share in Fondul Proprietatea, according to *Romania Business Insider.*

Since its listing in 2011, at least three major investors, including the hedge fund Elliott Associates – guided by board chairman Paul E. Singer, who also chairs the far-right Manhattan Institute, have invested in the Romanian Property Fund. Elliot Associates owns a 13 percent share.

That is, Singer has mixed Elliot Associates capital with the Holocaust-tainted Malaxa fortune – the lucre of heirs who seek "restitution" of genocidal assets from the government.

So much for "conservative principles" at the Manhattan Institute.

In the global investment sector, Singer himself operates with the ruthlessness of any Third World potentate. His strategy, according to *SourceWatch*, is to "find some forgotten tiny debt owed by a very poor nation." He then "waits for the US and European taxpayers to forgive the poor nations' debts; as well as offers of food aid, medicine and investment loans. At this point Singer grabs at every resource and all the money going to the desperate country." As a result, trade is severely limited, funds are frozen, and "an entire economy is effectively held hostage. Singer then demands aid-giving nations pay monstrous ransoms to let trade resume." For example, Singer demanded $400 million dollars from the Congo for a debt acquired for less than $10 million. "If Singer doesn't get his 4,000% profit, he can effectively *starve the nation.* In Congo-Brazzaville last year, one-fourth of all deaths of children under five were caused by malnutrition."

Back to the GOP: In 2007, the Democratic National Committee published a report on Republican money laundering and manipulation of the electoral process by the Rudy Giuliani campaign. The *Wizbang Blue* website notes that Singer, then chairman of the Giuliani Northeast fundraising apparat, was implicated in the illicit trail of campaign donations "to manipulate the 2008 election vote results."

He was accused of laundering $175,000 through the account of another key Giuliani donor, Charles A. Hurth III. Hurth is the leader of Take Initiative America, an ultra-conservative organization based in Missouri that launched a proposal to split California's electoral votes – despite the fact that Take Initiative America had no political ties to California: "This was intended to manipulate the overall electoral college vote and make it more difficult for a Democrat to win the national election in 2008 ... and further bias the electoral college towards the Republicans."

Singer is a generous donor to far-right causes. Recipients of his genocidal largesse, according to the *New York Times*, include Progress for America ($1.5 million in contributions), a political advocacy group set up to advance the policies of the Bush administration; Swift Vets and P.O.W.'s for Truth; and the Jewish Institute for National Security Affairs, which includes Vice President Dick Cheney and Richard N. Perle, an advisor to the former Defense Secretary Donald H. Rumsfeld, among its past and current advisory directors."

> Hedge fund money, which now exceeds $1 trillion, has emerged in the last several years as a potentially powerful force in politics, as underscored by the significant role it is playing in the presidential aspirations of Mrs. Clinton and Mr. Giuliani. During the 2006 election cycle, executives who work at the 30 biggest hedge funds made $2.8 million in contributions to political candidates or party committees, almost double the amount in 2000.

Some candidates consider hedge funds to be a smart alternative to the public financing of elections. "Money from Wall Street has long been a factor in Washington and has tended to flow, with a policy agenda, to the ascendant political party," reports the *Times:*

> Yet it is not just the money they donate directly that makes people in hedge funds attractive to campaigns. They also offer access to other potential donors in the financial

> world, which in recent election cycles has become one
> of the biggest sources of political contributions. ... Top
> candidates for the 2008 campaign are expected to raise a
> lot of money quickly — at least $100 million each by the
> end of this year by some estimates.

Given his macabre business connections and investment strategies, it's not all that surprising that the GOP benefactor "keeps a particularly low profile." Singer wouldn't want all of the above openly discussed by talk show ferrets and bothersome liberal Op-Editors. That could dent the bottom line and the increasingly conservative GOP.

CHAPTER SIX

ADNAN KHASHOGGI
AND AN AMERICAN PINAY CIRCLE

"...The sky burns, A copper roof over the shriveled corn.
Children and camels gasp in the noonday heat.
Enemies sweat in their steel, cry out at night,
And wake up trembling, wet with fright.
We squat and stare
Across the nervous barbs, tied by our common dreads..."
– Aubrey Hodes, "Hating"

Adnan Khashoggi's mercenary army of global corporate predators lives in Mafia mansions, basks in the political limelight, enjoys privileges of royalty in tyrannical desert dystopias, sips vodka in the shadow of gleaming Moscow spires. They are kings, Pentagon officials, priests, S&L thieves, assassins, prostitutes, Nazis, Big Oil execs, metals merchants, New Age cultists, drug barons, boiler-room con artists, mobsters and dictators by the horde.

And terrorists, of course.

Khashoggi is a Turkoman, the son of a doctor who tended to Abdul al-Aziz Ibn Saud. The Khashoggi brothers were classmates of the future King Hussein and several sons of the bin Ladens.[1] His career as an international "connector" began in the 1950s, while still an undergraduate at Chico State College. His purchase of fifty Kenworth trucks for resale to Saudi Arabia's bin Laden Group demonstrated his business savvy,

---

1. Roland Jacquard, *In the Name of Osama Bin Laden*, Duke University Press, 2002. http://print.google.com/print/doc?isbn=0822329913

and provided him the capital to launch his career as world-class death merchant.

In the early 1960s, he could be found lounging in the sun and/or plotting world domination at Edwin Pauley's Coconut Island estate in Hawaii. Pauley, then Democratic Party chairman, operated an oil company called Zapata with the son of Prescott Bush, the Nazi collaborator.[2]

Houston attorney Linda Minor sidelines as an investigator of banking and political malfeasance. Pauley, she says, was a slimy operator years before his alliance with Bush: "He was a spy within the White House, acting as a funnel for campaign funds to FDR, while at the same time gathering and transmitting information about oil policy and captured Nazi and Japanese assets back to his California business associates."

Pauley's political import stems from his participation in Gulf of Mexico oil explorations in the 1950's when, with an oil concession from Mexico, he threw in with Howard Hughes and George H.W. Bush.

"Pauley taught Bush how to launder money through corporate subsidiaries to be used for payoffs and the financing of political campaigns," Minor notes. "Both Pauley and Bush used this system to finance Richard Nixon's presidential campaigns."

The laundering scheme unraveled after the 1972 election, when a check drawn at a Mexican bank – the subsidiary of a Houston corporation controlled by associates of Bush the elder – surfaced in the Miami bank account of a Watergate plumber.[3]

Saudi shiekhs and domestic oil barons struck up alliances. Shiekh Kamal Adham and a circle of cohorts founded Arabian Shield Development Co. in Texas (since rechristened the Arabian American Development Company).

Sheikh Mohammad Salem Bin Mahfouz at National Commercial Bank was an Arabian Shield investor.[4] "During the

2. Bruce Campbell Adamson, letter to Congressman Sam Farr, September 15, 2001. http://www.mail-archive.com/ctrl@listserv.aol.com/msg96515.htm
3. Linda Minor, "Follow the Yellow Brick Road: From Harvard to Enron." http://www.newsmakingnews.com/lm4,30,02,harvardtoenronpt4.htm
4. Napa Valley financial researcher Lois Battuello, e-mail exchange with author, October 2, 2004.

1980's," reports Martin J. Rivers of the Center for Research on Globalization, the Mahfouz syndicate "performed major CIA-inspired banking operations for such former CIA assets as Osama bin Laden ... Saddam Hussein, Manuel Noriega and other drug dealing generals." G.W. Bush had "important business relationships ... with a total of nine prominent individuals central to Mahfouz's financial empire."[5]

The early 1970s also brought Saudi CIA recruits to train at American military bases, including Prince Bandar bin Sultan.[6] After September 11, 2001, Bandar drew the attention of the press when it was discovered that two of the terrorists involved were found to have received financing from the Prince's wife. Bandar trained at Ellington AFB near Houston.[7]

In the early '70s, the prince fell in with James A. Baker's social circle and struck up an alliance with Joanne Herring, who was instrumental in luring Texas Democrat Charlie Wilson to support Gul Hekmatyar of the Muslim Brotherhood chapter in Afghanistan.

The Big Oil-CIA-Saudi alliance was consummated with the establishment of the Safari Club of elite cutthroats, founded with covert Agency support on Sept. 1, 1976. George Herbert Walker Bush was then director of the Agency, and Nelson Rockefeller was vice president under Ford.

The Safari Club was a CIA cut-out: this clutch of intelligence agents, politicians and businessmen from three countries (Saudi Arabia, Egypt, and Iran) was founded with the express purpose of engaging in covert operations in Africa and the Middle East sans a CIA footprint.

Chicago Tribune book reviewer Padam Ahlawa neatly summarized the tensions that gave rise to the Safari Club:

> The origins of world terrorism go back to the cold war era. Moscow's monumental blunder in invading Afghan-

5. Martin J. Rivers, "A Wolf in Sheikh's Clothing: Bush Business Deals with Nine Partners of bin Laden's Banker," geocities.com, March 15, 2004. www.globalresearch.ca/articles/MAR403A.html
6. Anon., "Bandar bin Sultan, a CIA Agent," *House of Saud* website. http://www.geocities.com/saudhouse_p/irancont.htm
7. Battuello.

istan in 1979 set off a sequence of intrigue-laden events in Afghanistan.... High-profile military operations were out. Carter wanted a covert CIA operation like the one it had carried out in Laos, with no U.S. personnel directly involved. The Agency, it was decided, would co-opt specialized American military personnel with the support of the Pakistan military to train an army of Muslim zealots.

Anwar Sadat entered into an agreement to assist in the training and equipping of recruits for the coming Anti-Communist jihad.

> Russian weapons were flown to Afghanistan. Encouraging fundamentalism to grow in Egypt had its fallout when these Mujahadins turned hostile to Sadat for signing the peace treaty with Israel. It led to Sadat's assassination and the murder of 58 tourists. Zia ul Haq of Pakistan made the best of this opportunity by creating the ISI to train Pakistanis and Afghans. By doing this, Pakistan's economic and social instability increased and terrorist acts in Sindh grew.[8]

The Club's cover was blown when the Ayatollah Khomeini allowed an Egyptian reporter to peek into the archives of the exiled Shah of Iran – a Safari Club member.[9] The CIA/Safari Club left footprints in the destabilization campaign at Mengistu in Ethiopia, the unrest in Costa Rica, and all over Iran-contra, not to mention the funding of UNITA in Angola and the Afghan "freedom fighters," including bin Laden.[10]

The Central Intelligence Agency funded the Muslim Brotherhood and trained the Mujahadin to support Hekmatyar in Afghanistan. The Brothers served the CIA operationally for some 40 years, an arrangement rubber-stamped by Director Allen Dulles, Office of Policy Coordination/Nazi re-

8. Padam Ahlawat, "Journalists' account of terrorism," *Chicago Tribune*, May 5, 2002 (review of *Unholy Wars. Afghanistan, America and International Terrorism*, by John K. Cooley, Penguin.
9. Imad-ad-Dean Ahmad, review of *Unholy Wars, Journal of Islam and Muslim-Christian Relations*, Minaret of Freedom Institute, http://www.minaret.org/cooley.htm
10. Dr Samir Rihan, "Arms or democracy, but not both." http://www.globalcomplexity.org/Arms%20or%20Democracy.htm

cruiter Frank Wisner and Kermit Roosevelt. Airline hijacker Mohammed Atta was ID'd as a Muslim Brother by the *Wall Street Journal* and *New York Times* shortly after the 2001 air assaults on the World Trade Center. So were Khalid Shaik Mohammed and Ramzi Yousef (guided to a sacrificial pyre in the sky by Aman Zawahiri, al Qeada's second-in-command), in the period the Brotherhood operated under the aegis of the Agency, in the murder of Egyptian President Anwar Sadat and the 1993 World Trade Center bomb plot.

Richard Perle's "Narco-Terrorist" Business Partner

The House hearings on Iran-contra culminated in 1987 with a report that deftly mentioned Richard Secord's plan to construct an enterprise of his own in the bulk manufacture of "opium alkaloids."[11]

Opium? This curious detail floated by without comment and eventually drowned in a flood of perjury and hot air.

The committee didn't bother to follow up on that one. Better late than never to ask: "Opium alkaloids ... as in the base compound for the production of heroin?" It's doubtful we'll ever know the answer. And the explanation could be innocent, to be completely fair; Secord *may* have invented a cure for peptic ulcers or, perhaps, sexual impotence ... but heroin would appear the likeliest explanation given the cost of global conquest these days...

Even Adnan Khashoggi has financed wars with drug profits, the gist of a 1991 Pentagon report, declassified in July 2004 by the National Security Archives in Washington. The report details 104 "more important Colombian narco-terrorists contracted by the Colombian narcotic cartels for security, transportation, distribution, collection and enforcement of narcotics operations in both the U.S. and Colombia."

Pablo Escobar is on the list. Colombian President Alvaro Uribe is also on it.

Uribe, according to the document, is a "Colombian politician and senator dedicated to collaboration with the Medellin cartel

11. Jefferson Morley, "Iran-Contra's Unasked Questions, or the Case of the $400,000 Hamburger," *Los Angeles Times*, November 29, 1987.

at high government levels." He was "linked to a business involved in narcotics activities in the U.S. His father was murdered in Colombia for his connection with the narcotic traffickers." He has "worked for the Medellin cartel," according to the DoD report, and "is a close personal friend of Pablo Escobar Gaviria.... He has participated in Escobar's political campaign to win the position of assistant parliamentarian to Jorge [Ortega]..."

Adam Isaacson, a scholar at the Center for International Policy (CIP) in Washington, cast doubt on the Pentagon's intelligence. After all, the CIP scholar explained, Adnan Khashoggi's name was on it, so the list must be in error...

But the National Security Archives responded that the document is "accurate and easily verifiable. It is evident that a significant amount of time and energy went into compiling this report."

The term used by the Pentagon to describe traffickers listed in the report, including Khashoggi, was "narco-terrorist." So: Richard Perle, assistant secretary of defense under Bush, a business partner of Khashoggi's at TriReme Corp., boardroomed with a narco-terrorist, according to the Pentagon's own records.

President Uribe also denied the allegations regarding himself – not so easy to explain away, however, was the 1984 seizure of his father's helicopter by Colombian police on narcotics charges, or his brother's telephone number, stored in the memory bank of a cell phone belonging to Escobar.[12]

Ignoring the Pentagon's own intelligence regarding Colombia's narco-presidenté, Bush paid Uribe a call in August 2003. Anti-war reporter Jim Lobe wrote:

> The administration of President George W. Bush on Monday rallied behind Colombian President Alvaro Uribe in the face of allegations contained in a 13-year-old Pentagon intelligence report that he was a "close personal friend" of drug lord Pablo Escobar and had worked for his Medellin drug cartel.

12. Jim Lobe, "Bush Rallies Behind Colombian President, Despite Drug Allegations," Inter-Press Service, August 3, 2004.

"We completely disavow these allegations about President Uribe," said State Department spokesman Adam Ereli. "We have no credible information that substantiates or corroborates these allegations that appeared in an unevaluated 1991 report, linking President Uribe to the narcotics business or trafficking."

Isaacson: "It's something the left has been trying to pin on him for awhile, and this gives them new ammunition." However, he acknowledged, "in the big picture, almost everybody in Colombia's ruling class was mixed up in drugs until [former U.S. President] Ronald Reagan declared war on drugs in the mid-1980s."[13]

Narcotics have fuelled the flames of revolution and regime change, political assassinations and bomb plots – the "war on drugs" notwithstanding.

Another drug runner in this underground empire was Henry Asher, founder of DataBase, the ChoicePoint appendage. In a report by the Florida Department of Law Enforcement, Asher admitted to smuggling drugs in 1982. Police developed "corroborating information" that "during 1981 and 1982, Asher piloted five to seven plane loads of cocaine from Colombia to the United States." Asher admitted that he had shown "a lack of judgment," according to the report. The remorseful millionaire cooperated with the FBI and agreed to be a federal "informant." He was freed and went on to set up a total awareness surveillance operation.[14]

Another drug pilot on contra supply missions was Frank Moss who, according to the Kerry Report, "has been under investigation as an alleged drug trafficker since 1979." Moss has been investigated for drug offenses by ten law enforcement agencies. In addition to flying contra supply missions through SETCO, Moss formed his own company in 1985, Hondu Carib, which also flew supplies to the contras, including weapons and ammunition purchased from R.M. Equipment, an arms company controlled by Ronald Martin and James McCoy.

13. Ibid.
14. Multistate Anti-Terrorism Information Exchange, Jun 2003. http://www.google.com/search?hl=en&ie=ISO-88591&q=hank+asher+and+cocaine+and+biography

The Nicaraguan Democratic Force (FDN, the largest contra contingent) arrangement with Moss and Hondu Carib was pursuant to a commercial agreement between the FDN's chief supply officer, Mario Calero, and Moss, under which Calero was to receive an ownership interest in Moss's company. The Subcommittee received documentation that one Moss plane, a DC-4, N90201, was used to move Contra goods from the United States to Honduras. On the basis of information alleging that the plane was being used for drug smuggling, the Customs Service obtained a court order to place a concealed transponder on the plane.

A second DC-4 controlled by Moss was chased off the west coast of Florida by the Customs Service while it was dumping what appeared to be a load of drugs, according to law enforcement personnel. When the plane landed at Port Charlotte no drugs were found on board, but the plane's registration was not in order and its last known owners were drug traffickers. Law enforcement personnel also found an address book aboard the plane, containing among other references the telephone numbers of some Contra officials and the Virginia telephone number of Robert Owen, Oliver North's courier. A law enforcement inspection of the plane revealed the presence of significant marijuana residue. DEA seized the aircraft on March 16, 1987.[15]

Cable network opinion-shapers Ann Coulter and David Corn may insist that the CIA only "looked the other way" when its assets have been caught moving narcotics to finance assassinations, foreign coups, etc., but Khashoggi, Armitage and Asher weren't the only drug runners in the "family."

William Casey, CIA director under Reagan, created several large off-the-shelf networks to finance illicit covert operations. The first, dependent on opium profits, supported the Afghan Mujhaddin, with the CIA laundering funds through Pakistan's

15. Selections from the Multistate Anti-Terrorism Information Exchange, June 2003. http://www.google.com/search?hl=en&ie=ISO-8859-1&q=hank+asher+and+cocaine+and+biography. *Senate Committee Report on Drugs, Law Enforcement and Foreign Policy*, chaired by Senator John F. Kerry.

ISI and BCCI. The second channel, to support the Nicaraguan contra war, ran through BCCI, too. This channel also began with drug proceeds and ended in hot pockets of the Cold War. The same organizational chart – of CIA proxy armies funded by drug proceeds – was evident in KLA operations in Bosnia, complete with raping, pillaging, bombing al-Qaeda radicals.[16]

As a result, these networks, according to Peter Dale Scott, "have all aligned the U.S. on the same side as powerful local drug traffickers. Partly this has been from realpolitik – in recognition of the local power realities represented by the drug traffic. Partly it has been from the need to escape domestic political restraints: the traffickers have supplied additional financial resources needed because of U.S. budgetary limitations, and they have also provided assets not bound (as the U.S. is) by the rules of war."

The impact of all this trafficking in drugs, of course, is devastating. "These facts," Scott writes, "have led to enduring intelligence networks involving both oil and drugs, or more specifically both petrodollars and narcodollars. These networks, particularly in the Middle East, have become so important that they affect, not just the conduct of U.S. foreign policy, but the health and behavior of the U.S. government, U.S. banks and corporations, and indeed the whole of U.S. society."[17]

Al Qaeda, Abu Sayyaf & the CIA's Terror Incubator in the Philippines

Corporate press histories of al-Qaeda trace its roots to Saudi Arabia. Founder Osama Bin Laden reportedly pushed early funding through the International Islamic Relief Organization (IIRO), as arranged in meetings between al-Qaeda's inner circle and the charity's directors. (The Saudi government financed terrorist attacks on Israel in secrecy throughout most of the 1990's via charities in Virginia and Florida.[18]) Ayman al-Zawahiri, bin Laden's lieutenant, was employed by

16. Peter Dale Scott, *Drugs, Oil, and War*; and John Cooley, *Unholy Wars*.
17. Peter Dale Scott, "Afghanistan, Colombia, Vietnam: The Deep Politics of Drugs and Oil," http://socrates.berkeley.edu/~pdscott/qov.html
18. John Loftus, "What Congress does not know about Enron and 9/11," May 31, 2002. http://www.john-loftus.com/enron3.asp#congress

the IIRO in Albania. The Philippine branch office was run by Mohammed Jamal Khalifa, Osama's brother-in-law (1986-94), who made a lateral cash hand-off to the Abu Sayyaf – an al Qaeda offshoot.[19]

The DoD, CIA, other opaque branches of government, and the Mafia, drawn by the lure of Japanese and German gold, maintained a particularly busy presence in the Philippines as the Marcos kleptocracy declined and fell. Oliver North, Khashoggi's Iran contra ally, oversaw "back door" shipments of the recovered gold, much of it to Arab governments, some to Middle Eastern terrorists trading on the black market, according to the *Las Vegas Sun*. North met with Osama Bin Laden's moneymen frequently to negotiate exchange of the gold.[20]

The Abu Sayyaf Group (ASG), like al-Qaeda, owed its existence to the intelligence establishment. Abu Sayyaf was co-founded by Edwin Angeles, an undercover agent of the Defense Intelligence Group at the Department of National Defense, Republic of the Philippines. His Muslim name was "Ibrahim Yakub." As the organization's operations officer and chief recruiter, Angeles was largely responsible for the spread – and criminalization – of Abu Sayyaf.

In her history of the organization, Filipino television news reporter Arlyn de la Cruz writes that Angeles/Yokub "holds the key to the deep intricacies of how some government agencies manipulated the rawness of the Abu Sayyaf during its early years." The observation still applies and can also be said of al-Qaeda, the CIA-bred "freedom fighter" mutatant, as well.

It was Angeles who "introduced the idea of kidnapping as part of the fund-raising activities of the Abu Sayyaf," de la Cruz notes – beginning with the abduction of a wealthy woman in Davao. He planned and initiated the abduction. The victim was held not far from the Brigade Headquarters of The

19. Dore Gold, "The Suicide Bombing Attacks in Saudi Arabia: A Preliminary Assessment," *Jerusalem Issue Brief*, Vol. 2, No. 28, Institute for Contemporary Affairs, May 13, 2003. Hyperlink - http://www.jcpa.org/brief/brief2-28.htm http://www.jcpa.org/brief/brief2-28.htm
20. Gary Thompson and Steve Kanigher, *Las Vegas Sun*, Philippine gold series, 1993. Also see, Edith Regalado, "CIA whisks away Brit-Am blast victim; now in US," *Philippine Star*, July 9, 2002.

Philippine Marines in Tabuk. She was released only after her family paid a million-peso ransom to Abu Sayyaf.

The next to be kidnapped was Luis "Ton-Ton" Biel, a five year-old child, and his grandfather ... then Claretian priest Bernardo Blanco. Soon, the media were requesting interviews and "Yokub" stepped before the cameras to act the role of lethal but well-spoken religious lunatic. Angeles was a "good speaker, a good actor. He spoke like a Leftist leader espousing Fundamentalist principles."

An accidental blast at the Evergreen Hotel in Davao in May 2004 was a clear statement that the al-Qaeda offshoot still functions as an intelligence front, a proxy army of the U.S. National Security Council that exists to justify intervention in the Philippines.

The explosion, publicized in the United States as the work of Abu Sayyaf, was set off by a store of dynamite traced to one Michael Meiring, an African-born, naturalized, proverbial Ugly America citizen. Meiring claimed that Abu Sayyaf's mad dogs had lobbed a grenade into his hotel room, an alibi proved to be a fabrication upon examination of the scene by local police.

Meiring was so badly injured by the blast that both of his legs were amputated at the knees. The dynamite, *Manilla Times* reported, also tore off his "mantle of obscurity," exposing Meiring and "his numerous American and Filipino partners to the public limelight."

From the rubble at the Evergreen Hotel emerged the story of "a complex man, whose trail leads back to South Africa and boxes supposedly containing US Federal Reserve notes and bonds obtained from the Abu Sayyaf." The *Times* reported that employees of the hotel "claimed that while they were cleaning Meiring's room before the explosion, he warned them not to touch two metal boxes, which he said contained important documents. Police investigators said they recovered blasting caps and ammonium nitrate from the room where Meiring had stayed since Dec. 14 2001."

Meiring refused to talk to Philippine police. According Col. Lino Calingasan, a local immigration official, the American provocateur was "whisked out of the country on a chartered plane by agents of the FBI and NSC. American David Hawthorn, a close friend of Meiring, claimed the blast victim had confessed passing to Mandela's government the proceeds of a box of aged U.S. federal notes."

That box was one in a set of twelve, containing an estimated $500-million in counterfeit American notes.

Hawthorn was shown a letter from the South African government and a U.S. Treasury permit to support his claims. He also discovered a packing list that had "a cover sheet printed with the words 'US Army,' some numbers, and a group of upper-case letters." Meiring, he said, contended that "the list represented the serial numbers of the missing notes dating back to 1937. Similar boxes were recovered by the United States Secret Service and the Philippine Central Bank late last year. Other counterfeit bonds and currency were also recovered from a hotel in Davao a few months ago. It has been reported that these were to be ... shipped to Las Vegas, Nevada."[21]

Philippine police discovered that Meiring, the NSC amputee, had run with neo-Nazis and Islamic radicals alike, including Abu Sayyaf and other radical fronts. His key contact in Nevada was financier James Rowe, an executive producer for Wild Rose Productions, an independent documentary production company in New Green Valley, near Las Vegas. Rowe, in turn, ran with white supremacists and tax rebels in the United States and Germany. Another of Meiring's contacts back home was Chuck Ager, an ultra-conservative mining engineer in Colorado. Another was Nina North (possibly an alias), a CIA operative who took over "back door" financial transactions in black market gold formerly conducted by Oliver North at the NSC. Another was Filipino-American Bob Gould, a tax protester from Hayward, California in league with Fred Obado, leader of the Kodar Kiram terrorist cell and the son of Sultan Jumalul Kiram.

Meiring operated a shell company called PAROUSIA – a term used by right-wing Christian evangelicals referring to the second coming of Christ.

---

21. Anon., "Edwin Angeles: The spy who came in from the cold," INQ7.net, Hyperlink: http://www.inq7.net/specials/inside_abusayyaf/2001/features/spy_turns_bandit.htm

But Meiers wasn't the only home-grown terrorist running loose in the Philippines: "Three Vietnamese terrorists arrested last year for plotting to blow up the Vietnamese Embassy here were assets of the U.S. intelligence community," the *Times* reported bluntly.[22]

Adnan Khashoggi, Alexander Voloshin & the 1999 Moscow Apartment Bombings

Two years before the towers in Manhattan crumbled under the weight of global political corruption, a spate of bombings in Russia left relatives and victims, as CNN reported on September 10, 1999, "searching for answers."

At least 90 bodies, including seven children, were dragged from the wreckage of a bombed-out apartment building in Moscow in early September 1999. Russian Prime Minister Vladimir Putin, in a televised speech, said that he suspected Muslim terrorists; if so, he said, "we are facing a cunning, impudent, insidious and bloodthirsty opponent."

CNN:

> Russian President Boris Yeltsin declared a day of mourning on Monday for the victims of Russia's last three explosions and bombings – the Moscow blast, the bombing of a shopping center near the Kremlin and the September fourth car bomb that demolished another apartment building in Buinaksk, in the southern Russian region of Dagestan...[23]

By the third week of September, the death toll rose to over 200. Chechen forces were behind the bombings, proclaimed Yeltsin, a belief shared by Yuri Luzkhov, the mayor of Moscow. Interior Minister Vladimir Rushailo oversaw the investigation and announced that the Russian military "will consider itself within its rights to use all resources at its disposal to rebuff the aggression."[24]

22. *Manila Times* series written by Dorian Zumel-Sicat and Jeannette Andrade, May 29, 2002 through May 31, 2002. Also see, *Manila Time* reports to June 19, 2002.
23. Jill Dougherty, "At least 90 dead in Moscow apartment blast," CNN report, September 10, 1999.
24. STRATFOR.COM, "Who gains from the Moscow apartment bombings?" *Asia*

And none of this added up. The harried Russian pro-les were quick to accept the government's explanation that Chechens were responsible for the blasts in Moscow and the satellites. But as *Asia Times* editorialized, "it is highly unlike-ly." And no one stood to benefit by the outbreak of bombing but … well … Yeltsin…

In a statement of denial, Chechen leader Shamil Basayev stated, "We had nothing to do with the explosion in Moscow. We never kill civilians. This is not our style."

So who was behind the bombing rampage?

Provisions anticipating the Patriot Act were proposed. The Duma considered declaring a state of emergency. Until the bombings, the public had steadfastly opposed such measures, but even Yegor Stroyev, speaker of the Federation Council, the upper hall of Parliament, had to admit that he'd firmly opposed emergency measures in the past, but after the second Moscow explosion there was an obvious "need to consolidate the legal base for combating the rampage of terrorism and crime."[25]

Still, there were the inevitable skeptics and conspiracy theorists. Viktor Ilyukhin, a Communist leader, dismissed the bombings as provocateur actions: "Political hysteria is being fanned artificially, including by way of explosions to cancel parliamentary and presidential elections through a state of emergency."[26]

Day by day, the true, sordid details emerged in *Versiya*, *Novaya Gazeta* and UK's *Independent* to erode Yeltsin's cred-ibility. It emerged that there was more to the bomb plot than the government had revealed, that its true origins lay not in the insurrection but in a meeting of conspirators held at the flat of Saudi entrepreneur Adnan Khashoggi …

"It is clear that apartment explosions in Moscow would not have happened if somebody in the Russian political elite did not want them," *Novaya Gazeta* opined on January 24, 2000. "One by one, pieces of puzzle fit together. But there were

Times, September 14, 1999. Hyperlink: http://www.atimes.com/c-asia/AI15Ag01.html http://www.atimes.com/c-asia/AI15Ag01.html
25. Ibid.
26. Dougherty.

a few details that were lacking. They began to clear in January ... and at the same time, some of the participants started to tell their version of events. In the *Versiya* newspaper, there was an article about the meeting of [Alexander] Voloshin with [Shamil] Basayev in France."

Basayev was the radical Muslim leader who planned the violence in Dagestan. The planning "did not happen in Paris, as some of the newspapers reported later, but on the villa of Adnan Khashoggi, Arabic millionaire, on the Mediterranean."

French intelligence agents monitored the meeting and details surfaced in the public print. Khashoggi denied that he had attended the meeting in his own home, but his denial is irrelevant given the Turkoman's redundant role in acts of terrorism worldwide. The meeting's main participants – Anton Surikov, "formerly" of Army Special Forces, and Aleksandr Voloshin, Yeltsin's Chief of Staff – offered no comment. When reporters asked Surikov, he claimed that he hadn't traveled abroad in years, and certainly not to France. This did not quite square with the public record, however, Just a few months before, he was in Washington, D.C. to meet with Yuri Maslukov, Russia's deputy prime minister, and Michel Camdessus, managing director of the IMF. Surikov had also flown to France on a couple of occasions, once in December 1994 and again in the summer of 1999. Surikov was lying. He had, in fact, departed on June 23 aboard an Aeroflot bound for Paris, and returned from Nice on July 21, nearly a month later.[27]

A book on the Russian spy agency, Spetzsnaz GRU, written by former intelligence agents, reports that when the well-paid rebels entered Russia from Chechnya, the military was "commanded not to enter into battle with them and not to hinder the movement of the rebels."[28]

27. Boris Kagarlitsky, "We Don't Talk To Terrorists. But We Help Them?" *Novaya Gazeta*, (trans. by Olga Kryazheva, research intern, Center for Defense Information, Washington DC), January 24, 2000. Hyperlink: http://geocities.com/chechenistan/conspiracy.html http://geocities.com/chechenistan/conspiracy.html
28. John B. Dunlop, "The Second Russo-Chechen War Two Years On," presentation at U.S. and World Affairs Seminar, Hoover Institute, October 17, 2001. Hyperlink: http://66.102.7.104/search?q=cache:nGpCwJsA3z0J:www.freerepublic.com/focus/f-news/1233969/posts+Voloshin+and+khashoggi&hl=en&ie=UTF-8

The 1999 bombing campaign punctuated an uneasy period of calm. From August 1996 through August 1999, Chechnya had been relatively peaceful. "Hostilities resumed following a bold incursion from Chechnya into neighboring Dagestan by an 'international' force of Wahhabis," John Dunlop at the Hoover Institute reports, "whose titular leaders were the legendary field commander Shamil Basaev and the shadowy Arab commander Khattab. In September of 1999, there occurred the notorious terror bombings of large apartment complexes in Moscow, Volgodonsk and Buinaksk, which served to infuriate the Russian populace in a way similar to the American public's reaction to the events of 11 September in this country. On 23 September, Moscow once again commenced the bombing of Chechnya, and the second Russo-Chechen war of the past decade was on."[29]

Alexander Voloshin, who attended the meeting at Khashoggi's villa, is a singular political figure in Russia, outspoken in his support of the United States, in temperament comparable to an American Cold Warrior. On October 23, 2003, the *Guardian* reported that Vladimir Putin's chief of staff was at the center of "a furious row" between Moscow and Kiev "after he reportedly suggested Russia might bomb Ukraine if it did not back down in a diplomatic tiff over a small island between the two former Soviet states. Alexander Voloshin, the head of the president's administration, made the remarks while he was briefing Ukrainian journalists at the Kremlin.... The row is over 100 metres of sand..."[30]

Voloshin was subsequently forced out of government – not for his ties to the meeting at Khashoggi's villa, or to terrorists, but to Big Oil:

Putin's powerful chief of staff resigns
Pakistan Daily Times, November 1, 2004

Voloshin's resignation over arrest of top oil tycoon widens political scandal

---

29. Ibid.
30. Nick Paton Walsh, "Russian official condemned for joke about bombing Ukraine," *Guardian*, October 23, 2003. Hyperlink: http://www.rusnet.nl/news/2003/10/23/currentaffairs04.shtml

MOSCOW: Moscow press reported Wednesday that Kremlin's powerful chief of staff had resigned in protest of the arrest of a top oil tycoon in a widening political scandal on the eve of Russian parliamentary elections.

The Vedomosti business daily said that President Vladimir Putin had accepted Alexander Voloshin's resignation on Monday night after meeting for several hours with top Kremlin officials…

Newspaper reports said that Voloshin had handed in his resignation on Saturday only hours after Russia's richest man, Yukos chief Mikhail Khodorkovsky, was hauled in by secret service men at gunpoint in a Siberian airport and flown to Moscow for questioning.

Voloshin, 47, is seen as one of the last figures in the Kremlin to have hung on from the era of Putin's predecessor Boris Yeltsin and a leader of an administration clan known as "the Family" that battled the hawkish "siloviki" camp of former secret service agents that recently emerged in Putin's court. He was seen as a strong backer of big business and an instrumental Kremlin aide who managed to skillfully mediate between the various administration factions and parliament lawmakers on key economic reform issues.

His potential resignation had been rumored in Moscow for months as the Family – which supported big businesses including Yukos – was being squeezed out by the "siloviki" clan…. Western investors said that Voloshin's resignation – if officially confirmed – would mark an escalation of political instability on the eve of December 7 parliamentary elections.

"Assuming Voloshin's departure is confirmed today, this will only underline the seriousness of the political crisis resulting from Putin's decision to deal with the political problem of Khodorkovsky using KGB methods," the United Financial Group wrote in a research note. The investment house noted that Voloshin "seems to have made himself indispensable to Putin as a discreet but effective administrator with a good grasp of the reform policy agenda and adept at arbitrating between competing interests." Besides heading Putin's administration, Voloshin for the past four years has also served as chairman of the board of the United Energy System electricity monopoly that has been struggling to undertake reforms for the past four years.

But the United Financial Group predicted that Putin would probably try to seek a balance within his administration and was unlikely to give the post to any of the top members of the secret service Kremlin factions.

Voloshin became deputy head of Yeltsin's administration in 1998 and became chief of staff the following year. He was attributed with drafting economic portions of Yeltsin's speeches. Putin kept Voloshin on his post when he took the presidency following Yeltsin's abrupt resignation on December 31, 1999...[31]

Nazi Connections to the Khashoggi Syndicate

Old Guard Nazism is a recurring theme in post-WWII terrorism.

On November 7, 2001, Swiss authorities froze all accounts at Nada Management, a nondescript financial services/consulting house in Lugano, and stormed the premises.

The firm was accused by the U.S. Treasury Department of laundering funds for al Qaeda. Officers of the firm were detained for questioning, including Albert Friedrich Armand "Ahmed" Huber, a retired Swiss journalist and director of the Nada branch of the al-Taqwa ("Fear of God") syndicate, reportedly founded by ODESSA banker Francois Genoud.

Like Genoud, Huber was a repugnant study. On November 5, 2002, *Asia Times* published a thumbnail bio: "Huber [is] a high-profile neo-Nazi who tirelessly travels the far-right circuit in Europe and the United States. He sees himself as a mediator between radical Islam and what he calls the New Right. Since September 11, a picture of Osama bin Laden hangs next to one of Adolf Hitler on the wall of his study in Muri just outside the Swiss capital of Bern. September 11, says Huber, brought the radical Islam-New Right alliance together."[32]

Islamism and National Socialism have cursed democracy and shared political scapegoats since the 1920s, when they both emerged as ideologically driven political forces to serve their respective elites.

The Arab reflection of *Mein Kampf* was penned by Hassan al-Banna – founder of "al-Ikhwan al-Muslimun," an early in-

---

31. http://www.dailytimes.com.pk/default.asp?page=story_30-10-2003_pg4_1
32. Marc Erikson, "Middle East Islamism, fascism and terrorism," *Asia Times*, November 5, 2002. http://www.atimes.com/atimes/Middle_East/DK05Ak01.html. Also see, "Global Nazism and the Muslim Brotherhood Indicators of Connections," by Christopher Brown, *Anderson Report*: http://www.azanderson.org/anderson_report_geo_political_Global_Nazism_Muslim_Brotherhood_filesjuly_11.htm

carnation of the Brotherhood – a "supreme guide" who dwelt endlessly on "the sicknes" that has defiled the Muslim world and threatened to leave it spiritually drained.

Al-Ikhwan mustered a score of Islamist terror organizations in 1928. The organization received funding from the Saudis at about this time, and in the 1930s, Al-Ikhwan established a legation in Munich to assist in fund-raising for Adolf Hitler and his National Socialist Party.

Footholds were set up in dozens of countries to provide the vital network for al Qaeda. Meanwhile, the Brotherhood gathered up recruits and by the end of WW II there were a half-million in Egypt alone. By the late 1940s, the Brotherhood was so formidable that it vied for power over Egypt.

Al-Banna was martyred by the Government on February 12, 1949. His assassination incited a jihad.

Sayyad Qutb (pronounced KUH-tuhb), a propagandist who served up distorted religious instruction and Nazi-style anti-Semitism, assumed leadership of al-Ikhwan.

In the mid-1960s, Ayman al-Zawahiri, still a juvenile, was recruited into the ranks.

Zawahiri was born to a wealthy Egyptian clan. His grandfather was Grand Imam at the al-Azhar Institute, the Sunni hub of higher learning. Abdel-Rahman Azzam, Zawahiri's uncle on his father's side, was the Arab League's secretary general. In 1974, Zawahiri graduated from the medical college at Cairo university, where his father was on the faculty.

In the Middle East, the Grand Mufti of Jerusalem was the most influential Nazi collaborator. Another was Youssef Nada, board chairman of al-Taqwa on the day the files were impounded by the Swiss federal prosecutor's office.[33] Youssef Mustapha Nada was the president of the al Taqwa Bank Group.

Nada, a naturalized Italian, according to Paul W. Rasche in *Studien von Zeitfragen*, was "a member of the Egyptian Muslim Brotherhood and Jamaa-al-Islamiya, which is directly allied with al-Qaeda through Dr. Ayman al-Zawahiri." In 1970, Nada relocated to Saudi Arabia. With an assist from the

33. Ibid.

Muslim Brotherhood, he "established contact with members of the Saudi Royal family, and founded a construction company in Riyadh, much the same as the Bin Laden family. He remained active in Riyadh, and soon founded the first Islamic bank in Egypt, the Faisal Bank."

Combine this connection with Turki al-Faisal's business ties to Adnan Khashoggi, in cahoots with Sheik Kamal Adham, then director of Saudi intelligence (1963-79), brother-in-law of King Faisal and the a key CIA liaison in the Arab world.

Throw into the mix Saud al Faisal – brother of Turki – ever the cheerful optimist, an American ally in the war:

Royal Embassy of Saudi Arabia
Washington, D.C. Press Release, November 9, 2001

His Royal Highness Prince Saud Al-Faisal, Minister of Foreign Affairs, met with President George W. Bush at the White House today. His Royal Highness described the meeting, which covered a range of issues, and in particular the current situation in Afghanistan and the Middle East peace process, as "positive and productive."[34]

---

34. Saudi embassy press release: http://www.saudiembassy.net/2001News/Press/PressDetail.asp?cYear=2001&cIndex=22

CHAPTER SEVEN

THE BROTHER OF JAMES EARL RAY
LINKS THE CIA TO THE MURDER OF MARTIN L. KING, AND DETAILS ABUSE AT THE HANDS OF THE FBI

The following letter to Barry F. Kowalski, former special counsel at the Criminal Section of the Civil Rights Division, U. S. Department of Justice, was written by John Larry Ray, the brother of James Earl Ray, on March 8, 1999. I acquired the letter shortly after it was written. (The letter has been lightly edited for typographical errors.)

Joseph Paul Franklin, the "serial assassin" who makes a cameo appearance in the text, crippled Hustler publisher Larry Flynt for life with a gunshot – conceivably intended to terminate his journalistic interest in the John Kennedy assassination. Franklin has never been tried for the attempted murder of Larry Flynt, but was convicted for an unrelated homicide.

Greetings Barry F. Kowalski:

In 1998, U.S. Attorney-General Janet Reno put you in charge of conducting a limited investigation into the shooting of Rev. Martin Luther King. A few months later, I made copies of confessions of James Earl Ray, and John Larry Ray to you, and told you to make information from these confessions available to the public, such information as:

- That military policeman James Earl Ray, and the OSS/ CIA agents had connections to another racial shooting in Germany.

- That James Earl Ray accepted a sum of money from mobsters, and CIA agents in Illinois, and Canada to carry out some type of assignment.

- That since 1968, all the FBI directors, all the Attorney Generals, and members of Congress has buried this connection between Ray, and the CIA.

- That all the afore-mentioned FBI directors, Attorney Generals, and Congressmen carried out the following act of terrorism against John Larry Ray because he wouldn't join up with them in this Grand Conspiracy:

1. That the feds put John Larry Ray under custody for 18 years for supposedly picking a person up on a highway, who was not found guilty of robbing a bank in St. Peters, Missouri.

2. That the feds added an additional three (3) years to this sentence, because he was tardy about submitting a sample of his handwriting to the FBI.

3. That the feds ran John Larry Ray in and out of prisons, because he would not give testimony to Congress supporting their conspiracy.

4. That the feds tried to get serial-assassin Joseph Paul Franklin to give testimony that John Larry Ray was connected to the shooting of Urban-League president Vernon Jordan.

5. That the feds tried to put the SPECIAL DANGEROUS OFFENDERS ACT on the back of John Larry Ray.

6. That the feds beat on the head of John Larry Ray so much that he had to take two brain waive tests. Once at the Incarnate Word hospital in St. Louis, Missouri, and once at the St. Johns hospital in Springfield, Illinois. It's believed by some doctors that such injuries can cause Diabetes.

7. That the feds withheld Diabetic medication from John Larry Ray, which shortened his lifespan, and made a cripple out of him for life.

8. That the feds tried to put John Larry Ray in an Illinois insane asylum, because he would not go along with their Grand Conspiracy, but a sanity jury ruled, that there was nothing wrong with the sanity of John L. Ray.

9. That the feds accused, or charged John Larry Ray of committing more than 30 felonies in justifying holding him under custody for more than 25 years.

I am still waiting for you to make the afore-mentioned information available to the public. If you do not I will have to make such information available to the public. If I do not make such information available to the public, I might wind up in solitary confinement in some asylum in the united states, or stretched out beneath a tombstone before my time.

One reason I believe that the feds are involved in assassinations is that after each investigation, they seal up their findings for 50 years, thus, the feds investigating assassinations in the united states, would be like Jack the Ripper investigating who was carving up ladies of the night in England.

John Larry Ray,
Soulard City, Missouri

CHAPTER EIGHT

THE BIGGEST POLITICAL SCANDAL OF THE PAST DECADE:

LOCKHEED/SANDIA, BUSH'S STATE DEPT., PAKISTAN'S NUCLEAR BLACK MARKET & THE HIDDEN POLITICS OF THE PLAME AFFAIR

The Americans themselves sold us all kinds of computers for our use in Kahuta as well as electronic components, equipment, inverters, valves, leak detectors, materials and other nuclear-specific things.
– A.Q. Khan Interview, *Weltwoche Online*, Jan. 21, 2009

[American agents waged] one of the most reckless operations in the modern history of the CIA, one that may have helped put the nuclear weapons in the hands of a charter member of what President George W. Bush has called the 'axis of evil.'
–AP, January 10, 2011

A British nuclear expert who fell from the 17th floor of a United Nations building did not commit suicide *and may have been hurled to his death, says a doctor who carried out a second post-mortem examination. Timothy Hampton, 47, a scientist involved in monitoring nuclear activity, was found dead last week at the bottom of a stairwell in Vienna.... Under a year ago, an American died at the IAEA in strikingly similar circumstances, his body being found at the bottom of a stairwell.*
– *Daily Mail*, November 3, 2009

In 2011, *Foreign Policy* published the results of a poll in which 65 top experts in terrorism were asked: "Which country poses the greatest threat to the West today?" Four of five expressed the same opinion: "Overwhelmingly, the experts selected Pakistan as the country that posed the greatest threat," and a majority also selected it as "the country most likely to have its nukes end up in the hands of terrorists." Only two experts named Iran as the West's greatest threat or nuke proliferator to terror groups.

The Foreign Policy/Fund for Peace *Failed States Index 2010* ranked Pakistan in 10th place. To put this assessment in perspective, Somalia topped the list, while Sweden (175), Finland (176), and Norway (177) finished in the last three slots. Haiti (11), Nigeria (14), North Korea (19), Rwanda (40), and Guatemala (72) were all rated more stable than Pakistan.

Pakistan is politically polarized and boasts at minimum 100 fully-operational nuclear bombs.

The *Global Security Newswire* found that Pakistan's fissile materials have been "a leading security concern for the United States for some time. While outside experts believe it would be difficult for terrorists to seize an entire nuclear warhead, they say it would be easier for insiders working at one of Pakistan's many nuclear weapon sites to gradually smuggle out enough weapon-grade material to build a rudimentary atomic device."

The late Benazir Bhutto learned the details of her own country's nuclear capabilities, the strategic location of her own nuclear facilities, from the CIA on a visit to Washington, according to Duane Baughman, producer of the documentary *Bhutto.* The Agency knew all about Pakistan's nuclear capabilities because the Bank of Credit and Commerce International (BCCI), the drug cash laundry on intimate terms with the CIA, was instrumental in shaping them. In 1981, the bank set up a phony "charity," the BCCI Foundation, used it to shelter ill-gotten BCCI gains. Most of the money raised by the BCCI Foundation was "donated" to A.Q. Khan's nuclear initiative.

The father of Pakistan's atomic bomb began his paternity in the 1970s by stealing technology for the refinement of uranium-235 in the Netherlands while employed as a metallurgist at Urenco. Dutch Prime Minister Rund Lubbers told the BBC in 2005 that he had sufficient evidence to have Khan arrested on an Interpol warrant in 1975, but the CIA interceded. Khan was tried and convicted *in absentia* on charges of nuclear espionage in 1983. The conviction was dropped on a technicality.

On July 27 2006, *The Economist* acknowledge that it is unknown, "even to this day, how much Pakistan's leaders knew of the 'nuclear Wal-Mart' Mr Khan operated. The president, General Pervez Musharraf, is on record describing the moment the CIA handed him their detailed dossier of Mr. Khan's proliferation activities, bank accounts and the like as the 'most embarrassing' of his life – but whether because he knew and had been caught out, or because he was unaware of the scale of Mr Khan's nuclear state within a state, he isn't saying."

The CIA had intimate knowledge of Khan's prominence in the nuclear black market, yet his network was allowed to flourish. Intelligence concerning Iran's secret nuclear program, and Libya's, finally "brought Mr Khan down with a thud. But the damage he did was irreparable. Before his fall, he had been lining up a fourth (so far undetected) big customer for his full-service bomb-building package."

The Kahn distribution network, spanning "companies in at least a dozen countries," was coordinated by a front company in Dubai. Much of the technology in the supply chain is still unaccounted for, and "so are electronic copies of detailed, e-mailable designs for a uranium-enrichment plant. Mr Khan provided Libya with a virtually complete bomb design (given to Pakistan originally by China in its irresponsible days); were North Korea and Iran, and possibly others, sold that too? By turning the bomb into a marketable commodity, Mr Khan and his network helped sweep away the barriers to entry into the nuclear business. Parts of the network have been shut down. Others are still operating. And, as with any profitable venture, there will be imitators."

Nuclear proliferation in the Middle East continued apace while the CIA watched – and covertly assisted – because Pakistan played a significant role in the Cold War. "Pakistan was a frontline state in the East-West confrontation," Greenpeace notes in a report on the Khan network. "It was not in the interests of the West to confront Pakistan." The country was "an important strategic asset for the US as a counter to post-revolutionary Iran, communist China, and in the '80s the Afghan insurrection against the Soviets. Even Iraq was "given maximum leeway in arming itself for the 1980-88 war with Iran. The US countered the growing Iranian influence in the region by supporting Iraq in its invasion. ... This support extended to the export of sophisticated weaponry to Iraq, including the technology that country needed for its nuclear weapons program."

Khan was not, as the press would have us believe, merely a rogue agent. He was a vital chess piece in the CIA's geopolitical aims.

And it was a very dangerous game, as the *New York Times* reported on June 16, 2008: "Four years after Abdul Qadeer Khan, the leader of the world's largest black market in nuclear technology, was put under house arrest and his operation declared shattered, international inspectors and Western officials are confronting a new mystery, this time over who may have received blueprints *for a sophisticated and compact nuclear weapon* found on his network's computers."

Enhancements in Pakistan's nuclear explosive design make it "more efficient and easier to hide." Eventually, the compact nuke may well become a "terrorist issue."

"Working in secret for two years, investigators have tracked the digitized blueprints to Khan computers in Switzerland, Dubai, Malaysia and Thailand. The blueprints are rapidly reproducible for creating a weapon that is relatively small and easy to hide, making it potentially attractive to terrorists. The revelation this weekend that the Khan operation even had such a bomb blueprint underscores the questions that remain about what Dr. Khan ... was selling and to whom."

In January, the Nuclear Threat Initiative (NTI), a watchdog group, reported that the new, compact nuke design was sought by Indian terrorists: "The head of an Indian terror group reportedly has admitted to authorities that he wanted his superior in Pakistan to provide a compact 'nuclear bomb.' Indian Mujahideen leader Ahmad Zarar Siddibappa, also known as Yasin Bhatkal, has been in Indian custody since his arrest in late August. The terrorist commander and bomb expert told officials that he earlier asked in a phone conversation with his Pakistan-based superior, Riyaz Bhaktal, if he could be given an atomic device.... Bhatkal reportedly said Riyaz told him 'anything can be arranged in Pakistan.'

The Indian Mujahideen is believed to have a close alliance with the Lashkar-e-Taiba, the Pakistani-based group behind the November 2008 terror attacks on Mumbai. Should the group lay hands on weapon-grade materials from Pakistan, the result would be catastrophic.

On September 4, 2013, the Pak press published a summation of an American intelligence report on the country's nuclear weapons program. "Pentagon and CIA have focused on Pakistan's nuclear facilities that might come under attack by TTP [the Pakistani Taliban] and other extremist organizations.

In October, 2013, Pakistan's *Daily Times* warned that nuclear power plants and uranium enrichment facilities "may, at any time, come under potential attack from the TTP and its allies as they *have already established a strong network within the headquarters of the armed forces*. The possibility of a nuclear attack might be of several types – a commando type attack that might cause widespread dispersal of radioactivity, aircraft crash into an atomic reactor and cyber attack. All would be disastrous. *After several incidents of terror attacks on Pakistan nuclear facilities* (Wah, Kamra, Dera Ghazi Khan, Sargodha), it became clear that the TTP and other extremist groups can gain access to nuclear facilities with the help of their radicalized allies in the armed forces. In December 2011, an article in *Atlantic* Magazine labelled Pakistan as the 'ally from hell.' The article warned that Pakistan was transferring its nuclear weapons from one place to another in very low security vans to hide them from CIA. The inability of Pakistani armed forces was evident from the fact that instead of transferring nuclear weapons in armored vehicles, they were shifting them in unsafe vans."

The Cold War that motivated the CIA to give a nod-and-wink to A.Q. Khan and his atomic collaborators has shrunk into the past. But a far more disastrous hot war may hang on the horizon.

Introduction to Lockheed & the Cohen Group – "Peace" Candidate Howard Dean, Danny Sebright & the Afghan War

... Howard Dean wants the peace movement to believe that he is its best hope for bringing change in Washington. In television ads and presidential debates, Dean has emphasized his opposition to Bush's decision to launch a unilateral invasion of Iraq. ... Dean's earliest statements on foreign policy in the presidential campaign were written with the help of one of the architects of the war in Afghanistan, Danny Sebright, who held the Orwellian title of Director of the Executive Secretariat for Enduring Freedom at the Pentagon under Donald Rumsfeld...

When Sebright let the Pentagon in February of 2002, he went to work for his old boss, former Secretary of Defense William Cohen, at the Cohen Group, a Washington-based consulting company. The firm uses its political connections to help companies obtain contracts with the Pentagon and foreign governments...[1]

The Murder of Daniel Pearl Hovered in the Background ...

From the moment the WTC towers combusted, the press has made a willful mess of it. The reporting on accused 9/11 conspirator Omar Sheikh, a radical Islamist from England, and the Pakistani court decision to hang him for the 2002 murder of Daniel Pearl, for instance...

The Guardian, July 2002:

Both the U.S. government and Pearl's wife have since acknowledged that Sheikh was not responsible. But the Pakistani authorities refused to release Omar Sheikh 'for fear the evidence they produce in court might acquit Sheikh and reveal too much.... Sheikh is also the man

---

1. http://www.counterpunch.org/donahue10302003.html

who, on the instructions of General Mahmoud Ahmed, the then head of Pakistan's Inter-Services Intelligence (ISI), wired $100,000 before the 9/11 attaches to Moham-med Atta.[2]

The story was more than a shot at Pakistan by the inimical Indian regime. *Agence France Press* confirmed that a "high-ly-placed government source" maintained that the "damning link" between the General and "the transfer of funds to Atta was part of evidence which India has officially sent to the U.S.":

> "The evidence we have supplied to the U.S. is of a much wider range and depth than just one piece of paper link-ing a rogue general to some misplaced act of terrorism," the source said. The French report was quoted liberally in the Wall Street Journal, and Mahmoud was forced to step down as a result. The French report sank from view with the resignation of Mahmoud.

His closed conference with Marc Grossman has received scant mention, while attention has been slathered on others who met with the general on or shortly before September 11. The ISI director's meetings with GeorgeTenet, Richard Armit-age, and other ranking administration officials lit up the In-ternet, post-9/11.

And then FBI whistle-blower Sibel Edmonds "whispered cryptically" to AntiWar.com reporter Christopher Deliso some-thing about Grossman's little-known role in the Valerie Plame debacle. Grossman, she said, "has not been as high profile in the press," but "don't overlook him – he is *very important.*"[3]

His importance is multilateral. Fitzgerald considered Grossman to be a core leaker in the Plame investigation, but the prosecutor had his own subterranean conflicts of interest and was not likely to make substantive progress in the case against any ranking Bush administration official. A *Wikipe-*

2. Michael Meacher, "The Pakistan connection," *Guardian*, July 23, 2002. http://911re-view.org/inn.globalfreepress/Pakistan_connection.html
3. Christopher Deliso, "Lesser Neocons of L'Affaire Plame," AntiWar.com, Novem-ber 24, 2005. http://www.antiwar.com/deliso/?articleid=8137

dia entry explores his appointment, and when considered in context explains why the Plame investigation had no legs: "Fitzgerald was named by Deputy Attorney General James B. Comey after then-Attorney General John Ashcroft recused himself from the case due to conflicts of interest." Comey appointed Chicago's U.S. Attorney, "close friend and former colleague Patrick Fitzgerald, as Special Counsel to head the CIA leak grand jury investigation.... In August 2005, Comey left the DOJ and he is now General Counsel and Senior Vice President of Lockheed Martin."[4]

Lockheed/Sandia

The deputy AG has been richly rewarded in fraternal blood diamonds ... Why? How do Lockheed and its assets in the State Department pertain to Valerie Plame and her probings into nuclear smuggling in the Middle East? Another Lockheed connection: the Palmdale contractor owns Sandia's nuclear labs, and...

> Some corrupt U.S. officials of the Department of Defense and State Department facilitated the theft of US nuclear secrets [technology] from American national laboratories – Los Alamos and [Lockheed subsidiary] Sandia – to customers in several countries, including Pakistan. This procedure involved Israeli and Turkish intelligence and also Pakistan's ISI.[5]

A.Q. Khan's laboratory brokered nuclear materials to Algeria, Iraq, Iran, Libya, Syria, Myanmar, etc.

The Edmonds interview continued down a labyrinth of nuclear channels: "Is it correct that U.S. officials sold nuclear secrets not only to Pakistan but also to Israel and some Arab countries?"

"Of course, they did," she said. "The main recipient of most of the U.S. nuclear information was always Israel, specifically after the capture, sentencing and jailing of their main spy in

4. http://en.wikipedia.org/wiki/James_B._Comey
5. http://oraclesyndicate.twoday.net/stories/4677486

the USA. Jonathan Pollard's [handler] was a former top Israeli intelligence officer, Rafi Eitan [now] member of the Israeli government and former chairman of the Pensioners Party."

The Plame Game

This is the hidden, plausibly-denied background to the outing of Valerie Plame, her CIA assignment involved investigating the nuclear black market in Pakistan. High-ranking officials of the State Department and CIA were implicated. In Switzerland, an American was the subject of some public interest in a trial of cut-outs in the AQ Khan network.

The State Department officials involved *happened* to be the very same ne'er-do-wells who blew Valerie Plame's CIA cover. She was effectively neutralized by Grossman, Richard Armitage, and other Lockheed/Cohen Group/State Department jacked-nuke dealers. The submerged nuclear scandal and its ties to Lockheed/Sandia/Cohen Group are transparent when taken together: Grossman is a Cohen Group (remember Danny Sebright?) director – Cohen interlocks neatly with Lockheed's board. As mentioned, James M. Loy, senior counselor at the Cohen Group, also directs Lockheed, and so does Joseph W. Ralston, vice chair the Cohen Group – a Lockheed Martin sub-contractor.

Lockheed influence on the prosecution ... Lockheed influence on the defense ... Lockheed "loses" nuclear secrets ... Lockheed peddles them in Pakistan ... Lockheed here, there, and everywhere in the Scooter Libby case...

It wasn't only Ashcroft who should have recused himself, but also Fitzgerald – whose boss, succeeding Comey, was Robert D. McCallum, a former tobacco industry attorney and a member of the Skull & Bones fraternity at Yale, no less, and of course, a crony of G.W. Bush. The moment of recusal came when Comey went to work for Lockheed and McCallum assumed supervision of the Plame investigation, because Grossman represents none other than ... Lockheed – and lobbies contractually on its behalf.

Lockheed's sudden interest in Comey was a quid-pro-quo. The many interlocking scandals that involving Scooter Libby – including Grossman and his meeting with the director of

Pakistan's ISI preceding 9/11 – were ignored both by Fitzgerald and his predecessor in the case. All of this tainted Libby's prosecution severely.

The name Cheney was excluded from the loop. So were the names Grossman, Mahmoud Ahmed, Daniel Pearl, the Lockheed board of directors, Armitage, and a certain executive branch nuclear black marketing enterprise.

Grossman entered the Plame picture when a memo written on June 10, 2003 turned up, written by a staffer at the State Department's Bureau of Intelligence and Research (INR) on behalf of the undersecretary of state.

In the memo, Marc Grossman requested a briefing on INR's opposition to the administration's contention that Saddam Hussein had sent out feelers toward securing uranium from Niger. The *Washington Post* reported that Grossman – in the role of acting secretary of state, "since Secretary of State Colin L. Powell and Deputy Secretary Richard L. Armitage were out of the country – wanted the letter marked 'secret' preceding a meeting at the White House where the discussion was focused on then growing criticism of Bush's inclusion in his January State of the Union speech of the allegation that Hussein had been seeking uranium. Grossman has refused to answer questions about the letter."[6]

Researcher Michel Chossudovsky:

> Lt. General Ahmed as head of the ISI was a 'U.S. approved appointee.' As head of the ISI since 1999, he was in liaison with his U.S. counterparts in the CIA, the Defense Intelligence Agency (DIA) and the Pentagon. Also bear in mind that Pakistan's ISI remained throughout the entire post-Cold War era until the present, the launch-pad for CIA covert operations in the Caucasus, Central Asia and the Balkans. ... The Bush Administration had sought the "cooperation" of those who were directly supporting and abetting the 9/11 plotline. Absurd, yes, but at the same time consistent with Washington's broader strategic and economic objectives in Central Asia.[7]

6. Deliso.
7. Michel Chossudovsky, "Cover-up or Complicity of the Bush Administration?"

Step back in time, slip on the wing-tipped shoes of a Lockheed director, and ask: Is this all that preoccupied Grossman as he gazed across his polished desk at Atta's generous benefactor – *or* was it a money trail for the press and FBI to follow – a few days before the terror strikes?

What were the objectives? State Department dictates or those of the Cohen/Lockheed group? Lockheed was in step with the Scooter Libby song-and-dance cover story all along. This was the backdrop of the Plame case – and a commuted sentence was waiting at the end of trial. When it was granted by Bush, the opportunity to expose the many scandals intersecting at Grossman's office – with Cohen and Lockheed and all hidden safely away in filing cabinets – was buried, a smoking carbine under wraps.

Well, not entirely. Before returning to power in Pakistan, former Prime Minister Benazir Bhutto offered to allow investigation the Khan network in the West, with foresight that foreign inquiries "might produce terrible results" for several ex-generals of the Pakistan Army who were allegedly part of the infamous proliferation network of AQ Khan, but "were conveniently let off the hook as part of a secret deal between General Pervez Musharraf and Richard Armitage in 2004."

"Dr AQ Khan," Pakistan's *International News* reports, "is on record having said that all the top army generals since 1985 knew about the proliferation activities of his network." Musharraf agreed to jail Dr. AQ Khan "only after striking a secret deal with the US Deputy Secretary of State Richard Armitage in 2004 that his own army generals involved in the illegal nuclear trade would not be touched, and most importantly that he himself would be accepted by the Americans *to rule Pakistan in his military uniform.*"

Bhutto herself stood in the way of General Musharraf's ambitions, however, but it is not known if assassination – a foreign policy function that Armitage had some experience in – was a term of the secret agreement, but it was a necessary one if Pakistan was to have a prime minister who ruled in military

Centre for Research on Globalisation, November 2, 2001. http://www.globalre-search.ca/articles/CHO111A.html

plumage. Benazir Bhutto was murdered on December 27, 2007 in Rawalpindi. Mark Siegel, an American lobbyist, former director of the Democratic National Committee and a Bhutto confidante, has testified, in a statement recorded by Pakistan's Federal Investigation Agency, that Pervez Musharraf threatened Bhutto with "dire consequences" if she returned before the 2008 elections. Bhutto was with Siegel when she received a call from Musharraf, he told investigators. In that conversation, Musharraf informed Ms Bhutto that "he would not be responsible for her security if she returned before the elections."[8]

After the deal was consummated by Armitage and Musharraf, "the role of Pakistani generals in nuclear proliferation was ignored by the Americans and they focused on AQ Khan alone." Khan was "made a scapegoat in the name of 'national security interests.'"

A dossier on the Khan network released in the UK states that AQ Scapegoat was "put under detention after he threatened the former ISI chief General Ehasanul Haq that he would tell the names of all the military generals who were part of this network if he was touched by the Musharraf government." Before he could make good on his threat, however, "he was arrested and put under house arrest without any access to the media and the courts. The same dossier had revealed that Dr AQ Khan had told his investigators that all the chiefs of Pakistan Army since 1985 knew about the activities of his illegal network."[9]

Five years after Benazir Bhutto was murdered by a suicide bomber...

Musharraf wanted to 'eliminate' Bhutto considering her 'threat': Pak authorities
ANI, December 15, 2012

Islamabad: Pakistan's Federal Investigation Agency (FIA) has told Interpol that of former President Pervez Musharraf

---

8. Khalid Iqbal, "Mark Siegel Among Six Summoned by ATC," *The International News*, December, 16, 2012.
9. "Access to AQ Khan to Expose Many Sacred Cows," The International News, (available at the "Back Issues" section of the IN site, not in the archives, but it was reposted on October 10, 2007): http://www.constantinereport.com/allposts/access-to-aq-khan-to-expose-many-sacred-cowsrichard-armitages-secret-deal/

wanted to eliminate Benazir Bhutto considering her a threat to his rule, it has emerged.

The statement was apparently made after the world police rejected Pakistan authorities' request to arrest Musharraf, who is currently in exile in London. According to the Dawn, in September this year, the FIA sent the request to Interpol for the arrest of Musharraf, but the latter rejected it, stating it was moved under political pressure.

The FIA recently dispatched another letter to Interpol, requesting them to arrest Musharraf, a prime accused in the Bhutto murder case.

FIA attached arrest warrants for Musharraf as well as some pieces of evidence, with the letter.

The evidence dispatched with the letter on Thursday included a statement by US Journalist Mark Siegel and records of emails sent by Musharraf to former premier Benazir Bhutto.

Back home, the prosecution's epidermal probes and Bush's commutation smoothed over a bullet-perforated trail of offenses and war crimes that kept returning to the Cohen Group.

"Access, Insight and Intelligence" is the firm's motto.

"Access," "Insight": "In December 2000, shortly before Cohen left office, the Pentagon awarded Iridium Satellite LLC a $72 million contract, sans competitive bidding. David R. Oliver, Jr. (current director of business development and technology for Naval Systems, Northrop Grumman Electronic Sensors and Systems Division), then a senior procurement official, said that he and Cohen were the Pentagon's key lobbyists in the Iridium deal. In two years, Iridium paid the Cohen Group some $400,000 to lobby legislators and the DoD. [10]

"Intelligence" for profit: Conflict-of-interest runs rampant: "At the hub of the Cohen network, the former secretary makes frequent appearances on CNN, where he is a commentator on world affairs. He has served as a director of several corporations, some of which made arrangements to pay the Cohen Group for bringing in business.[11]

An alert blogger, "Cmdr. Salamander," asks: "Is this a business meeting or war strategizing?"

---

10. See http://cdrsalamander.blogspot.com/2006/05/bill-cohen-and-making-of-beltway-whore.html
11. Ibid.

Nowadays, most of Cohen's mornings begin with an 8:30 staff meeting in the "Pentagon." That's the Cohen Group's name for the conference room where the daily meeting is held. On any given day, the gathering may include Joseph W. Ralston, a retired Air Force general and former vice chairman of the Joint Chiefs of Staff; James M. Loy, who finished a long public career as deputy secretary of homeland security; and Marc Grossman, a former undersecretary of state. Another prominent member of the firm, former NATO secretary general and British minister of defense George Robertson, is based overseas. They form an elaborate network.[12]

This is the network that (Russian theory) "suicide" Charles Reichers. *Pravda*:

> Charles D. Reichers, USAF, Retired. Previous member of the Senior Executive Service of the AF, Principle Deputy Assistant Secretary of the Air Force for Acquisition and Management. Also a master navigator and electronic warfare specialist. Found dead of apparent suicide on October 14.

However, Russian Intelligence analysts reported in *Pravda* that the ruling of suicide was a cover-up, that Reichers was murdered because of his involvement in the Minot affair. According to the *Pravda* article, the incident was linked to an operation to smuggle nuclear weapons away from the U.S. military in connection to launching a war against Iran. A principal in that operation was said to be Daniel Richard DeVos, who runs the Commonwealth Research Institute, a non-profit organization and Pentagon contractor.

Deaths Related to NukeGate

There have been a number of mysterious deaths of USAF personnel shortly before and shortly after the incident.

Airman 1st Class Todd Blue: Attached to the 5th Security Forces Squadron at Minot AFB, specifically the Weapons System

---

12. Ibid.

Security section responsible for the security of all "priority res-sources" – including nukes. Returned home on leave immediately after the incident and died on September 10th at the age of 20.

USAF Captain John Frueh: Attached to the USAF Special Operations Command. Last seen with a GPS device, camera and camcorder in a backpack. Found dead on September 8 in Washington State. Last call from his cell at 12:28 p.m. on August 30, the day of the Minot incident. The Air Force refused to allow Washington state police to investigate his disappearance as a missing person case until they had completed a military investigation. Did they know that he was dead?

Clint and Linda Huff: Clint Huff was attached to the 26th Operational Weather Squadron at Barksdale AFB. He and his wife were killed on their motorcycle on September 15th after an SUV they were passing swerved hard left into them.

First Lieutenant Weston Kissel: B-52H Stratofortress Bomber pilot. Also died in a motorcycle accident on July 17, less than two months before the Minot incident.

Adam Barrs and Stephen Garrett: Attached to the 5th Aircraft Maintenance Squadron, responsible for loading and unloading weaponry on the B-52H Stratofortresses at Minot. They were killed in a single vehicle accident on July 3.

The Huffs, Kissel, Barrs and Garrett perished before the incident. But if there was advanced planning – and any significant operation takes advanced planning – they might have been involved.

DeVos

Daniel DeVos, identified as a nuclear kingpin in the *Pravda* article, CEO of Concurrent Technologies Corp., is, naturally, a Lockheed contractor. From conservative *NewsMax*: "A top Clinton administration official, former Defense Secretary William Cohen, sits on the board of Global Crossing. This is the telecom giant that went belly up, the fourth largest bankruptcy in U.S. history, leaving a trail of inflated revenues, top executives enriching themselves, employees and shareholders holding the bag, and Arthur Andersen acting as both consultant and auditor."[13] GHW Bush addressed directors of the Global Crossing start-up, and as payment received stock worth $13 million when the company went public. Global Crossing employees staked another $1 million in GW's campaign.[14]

Postscripts

Book accuses U.S. and Swiss of nuclear cover-up

By Louis Charbonneau
UNITED NATIONS, January 14, 2011

UNITED NATIONS (Reuters) – The CIA persuaded Switzerland to destroy millions of pages of evidence showing how a Pakistani scientist helped Iran, Libya and North Korea acquire sensitive nuclear technology, according to a new book. "Fallout" by Americans Catherine Collins and Douglas Frantz tells the story of the illicit nuclear procurement network created by Abdul Qadeer Khan, a metallurgist who is widely considered the father of Pakistan's nuclear weapons program.

In 2004, Khan admitted to selling Iran, North Korea and Libya uranium enrichment technology that can be used to produce fuel for civilian reactors or atomic weapons. Khan's movements have been curtailed since his public confession.

Analysts and U.N. officials have said that Khan's illicit network, which specialized in helping countries skirt international sanctions, created the greatest nuclear proliferation crisis of the atomic age.

"Fallout" is the second book on the Khan network by Frantz and Collins, a husband-and-wife team of investigative journalists.

They say the United States pressured the Swiss government to destroy evidence that could have helped U.N. investigators determine the full extent of Khan's black marketeering and say they did it to cover up CIA mistakes that had enabled Khan's network to flourish...

The CIA tried to sabotage Iran's nuclear program while monitoring Khan, but it appears the Iranians discovered the problems with equipment that had been tampered with and repaired it, the authors write.

13. Wes Vernon, "Global Crossing Tied to Clinton Defense Secretary," NewsMax.com, February 16, 2002. http://www.the-catbird-seat.net/GlobalCrossing.htm
14. Greg Palast, "Poppy Strikes Gold," *UTNE Reader*, April 8, 2003. http://gregpalast.com/detail.cfm?artid=207&row=1

"STUPIDITY"

A Swiss investigator of the Khan case maintains that the Bush administration wanted evidence seized in raids on the Tinners' home and offices, including computer files, hard drives, disks and documents, to disappear and *"hide their own stupidity."*

In addition to the discovery of more than 300 schematics for two types of Pakistani atomic weapons in the Tinners' possession, *hard drives belonging to the family were found in Thailand, Malaysia and South Africa. Classified information useful in constructing nuclear bombs has traveled the globe.*

Swiss Court Finds "NO AQ Khan Network, Only WESTERN Suppliers"

Shahidur Rehman
International Herald Tribune, January 6, 2011

ISLAMABAD: There was no AQ Khan nuclear proliferation network; there were only Western suppliers of nuclear wares. This is borne out by the report submitted recently by a Swiss Magistrate into the affairs of three members of Tinner family.

The report has spelt out that there was as such no AQ Khan network but several members of the so-called network (actually suppliers) were collaborating with CIA and MI6.

The report submitted by a Swiss Magistrate into the affairs of three members of Tinner family last month has spelt out in words what previous accounts of Dr. A.Q. Khan saga had stated between the lines i.e. – *several members of the so-called network were collaborating with CIA and MI6.*

It has been established beyond doubt that three Tinners – father Frederick Tinner and his two sons Marco and Urs Tinners were working for CIA at least since 2000 till Dr. Khan's fall from high pedestal on February 4, 2004 on charges of proliferation to Libya, Iran and North Korea.

Magistrate Andreas Muller has recommended that charges be brought against three Tinners for violation of Swiss laws and obstructing justice.

"They massively interfered in the wheels of justice," the judge said.

Muller investigated proliferation activities of Tinners for four years, and the reports that *a huge drove of documents and electronic files including allegedly "a highly sophisticated*

Pakistani bomb design" were destroyed by the Swiss authorities on pressure from CIA.

Tinners played a central role in Pakistan's nuclear program since its inception in the 1970's, till the disgraceful fall of Dr. Khan in February 2004.

In February 2008, when the Swiss president acknowledged that files related to the Tinners were shredded by Swiss authorities. The Pakistan government was not informed. Dr. Khan told Kyodo News Agency that *the shredded files took with them proof that "he was innocent of the wrongdoing heaped on his doorstep."*

The decision of the Swiss judge regarding the CIA's complicity in the whole affair takes some heat off of the Pakistanis and Dr. Khan.

A.Q. Khan Interview:
"The U.S. Sold Us Nuclear-Specific Components of the Bomb"

www.weltwoche.ch, January 21, 2009

...The Americans themselves sold us all kinds of computers for our use in Kahuta as well as electronic components, equipment, inverters, valves, leak detectors, materials and other nuclear-specific things...

CHAPTER NINE

THE EARLY HISTORY OF THE JOHN BIRCH SOCIETY

The new America will not be capitalist in the old sense, nor will it be socialist. If at the moment the trend is toward fascism, it will be an American Fascism, embodying the experience, the traditions and the hopes of the great middle-class nation.
　　　　　　　– E.F. Brown, *Current History*, July 1933

We have absorbed into our own legal system the German tyranny that we fought and inveighed against. The approach, copied from the Nazis, works this way: The press and radio first lay down a terrific barrage against the Red Menace. Headlines without a shred of evidence shriek of atom bomb spies or plots to overthrow the government, of espionage, of high treason, and of other bloodcurdling crimes. We are now ready for the second stage: the pinning of the label "Red" indiscriminately on all opposition.
　　　　　　　– Abraham Pomerantz, U.S. Deputy Chief Counsel,
　　　　　　　　　　　　　　　　　　　Nuremberg Trials

An Ornery Bunch Lays Down a Terrific Barrage

If you lived in southern California and traveled with any liberal organization in the early 1980s, odds are that your name could be found in a secret police computer file. On May 25, 1983, L.A.'s Public Order Intelligence Division (PDID) was exposed to the world as a clearinghouse of spies gathering intelligence on the left in Southern California. The PDID stored data on thousands of law-abiding liberals at a cost of $100,000 in tax revenue, utilizing a computer dossier system designed by the late Representative Larry McDonald's Western Goals organization, the intelligence branch of the John Birch Society.

McDonald was national leader of the JBS. Late political researcher Mae Brussell noted in "Nazi Connections to the John F. Kennedy Assassination," that the Society's chief executive officer [killed in the downing of Flight 007] was *a powerful political force in Dallas preceding the murder of John Kennedy.* "*Western Goals has offices in Germany run by Eugene Wigner [a Hungarian-born scientist who worked on the atomic bomb at the University of Chicago] that fed data to the Gehlen BND [post-WW II Nazi intelligence division mustered by the CIA]. On the board of Western Goals sat Edward Teller, Admiral Thomas Moorer [Bob Woodward's superior officer in the Naval wing of the Pentagon within a year of the Watergate series published by the Washington Post], and Dr. Hans Senholt, once a Luftwaffe pilot.*"

The Birchers had everything in common with their Nazi contacts in Germany. Fred J. Cook, in *The Warfare State* (MacMillan, 1962), writes that the JBS was named after John Morrison Birch, the son of Christian missionaries. Birch himself was an obscure evangelical missionary hailing from the Theological Bible Baptist Seminary in Fort Worth, Texas, and an OSS captain executed by Chinese Communist guerrillas ten days after World War II ended for refusing to disarm.

From the JBS website: "Shortly after America's entry into the war, John Birch volunteered to join General Claire Chennault's 14th Air Force, known also as the Flying Tigers. Birch was of particular value in the war because of his facility with various Chinese dialects and it was thus that he was assigned primarily to intelligence work."

The associative pathways of any CIA historian's brain will instantly link "Chennault" with "opium." The OSS entered the narcotics trade with an airline front, the Flying Tigers, vanguards in the struggle to stop Mao Tse Tung from rising to power. (The Tigers were OSS mercenaries mustered by Allen Dulles, who figures prominently in *Bitter Fruit*, by Schlesinger, Kinzer & Coatsworth, which details the transnational financing of Dulles's secret wars.)

The early Birch Society, per Cook, was a "monolithic organization, as authoritarian in its own way as any communist dictatorship.... Welch's John Birch Society is as secret as the Ku Klux Klan" and as "unbalanced as the Nazi Party of Hitler, with many of whose ideas and methods it would find itself quite compatible."

What would the Cold War have been without the jingoistic histrionics of the Birchers, dismissed as silly "yahoos" by most observers, a fascist revival by those who looked into them closely?

The Society was founded in 1959 by Robert Welch. Welch attended the U.S. Naval Academy and studied law at Harvard for two years. He was vice president of the James O. Welch Candy Co. in Cambridge, Massachusetts, and in 1948 vice chairman of the Massachusetts Republican Party's Finance Committee.

Welch made an unsuccessful bid for the office of Lt. Governor at the 1950 Republican primary. He was a ranking director of the National Association of Manufacturers, the subject of many a rancorous essay by George Seldes, who found NAM, in the 1950s, to be a hive of domestic fascist intrigue.

In *Roads to Dominion: Right-Wing Movements and Political Power in the United States*, Sara Diamond writes: "Before and after the formation of the John Birch Society, corporations played a major role in rallying the public to the anticommunist cause." They did this by cranking out books, pamphlets, radio and television programs, often with the aim of crippling organized labor. Non-profits like the Birch Society were sought to lower propaganda costs;

> By 1963, corporations were spending an estimated $25 million per year on anticommunist literature.... Some

169

corporations circulated print and audio-visual materials produced by the John Birch Society; other corporations produced their own in-house literature.... By the early 1960s, the Nation magazine reported that there [were] a minimum of 6,600 corporate-financed anticommunist broadcasts, carried by more than 1,300 radio and television stations at a total annual budget of about $20 million.... Leading sponsors included Texas oil billionaire H.L. Hunt and Howard J. Pew of Sun Oil The corporate sector's massive anticommunist propaganda campaigns created a favorable climate for the mobilization of activist groups like the John Birch Society.

The JBS website boasts that in Welch's time, "self-reliance, good manners, moral uprightness, respect for hard work, and especially rigorous honesty were as pervasive among Americans then as watching television and collecting welfare are for a great many of them today." Welch's funding originated largely with Texas oil billionaire H.L. Hunt, a Texas "patriot" and sponsor of *Lifeline,* a fuming ultra-conservative radio program that aired in 42 states, sponsored by Sunoco and NAM's corporate constituents.

Welch learned, according to the JBS site, that "The Conspiracy" was more "deeply rooted than he had previously thought, and supported this thesis by tracing its origins back over a century to an occult group known as the Illuminati, founded on May 1, 1776 by a Bavarian named Adam Weishaupt." Tenaciously tracking back through the pages of obscure political tracts, Welch claimed that he found this "Satanic" conspiratorial cabal had participated in the French Revolution of 1789, "which infamous uprising, as we know, struck out with intense savagery against God and civilization and resulted in the murder of roughly a million human beings. Clearly, the upheavals and atrocities of 1789 served as a model for revolutions to come, especially the Bolshevik Revolution."

Welch introduced his vision of the Society at a meeting of twelve "patriotic and public-spirited men" in Indianapolis on December 9, 1958. The first chapter formed two months later.

THE EARLY HISTORY OF THE JOHN BIRCH SOCIETY

"The core thesis of the society," reports Political Research Associates in Somerville, Massachusetts,

> ...was contained in Welch's initial Indianapolis presentation, transcribed almost verbatim in The Blue Book of the John Birch Society, and subsequently given to each new member. According to Welch, both the US and Soviet governments were controlled by the same furtive conspiratorial cabal of internationalists, greedy bankers and corrupt politicians. If left unexposed, traitors inside the U.S. government would betray the country's sovereignty to the United Nations to form a collectivist new world order managed by a "one-world socialist government."

The Birch Society "incorporated many themes from pre-WWII rightist groups opposed to the New Deal, and had its base in the business nationalist sector."

On hindsight, Bircher G. Edward Griffin, writer and narrator of the 1992 quack documentary *The Discovery of Noah's Ark*, is critical of the "fascists" who made up the Society's National Council:

> Members of the Society's Council included a few regional directors of the Federal Reserve System, members of the Council on Foreign Relations, and some of them worked closely with operatives of secret government agencies. For example, William J. Grede, an industrialist on the Executive Committee of the JBS Council, was a director of the Federal Reserve Seventh District. Coleman T. Andrews was a member of the Bohemian Club. Spruille Braden, an ambassador to numerous countries who helped to topple their regimes, was an agent of The United Fruit Company, director of the W. Averell Harriman Securities Corporation, an agent of Standard Oil, and a member of the Council on Foreign Relations. Ralph E. Davis was a director of the Wackenhut Corporation, a private security firm that has contracts for security and paramilitary services of various government agencies including black-[bag] operations. Other Wackenhut board

members included former FBI Director Clarence Kelly, former Defense Secretary and CIA deputy director Frank Carlucci (later known for his leadership role in the Carlyle Group), former Secret Service director James J. Rowley, and many others from the military and CIA. George Wackenhut boasted that his company maintained files on 2.5 million Americans who were suspected dissidents."

("WAS MR. GRIFFIN A MEMBER OF THE JOHN BIRCH SOCIETY, AND ISN'T THAT AN EXTREMIST GROUP? – A reply by G. Edward Griffin," Freedom Force International website, October 28, 2007.)

Fred Koch, founder of Koch Industries, was a founding board member of the nascent Birch Society. Koch was instrumental in launching hateful propaganda assaults on conspiratorial Marxist threats to the Republic: organized labor, liberal clergy, intellectuals and public education. The *New American*, the Society's online propaganda organ, reports that the Kochs played a seminal role in the group's political direction:

"Koch warned that American institutions were honeycombed with communist subversives, from labor unions and tax-free foundations to universities and churches. Art and newsprint, radio and television – all these media had been transmuted into vehicles of communist propaganda." Koch was no "fly-by-night pamphleteer. He spent a generous portion of his later years using his wealth and influence to fight the communism he abhorred. He was an early member of the John Birch Society's National Council, an advisory group to JBS founder Robert Welch."

Lee Fang at the ThinkProgress website fills gaps in the *New American* portrait with Fred Koch's "record of bigotry." In a booklet written by the industrialist, Koch screeched against civil rights leaders, and claimed the movement against racial segregation was a communist plot to manipulate African-Americans into destabilizing the country. Birchers bankrolled by Fred Koch hosted numerous rallies during the '60s warning that racial integration would lead to a 'mongrelization' of the races.

THE EARLY HISTORY OF THE JOHN BIRCH SOCIETY

The legacy of Fred Koch is a quiet race war. Although his sons, the notorious Koch brothers, "try to eschew explicit racism," their leading Tea Party front, Americans for Prosperity, "is currently pursuing similar racial segregation goals. In North Carolina, the Americans for Prosperity chapter led a campaign to end a highly successful public school integration system." ("John Birch Society Celebrates Koch Family For Their Role In Founding The Hate Group, *ThinkProgress*, June 10, 2011.)

The JBS had a corporate foundation – mainly oil companies and military contractors. The leadership boasted that Birchers served as a first line of "defense" against the creeping encroachments of communism. But some feared that the American Dream was doomed. Palme Dutt, in *Fascism and Social Revolution* (International Publishers, 1935), caught on early. Twenty years before the formation of the Birch Society, he found that capitalism "can no longer maintain its power by the old means." Crisis was "driving the whole political situation at an escalating pace." The rise of the labor unions and social movements threatened to usurp the power, wealth and privilege of the ruling class.

Every sector of society was affected by the clash.

The Lords of Industry, with one eye askance at developments in the East, was "driven to ever more desperate expedients to prolong for a little while its lease on life." Rabidly nationalistic fronts like the John Birch Society were a "desperate expedient" of social control, undermining any attempt to trespass on the self-serving authority of the country's military-industrial plutocrats. In the wings of the Birch Society, with its insistent rejection of "collectivism," lurked corporate sponsors keen on mass perception management.

In an address to the Cooperative League of the United States, T.K. Quinn, a former vice president of General Electric, shared a dissident view of the corporate underpinnings of the Birch Society:

> In forms of organization and control, these giants are essentially collectivistic, fascist states, with self-elected

and self-perpetuating officers and directors, quite like the Russian politiboro in this respect. Their control extends directly over production, over tens of thousands of small supplying manufacturers and subcontractors, and over thousands of distributors and dealers. Indirectly, the control of these giant corporations influences legislation through paid lobbies in state capitals and Washington, and it is seen and felt in the magazines, newspapers, radio and television stations, all dependent upon these giants and their associates for their existence.

By comparison, liberal lobbyists were given the political heave-ho. The American Federation of Labor may have won three lobbying campaigns, but lost seven. The Farmers' Union scored one in eight. Veterans of Foreign Wars, one in five.

Anti-fascist journalist George Seldes discovered that National Association of Manufacturers (NAM), "the richest and most powerful lobby in the nation, got all the laws it sponsored passed by Congress." The Committee for Constitutional Government, called "America's Number One fascist organization" by Congressman Wright Patman, won seven in eight that it sponsored.

Unquestionably, favoritism at the legislative level fell to right-wing corporate fronts, not the left. The Birch Society was an arm of NAM and its corporate constituents – General Motors, DuPont, Sunoco, U.S. Steel, etc. "Another organization," Seldes wrote, "apparently founded with the intention of the Birch Society to unite reaction in a vast and powerful political weapon, calls itself Americans for Constitutional Action and unites NAM leaders, the owners of the *Reader's Digest*, and Birchers; it is reaction's answer to Americans for Democratic Action."

Reader's Digest? The ubiquitous "funny little magazine" calls to mind another sponsor of right-wing extremist front groups – the CIA. In the Eisenhower period, propagandists on the Agency payroll contributed regularly to the *Digest*, including Allen Dulles, Carl Rowan, James Burnham, Brian Crozier, Stewart Alsop and other ultra-conservative propagandists.

Another right-wing headshrinker was the *National Review*, in its early days indistinguishable from Birch Society fulminations. The magazine was edited by the CIA's William F. Buckley, a close friend of Welch's. The first issue appeared on the stands in November 1955. Buckley opened with a "Publisher's Statement" in which he declared war on "the Liberals who run the country." The *Review*, Buckley boasted, "stands athwart history, yelling Stop!"

In March, 1956, John Fischer, editor of *Harper's*, spat: "Last November, newsstands throughout the country offered the first issue of a new magazine, *National Review*, which described itself as 'frankly, conservative.'" But the magazine's first half-dozen issues demonstrated clearly that it "was an organ, not of conservatism, but of radicalism ... [and] like most of the extremist little magazines, it seems to be aimed at an audience of True Believers." The readership of the *National Review* were "emotional people who throw themselves frantically into a cause – often to make up for some kind of frustration in their private lives. They form the hard core of many religious, nationalist and revolutionary movements: they have great capacity, in Hoffer's words, for 'enthusiasm, fervent hope, hatred and intolerance ... blind faith and single-hearted allegiance.' They are the opposite of conservatives."

Dwight MacDonald, a staff writer for the *New Yorker*, cautioned: "*NR* seems worth examining as a cultural phenomenon: The McCarthy nationalists call themselves conservative, but that is surely a misnomer – they have never before made so heroic an effort to be intellectually articulate. Here are the ideas, here is the style of the lumpen-bourgeoisie, the half-educated ... who responded to Huey Long, Father Coughlin and Senator McCarthy.... These are men from underground, the intellectually underprivileged who feel themselves excluded from a world they believe is ruled by liberals (or eggheads — the terms are, significantly, interchangeable in *NR*)."

The CIA's William F. Buckley passed himself off as an independent thinker, journalist and publisher. But documents declassified by the Assassination Records Review Board debunk this profile. In Watergate "Plumber" Howard Hunt's Office of Security file, Dan Hardway of the House Select Committee found a pile of documents concerning Buckley. He was not merely a spook. Buckley was a ranking intelligence officer stationed in Mexico City to direct covert ops. Thereafter, he attempted to conceal his CIA status with Hunt's assistance.

Documents subpoenaed by Congress note that some articles published by the *National Review* were in fact written by E. Howard Hunt – a review critical of *The Invisible Government,* by David Wise, for instance. When Buckley left the CIA to publish *National Review*, he maintained a covert relationship with Hunt.

Buckley also distanced himself publicly from Welch in the April 21, 1961 issue of the *Review*. There was growing interest in the organization, Buckley claimed, because "liberals, and to the extent their programs coincide, the communists, feel threatened by the revived opposition. Accordingly they have taken hold of a vulnerable organization and labored to transform it into a national menace." It might be argued that the Society had something to do with its own reputation, that liberals did not have to "labor" too strenuously, after all. Buckley himself admitted in his next breath that the Birch Society was "an organization of men and women devoted to militant political activity."

"I myself have known Robert Welch since 1952," Buckley acknowledged. "I have read all his books, and most of his articles and editorials. He bought stock and debentures in *National Review* in its early years (less than one percent of our original capital). We have exchanged over a dozen letters, and spoken from the same platform on two occasions. I have always admired his personal courage and devotion to the cause."

But, wrote Buckley, he had to part with Welch's conclusion that Dwight D. Eisenhower was a "willing agent of the Soviet Union," though he believed "most definitely" that the "communist conspiracy" was a "deadly serious matter." In the future, he hoped that the Birch Society "thrives," so long as "it resists such false assumptions as that a man's subjective mo-

tives can automatically be deduced from the objective consequences of his acts."

Buckley hoped to salvage the organization's political usefulness to the far-right cause by plotting to distance his "old friend" Welch from the Birch Society.

George Seldes noted that Welch's "paranoid and idiotic libels" of President Eisenhower caused a stir in the Republican Party: "It resulted in an attempt to separate Welch from Birch and set Welch adrift. Editor William Buckley of the *National Review*, and a highly popular Birch radio orator, Fulton Lewis, Jr. (who outdid the Birchers by favoring *lynching*, not merely indicting, the Chief Justice), joined in the chorus calling for Welch's resignation. Then the John Birch Society would survive to serve their own interests. They did not succeed" (Seldes, *Never Tire of Protesting*, p. 220).

Welch was not one to forget a minor slight like a coup attempt. He'd been betrayed by the Skull-and-Bones CIA Yalie, snooty Bill Buckley, and he was bitter. His business affairs were tangled up with Buckley's, however, and the connection went far beyond a minor stock holding. Welch wielded influence at Young Americans for Freedom, founded in September 1960. YAF was a fascist front crawling with Birchers. It also served as an enclave for German spies arriving from Munich, Germany (Dick Russell, *The Man Who Knew Too Much*, Carroll & Graf, 1992).

And YAF leadership was loyal to Buckley. In the summer of 1961, Welch enlisted the aid of Nelson Rockefeller (in Birch lore, the country's most powerful closet "Communist") and launched a counter-coup of the student organization. Together, *National Review* publisher William Rusher recalls in *The Rise of the Right*, an incredible, unlikely alliance, "Welch and Rockefeller, in league, through their youthful agents, [attempted] to wrest control of the national board of YAF from the friends of *National Review*." In the end, the Birch faction was outvoted and the Buckley crowd maintained control of the radical right student union (Rusher, pp. 115-116).

Birchers have never been content to sit idly by, swapping tales of phantom communist conspiracies. They took an active hand to throttle the amoral, anti-capitalist "imperialists" threatening to destroy God's chosen people.

General Edwin A. Walker resigned from the Army in November 1961 after he was chastised by the Pentagon for distributing Birch Society propaganda to his troops. He was temporarily relieved of command pending an investigation. Walker, a Bircher to the bone, chairman of Committee for the Defense of Christian Culture (a group with chapters in Bonn, Germany established by a Nazi), ultimately blustered his way into a number of footnotes in Camelot history. Lee Harvey Oswald reportedly attempted to shoot him, and the general once made a bid for governor, but finished last in the 1962 Democratic runoff. Dick Russell:

> Late in September, 1962, the general made headlines around the world. James Meredith was seeking to become the first black ever admitted to the University of Mississippi. It was a landmark moment in the fight against racial segregation. Meredith's entry was mandated by a federal court order, and when Mississippi governor Ross Barnett set out to block it, Kennedy ordered National Guardsmen deployed on Meredith's behalf. That was when General Walker called for ten thousand civilians to march on Oxford, Mississippi, in opposition. Walker was on the scene when rioting erupted against four hundred federal marshals escorting Meredith onto the campus.

Two people were killed in the melee, 70 wounded. The next morning, "Walker was arrested by federal authorities on four counts, including insurrection, and flown for psychiatric observation to the Medical Center for Federal Prisoners at Springfield, Missouri."

The Liberty Lobby, another fascist corporate front, hastened to General Walker's defense and blamed the Kennedys for waging a campaign against Walker to "reduce his prestige" and "asset value to the anti-Communist cause" (p. 309).

Back in 1957, General Walker made the cover of *Time* magazine and was actually credited with furthering the cause of racial equality after he led federal troops integrating the schools in Little Rock, Ark. Actually, Gen. Walker led the troops only after President Eisenhower refused his resignation, historian Don E. Carleton, author of *Red Scare*, told the *Fort Worth Star-Telegram.* "He did not want to carry out that order," Mr. Carleton said. "He did not believe in racial integration" (General Walker obituary, AP release, November 2, 1993).

Walker flew the U.S. flag upside down to express his rage over the perceived "communist" leanings of Kennedy and sundry federal officials, according to Darwin Payne, a former Dallas newspaper reporter. "He was not a good speaker. He was a poor campaigner and finished last in a field of six [in the gubernatorial race], which was a surprise because he had so many ardent followers in the rightwing," Mr. Payne said in Walker's obituary.

General Walker loudly declared himself a martyr in the war against communism. At a hearing of the Senate Armed Services Committee in 1962, he testified that the "Conspiracy" was, in the words of columnist Jack Anderson,

> ... clearing the way for world communism by systematically slandering and discrediting its effective opponents. The cast of victims of this 'hidden policy' ran to thousands ... and he undertook to name the brightest of the fallen: General Douglas MacArthur, Defense Secretary James Forrestal, Generalissimo Chiang Kai-shek, Senator Joseph McCarthy, General George Patton, Congressman J. Parnell Thomas. Walker's litany of martyrs was standard among the 'anti-communist' right; it could have been lifted intact from the speeches of Senator Joseph McCarthy or Gerald L.K. Smith a decade earlier, just as it would be reproduced a decade later in the pamphlets on the fanatical fringe, except that in the latter case the roster of unheeded prophets would be updated by the addition of Senator Thomas J. Dodd of Connecticut and Representative Michael Feighan of Ohio (Jack Anderson, *Confessions of a Muckraker*, Random House, 1979, pp. 100-101).

Even liberals within the GOP were smeared by the Birchers. Thomas Kuchel, a U.S. senator for 16 years and the last major liberal Republican to hold office in California, was one of them. Kuchel expressed particular pride in his support of civil rights bills for enfranchisement of blacks, and desegregation of public facilities under the Johnson administration. In 1994, the *Los Angeles Times* reported that Kuchel

> ... said with characteristic disdain, the main feature of "right wing Republicans," as he understood them, "was militant anti-Communism. They seemed convinced we were about to be invaded by the Communists." Mr. Kuchel always traced his trouble with the political right to his response to a surge of mail he got from members of the then-obscure John Birch Society shortly after John F. Kennedy became president. "I got thousands of letters telling me that Chinese Communists were in Mexico preparing to invade California," he recalled. After checking with military authorities, Mr. Kuchel wrote a short form letter in response: "We have no evidence of Communists gathering in Mexico, Chinese or otherwise." Shortly thereafter, Mr. Kuchel learned that he was being labeled a "Comsymp," a term he had not heard of until that time. "I got a little tee'd off, and prepared a carefully researched speech critical of the John Birch Society and that kind of mentality," he remembered. "I kicked them around, and they never forgave me." (Kuchel obituary, *Los Angeles Times*, November 23, 1994).

An editorial writer for the *Times Record News* in Witchita Falls followed the political machinations of the Birch Society from an early age ("A Society of Hate," Oct. 25, 1998), and observed that JBS founder Robert Welch "was not in government but despised most of those inside it, was never stopped, and his influence grew even as McCarthy's bulb dimmed and died out."

Birchers down in Texas were hyperactive. They gained a foothold in local politics

> ... and that's how I know they were an ornery bunch. The first person I actually came to know as a Bircher was a

kid I'd gone through school with who showed up one day outside the schoolhouse with the trunk of his car loaded down with boxes of paperback books. He was standing there with the trunk lid up handing out free books to anybody who'd take one. I could kick myself now for not taking one then because it would be interesting to have it just to show my kids what mean times those were. If you think the Starr Report made President Clinton look bad, you should've seen this book. The name of the book was *A Texan Looks at Lyndon*. I came to know quite a number of Birchers in various contexts, some through church, some through groups my parents socialized with, some through my job as a journalist, but I didn't know them as Birchers until I started connecting the dots.

They were a sneaky bunch, and mean, and at one time they ran the government in my hometown, and used their offices to preach against communism and socialism as though evil was right there at the city limits threatening to come in and take over. I never ran across a communist or socialist back then, so maybe the Birchers were successful. I dunno. A little later, they tried to take over the entire Republican Party in the county where I lived by putting stealth candidates on the ballot for every position at the last minute. I guess they knew so much about communist infiltration that they'd become experts at it. The ones I knew were a humorless bunch, sullen, suspicious and stiff-necked. They saw America going straight to hell right before their eyes, and they resented the fact that so few heeded their doomsday predictions.

Welch's disdain for government officials didn't deter Representative Howard Buffett, an Omaha investment broker before his run for congress and father of "Sage" Warren Buffett, from joining the JBS. "By the late Eisenhower years," Alice Schroeder wrote in her biography of the Omaha billionaire (*The Snowball: Warren Buffett and the Business of Life*), felt the country had "grown soft and fat in its prosperity" and "was losing the arms race." Buffett senior joined the JBS "with what he described as 'concern' for the 'moral and spiritual problem of America, which would be with us even if Communism were stopped tomorrow. He covered his office walls with maps showing the menacing red advance of Communism."

Howard Buffett was instrumental in bringing the Christian Anti-Communist Crusade to Omaha, and ran with a movement of "ideological conservatives that was coalescing around Arizona Senator Barry Goldwater. Howard was respected as a philosophical purist among libertarian-leaning wing of the Republican Party, but anyone associated with the Birchers attracted both alarm and ridicule. After he went to the local press to defend his Birch membership, people instinctively wrote him off as an eccentric. That Omaha snickered at his revered father was painful to Warren."

An exception to the sneering that met Welch's cultic bund was William Kintner, a former CIA officer who castigated critics of the extreme right in the May, 1962 issue of *Reader's Digest*. Kintner maintained that the "campaign" waged against radical right havens like the John Birch Society began when "dossiers in Moscow's espionage headquarters were combed for the names of unsuspecting persons in the United States who might do the Kremlin's work." Anyone castigating the home corporate-military state was a suspected Soviet agent peddling subversive "disinformation."

"Hey, Hey, JFK – How Many Birchers Gunned You Down Today?"

But the Society's ambitions went far beyond control of small-town politics. Members who objected to Kennedy's communist "appeasement" policies went so far as to plot the overthrow of the government.

In 1962, Dallas officials of the John Birch Society attended a meeting with H.L Hunt, General Edwin Walker, Robert Morris (leader of the Defenders of American Liberty, president of Plato University in New Jersey and former chief counsel for the U.S. Senate Internal Security Subcommittee), and Larry Schmidt, a veteran of two tours of Army duty in Munich who idolized Hermann Goering. Back home, Schmidt, his head wheeling with Bircher propaganda given to him by General Walker back in Germany, took a position at United Press International. He had made plans while stationed in the Rhineland to start an organization he called CUSA, short for "Conservatism U.S.A."

By the summer of 1962, Schmidt organized a platoon of zealots from the Military Police and Counter-Intelligence Corps. *Look* magazine (January 26, 1965) reported that Schmidt "trained a small, disciplined band of soldier-conspirators to follow him stateside and do, he hoped, 'whatever is necessary to accomplish our goal.'" Schmidt's coup plan called for infiltrating conservative organizations around the country, and marshaling them to overthrow the Kennedy government. The core of this seditious secret army was to be the first organization drawn into Schmidt's plan – Young Americans for Freedom, the Birch Society offshoot with some 50,000 members – by arrangement with Heidelberg-born Major General Charles Willoughby (true name Weidenbach, a YAF founder, alleged by Dick Russell to be one of the central participants of the John F. Kennedy assassination).

The coup plan was exposed when Warren Commission investigators happened upon Schmidt's role in the purchase of a newspaper ad framed with a thick, black border that ran in the *Dallas Morning News* the morning Kennedy was shot, condemning a president guilty of treason for alleged diplomatic dalliances with the Russians (Russell, pp. 320-24).

The name Kennedy irritated the colons of good Birchers everywhere. Ronald Reagan, president of the Screen Actors' Guild and FBI snitch, under secret contract with MCA management, emerging political star in Hollywood, was closer to the mark. After the 1964 presidential election, Democratic Party officials crafted a plan to take on right-wing extremists in the public arena, including one of Reagan's support groups, Citizens for Constitutional Action, a "conservative grassroots" organization that had backed Goldwater in his presidential run and thereby splintered the Republican Party. Both Goldwater and the John Birch Society received lavish support from J. Howard Pew, owner of the Sun Oil Company (Colby and Dennett, *Thy Will Be Done*, HarperCollins, 1995, p. 453).

The Republicans countered with measures tailored to inspire party unity. Reagan was cautioned not to allow himself to be defined as either a moderate or conservative. "During one secret strategy meeting," Curt Gentry (in *The Last Days of the Late, Great State of California*, Putnam's, 1968) wrote, "John Rousselot, national public relations director of the John Birch Society, approached Stuart Spencer with a coldly pragmatic offer: the society would be glad to endorse Reagan or denounce him, whichever would help most" (p. 125). When Reagan was sworn in as governor of California on January 2, 1967, he was congratulated by Robert Welch himself. Welch proudly proclaimed that the Birch Society was, "in large part," deserving of credit for Reagan's electoral victory.

"We had chosen California as a state in which to concentrate, practically since the beginning," Welch said. "As a rule, about fifteen percent of the total field staff we could afford, and hence at least fifteen percent of our total membership has been in California" (Gentry, p. 285).

The rise of Ronald Reagan occurred in the Society's halcyon period, before public opinion forced conservative politicians to distance themselves from Welch's hyper-vigilant red-baiters. But the Birch Society remained symbiotic with the very corporate-military elite it denounced. The editorial advisory committee of Welch's *American Opinion* magazine claimed four past presidents of the National Association of Manufacturers were communist infiltrators. Other editorial advisors of the JBS's house organ: General A.C. Wedemeyer from the Pentagon's War Plans Division under the Joint Chiefs of Staff; Colonel Laurence Bunker, formerly the ranking aide-de-camp to General Douglas MacArthur; and the Honorable Spruille Braden, a shoo-in for "Insider" as former undersecretary of state (Mike Newberry, *The Yahoos*, Marzani & Munsell, 1964, p. 21).

The Birch Society identified the Council for Foreign Relations (CFR) as the heart of the world Marxist conspiracy. Ironic, again, that many of the leaders of the JBS also sat on the CFR, according to *Who's Who*, including William Grede, founder of the Birch Society National Council, director of the 7th Federal Reserve Bank, an arm of the much despised CFR; William Benton McMillan, the first Life Member of the Birch Society and ramrod of the St. Louis Committee of the CFR; Robert Waring Stoddard, a JBS Council member and chairman of the Board of the *Worcester Telegram and Gazette,* a newspaper that employed editors belonging to the local committee of the JBS National Council. Braden was a fixture of the CFR, sat on the Council, and was a director of the W. Averell Harriman Securities Corporation.

The Birch Society Salon

"I've always been opposed to the secret government."
– John F. Kennedy, 1958

Society leader Thomas Anderson, a hardened advocate of racial segregation, gave the game away when he whined in *Straight Talk*: "Invariably, hiding behind the sanctimonious cries of 'freedom of the press,' and 'academic freedom' are defenders of Alger Hiss, Fifth Amendment addicts, attackers of the House Committee on Un-American Activities, people who urged barring *Mein Kampf* from distribution. In short, the enemies are: Criminals, Socialists and Communists."

Hitler was now a cause celebré.

Of critical importance to the anti-communist wars of the Birch Society was Welch's relationship with Dr. J.B. Matthews, former chief investigator for the House Un-American Activities Committee (HUAC). When Joseph McCarthy announced that he held a list of Soviet agents in his hands, he referred to one of Matthews' compilations. When McCarthy fell into disrepute, J.B. strolled off into the sunset, taking his files on known "communist subversives" with him, moved on to become Robert Welch's aide-de-camp. "My opinion of various characters," Welch wrote in his *Blue Book of the Birch Society,* "formed entirely independently, has [proven] to coincide with the opinion of J.B. Matthews." Welch boasted that he had "a fairly sensitive and accurate nose" for rooting out agents of the communist underground.

Dr, Matthews pushed the number of "agents," "subversives" and "travelers" among the nation's clergymen in Birch Society files from 1,000 to 7,000 names. America's parishes evidently swarmed with spies and dupes of "The Conspiracy." In July 1961, the *Birch Society Bulletin* claimed that there were no less than "300,000 to 500,000 Communists in the United States" (Newberry, p. 89). Welch and Matthews dreamed of assembling files on every one of them.

The American Opinion reading room was the place to learn all about these subversives, an alternate universe of fanatical right-wing lectures devoid of recognizable reality. Medford Evans, formerly editor of the *National Review* and the Birch Society's Texas coordinator, published a critical tour-de-force in *Human Events* magazine (January 26, 1957), a CIA-subsidized publication: "Why I Am An Anti-Intellectual." Evans once served under Admiral Lewis Strauss at the Atomic Energy Commission. The dossiers of J. Robert Oppenheimer and Edward Teller were cleared by the AE's proud anti-intellectual chief of security (Newberry, p. 138).

Early on, Welch's Society was allied with William Regnery, whose name appears on American Security Council (ASC) incorporation papers. The ASC was a domestic covert operations arm of the military-corporate complex, closely aligned with the JBS, Libery Lobby and other sons of the fascist revolution. Regnery and a pair of pre-war America First isolationists initiated the *Human Events* radio program and the Regnery publishing firm in the mid-'50s. The first two books published by Regnery were critical of the Nuremberg Trials, and the third found fault with allied bombing campaigns during WW II.

In 1954, Regnery turned out a couple of tracts for the Birch Society. The nascent publishing concern also printed up William F. Buckley's *God and Man at Yale*, subtitled, *The Superstitions of Academic Freedom*. "In light of the publishing of the pro-Nazi books," SpritOne Information Services comments, "it is interesting to note that Regnery Publishing was subsidized by the CIA, according to Howard Hunt. The reader is reminded to remember [the] point ... concerning the CIA and its involvement with Nazi war criminals. Henry Regnery, along with Bunker Hunt, funded Western Goals." The Western Goals spying operation was organized by the Birch Society.

In 1986, President Ronald Reagan "appointed Alfred Regnery to help dismantle the Justice Department's Office of Juvenile Justice. In the 1990s, [Regnery] has been the publisher of numerous venomous smears (I would use the word 'books' but that would be a lie by any measure) attacking President Clinton. [A] direct linkage between the past pro-Nazi groups of the 1930s and today's right wing has been fully established" (www.spiritone.com).

Gary Allen, among the oiliest propagandists in the Birch pantheon, was the author of *None Dare Call It Conspiracy*, a '76 Press release, Birch Society bible and stunning success that has sold over four million copies, according to a publisher's blurb.

Picture the nation's corporate elite driving for a "Great Merger" with the Kremlin, poisoning the air with Stalinism. This is among the central themes of *The Rockefeller File* (1976), Allen's critique of the most powerful family in the world, the dreaded CFR and United World Federalists, those One World people. At first glance, Allen's books may appear a confused clot of paranoid political fantasies. He claims that the Carnegie and Rockefeller money machines have "jumped into the financing of education and the social sciences with both Left feet" – as though these foundations traveled with Marx, when in fact they have proven time and again to serve as funding conduits of the CIA, an agency with interests that do not exactly correspond with Marxist principles. The result, Allen laments, has been "a sharp Socialist-Fascist turn" (p. 45). Decipher this one, and you have washed onto the eerie island of ultra-conservative conspiracy theories, teeming with nationalistic puffery and Bible-thumping "moral" sentiment. The Union Theological Seminary supposedly turned out armies of "Christian-Communists." Dan Smoot, an infamous fascist organizer, "scholar," a former FBI agent, was, from Allen's perspective, a heroic David who stood his ground against the evil EPA (p. 142). The *New York Times*, per Allen, was a cabalistic haunt of left-wing thought control (p. 66).

Gary Allen's oblique reasoning was often identical to Adolph Hitler's anti-democratic snits. "The present democracy of the West," wrote Germany's Fuhrer, "is the forerunner of Marxism which would be unthinkable without it. It is democracy alone which furnishes this universal plague the soil in which it spreads."

How many communists poisoned the soil of democracy? The John Birch Society *Bulletin* on July 1961 let on that there were "not more than a million allies, dupes and sympathizers." Welch proposed compiling a list of these internal saboteurs, "the most complete and most accurate files in America on the leading Comsymps, Socialists and liberals" (Newberry, pp. 89-90), presaging the Western Goals database of known leftists.

Another scholar of the extreme right was Antony Sutton, author of *National Suicide: Military Aid to the Soviet Union*, and a series of chapbooks on Yale's Skull and Bones fraternity. He was an advocate of separation between the races in South Africa. Sutton, who published a newsletter, *The Future Technology Intelligence Report*, contended that "possible advanced alien technology" has been reverse-engineered and is squandered by the federal government. (The "reverse engineering of ET technology" schtick was whistled up by Phillip Corso in the 1960s. Corso was a charter member, under Charles Willoughby, the aforementioned YAF co-founder, of the Shickshinny Knights of Malta in Pennsylvania, a conspiratorial fraternal order patterned after the military order of the Vatican.) Sutton was once employed as a research fellow at the arch-conservative Hoover Institute. He was a frequent contributor to *The New American* and the '76 Press, a small publisher featuring the "America First"-style manipulations of W. Cleon Skousen, the former FBI agent and author of *The Naked Capitalist*, a revival of Carroll Qugley's views of worldwide economic subversion by British elitists.

Skousen was the chief of police in Salt Lake City until the mayor, a Bircher himself, dismissed him in 1960, explaining that the outgoing chief was "an incipient Hitler" (Group Research Reports, 1980, Washington, D.C., Group Research, Inc., p. 20). Skousen had no qualms about publishing in Sun Myung Moon's *American Freedom Journal*, despite his "America for Americans" posturing. Other '76 Press writers included the vigorously anti-feminist Phyllis Schlafly, founder of the Eagle Forum – who, in 1960, hotly denied that she was a member of the Birch Society ... after Welch announced that she was "one of our most loyal members" (Carol Felsenthal, *Phyllis Schlafly*, Doubleday, 1981, p. xviii). Then there was nuclear strategist Admiral Chester Ward, a former law school professor, architect and Naval Judge Advocate, commended by President Eisenhower for his courageous opposition to the Communist conspiracy. (Felsenthal, p. 221).

Guy Bannister, a Birch Society pamphleteer, was Lee Harvey Oswald's handler at 544 Camp Street in New Orleans. Bannister employed an investigator, Jack S. Martin, a fascist co-conspirator with his boss and Charles Willoughby/Weidenbach (formerly General MacArthur's intelligence chief in Korea), a core strategist in the Kennedy assassination, according to Mae Brussell, Dick Russell and others. Bannister was a drunkard, a former FBI agent and Naval Intelligence officer. He published a racist newsletter. He choreographed the activities of a group of anti-Castro Cubans in New Orleans. He died nine months after the murder of John Kennedy.

Jim Garrison investigated Oswald's connection to Bannister and CIA pilot David Ferrie. The devout, alcoholic anti-communist had Oswald passing out Fair Play for Cuba flyers on street corners.

What would Bannister and his fellow Birchers say if they could speak openly, dropping the Jeffersonian platitudes and geopolitical tirades? In a privately-published paper concerning Charles Willoughby-Weidenbach, "Looking for 'Hate' in all the 'Right' Places," political researcher William Morris McLoughlin can't resist speaking for the Birchers: "We have been sitting on our hands and 'gnawing the rug' since 1945, when, as far as we are concerned, World War III actually began, with the murder of our hero, John Birch in Manchuria, China." The war was waged "entirely by members of various national and international right-wing, militantly extremist groups still united under the auspices and control of the World Anti-Communist League. Its U.S. affiliates include the U.S. Council for World Freedom and the American Security Council, part of the Liberty Lobby, as well as other organizations," including the Birch Society.

The JBS waged its grassroots, populist approach to psychological warfare with bullets of scapegoating literature. In *The Radical Right* (Random House, 1967), authors Epstein and Arnold offer that at the 1965 convention of the Christian Crusade, another fascist front, General Walker, "in speaking of the man who killed Lee Harvey Oswald, President Kennedy's assassin, urged his listeners not to forget that Ruby's name was Rubenstein, and they can't change that fact no matter how often they refer to him as Ruby."

Overall, Robert Welch tried to keep the race question out of the discussion. He insisted that the enemy was the left, not the Jews. Nevertheless, there was no holding back the anti-Semitism that many Birchers, cryptically or not, felt the need to convey. There was Florida Bircher Bernard "Ben" Klassen, author of *The White Man's Bible*. And there was William Pierce, author of *The Turner Diaries*, who cut his ideological teeth as a dues-paying member of the John Birch Society. Pierce left the Society to shift the thrust of his "research" to the "international Jewish conspiracy," the very fountainhead, he maintained, of communist subversion, the true Insiders behind the Insiders. (Pierce, "Enemies on the Right," *National Vanguard Magazine*, August 1996).

Pierce:

> One thing I am grateful to the Birch Society for is that it directed me to a number of books on Communism, and from those books I learned enough about the nature and background of Communism that I knew I wanted to

learn much more. That was really the beginning of my education: the start of my quest for understanding about history, race, politics, and, in fact, nearly everything except the physics and mathematics to which I had devoted myself until that time. The half-dozen or so other members of the chapter seemed to be decent enough, if not very stimulating, fellows. The term that best characterizes them is "middle class." They were pretty much the sort one can meet in any American Legion hall, except they were a little more intense – especially when talking about the Communist Conspiracy, which was practically the only thing they talked about.

The world certainly seemed to be going to the dogs. Thanks so much, communist conspiracy. General Albert Wedemeyer, a guest on the *Manion Forum*, a radio program hosted by Clarence Manion of the Birch Society's National Council, claimed the seeds for the advancing Red Tide were planted when Roosevelt entered the war against the Axis: "The Soviet colossus would not now bestride half the world had the United States kept out of war – at least until Soviet Russia and Nazi Germany had exhausted each other." (A realistic expectation? One side, perhaps the Germans, would have prevailed, or so some pre-war isolationists hoped.) "But Franklin D. Roosevelt, the proclaimed champion of democracy, was as successful as any dictator could have been in keeping Congress and the public in ignorance of his secret commitments to Britain. Commitments which flouted the will and the wishes of the voters who had re-elected him only after he had assured them that he would keep us out of the war" ("Historical News and Comment," *Journal of Historical Review*, undated, vol. 11, no. 4, pp. 495-499).

But a social backlash against the antics of JBS yahoos was mounting. In 1965, a group of moderate Republican governors met with the Party's coordinating committee to urge a statement denouncing the John Birch Society. On December 24, the *New York Times* reported that the committee voted in the interest of party unity to adopt a "diplomatic resolution." The GOP would "reject membership in any radical or extremist organization ... which seeks to undermine the basic principles of American freedom and constitutional government." Former House Representative John Rousselot, a Christian Scientist – also the John Birch Society's national director of public relations – told the press that the resolution meant communists and the KKK would be denied access to the Republican Party, but not members of the Birch Society.

The GOP, after all, had scores of Birchers in its ranks, and many of them were "high-minded" loyalists to the Party. The JB Society bestowed awards on policemen who acted heroically in the line of duty. This endeared police officers around the country to the front organization. A reporter in New York noticed that most of those attending one Birch Society rally sported "Police Benevolent Association" badges. Well-known law enforcement officials were drawn to Society-sponsored media events, including L.A. Police Chief Willam Parker, who turned up for an interview on the *Manion Forum*. In 1966, Sheriff James Clark, a Bircher who found fame for his resistance to the civil rights movement, was voted president of the national sheriff's organization by the rank-and-file. (Seymour-Martin Lipset and Earl Raab, *The Politics of Unreason*, Harper & Row, 1970, pp. 317-18).

Not publicized were the lives they led behind the hoopla. General Walker, one of the most visible Birchers, kept up his relationship with Nazi Gerhard Frey back in Germany. Walker phoned Frey's newspaper after Oswald was identified as the poor marksman who fired four shots through his window. Frey was the publisher of the *Deutsche National-Zeitung* und *Soldaten-Zeitung*. The *Brown Book: War and Nazi Criminals in West Germany* mentions that Frey's weekly newspaper

... has become a central organ of all ultra-right neo-fascist forces in West Germany and defames each and every movement advocating a realistic policy. Thus von der Heydte, SS man and parachute officer of the nazi Wehrmacht, called for long sentences of penal servitude for 'renunci-

> ation politicians,' meaning those forces striving for nor-
> mal relations with the neighboring peoples in the east and
> south-east of Europe. This paper advocates with peculiar
> zeal a general amnesty for nazi and war criminals.

Frey's press applauded the acquittal of Erich Deppner, an SS storm trooper who ordered the murder of 65 Russian prisoners, a "turning point in the trials of war criminals" (*Brown Book*, p. 338-39).

Another prominent Bircher with a secret life was Edward Hunter, the CIA mind control operative who coined the word "brainwashing" back in 1950. The word quickly, John Marks observed in *The Manchurian Candidate: The CIA and Mind Control*, ""ecame a stock phrase in Cold War headlines." Hunter, an OSS veteran and CIA propagandist employed as a "journalist," wrote scores of books and articles on the emerging science of mind manipulation. His many readers responded with outrage at the communist menace he exposed in his articles, and its insidious mind control tactics. The enemy had developed methods "to put a man's mind into a fog so that he will mistake what is true for what is untrue," Hunter reported, "what is right for what is wrong, and come to believe what did not happen actually had happened, until he ultimately becomes a robot for the Communist manipulator" (p. 125-26).

The country's elected representatives had no choice but to allow the CIA to conduct its own inhumane experiments on nonconsenting human subjects. But there was no brainwash like the Birch brainwash.

In 1962, Dan Smoot's *The Invisible Government* exposed as fronts for international Bolshevism a number of policy groups. Democracy was teetering. Smoot had unearthed the enemies in our midst: the Committee for Economic Development, the Advertising Council, the Atlantic Council (formerly the Atlantic Union Committee), the Business Advisory Council and the Trilateral Commission. Smoot, incidentally, reported to FBI headquarters in Washington before he was bitten by the bug to publish his neo-fascist newsletter, *The*

Dan Smoot Report. "Somewhere at the top of the pyramid in the invisible government," he wrote, "are a few sinister people who know exactly what they are doing: They want America to become part of a worldwide socialist dictatorship under the control of the Kremlin" (Political Research Associates).

The rabble rousing of Welch, Manion, Smoot and other Birch Society celebrities was understandably disturbing to some of the political targets of the abuse.

President John Kennedy responded to the noisy extremists of the Birch Society in an address delivered at a fund-raising dinner hosted by the Democratic Party at the Hollywood Paladium on November 18, 1961. "In recent months," Kennedy said, "I have spoken many times about how difficult and dangerous a period it is through which we move. I would like to take this opportunity to say a word about the American spirit in this time of trial. In the most critical periods of our nation's history, there have been those on the fringes of our society who have sought to escape their own responsibility by finding a simple solution, an appealing slogan or a convenient scapegoat." Political extremists, he said, sought the easy explanation for every national crisis and ignored political complexities. A downturn in the economy "could be explained by the presence of too many immigrants." Wars are orchestrated by "international bankers." China ended trade relations with the world not as a result of internal conflicts, but due to "treason in high places." With their rhetoric, "these fanatics have achieved a temporary success among those who lack the will or the vision to face unpleasant facts or unresolved problems."

Cold War is oppressive, Kennedy acknowledged, and "the discordant voices of extremism are heard once again in the land. Men who are unwilling to face up to the danger from without are convinced that the real danger comes from within. They look suspiciously at their neighbors and their leaders. They call for 'a man on horseback' because they do not trust the people."

The extreme right equated the Democratic Party with "the welfare state," said Kennedy. They object, "quite rightly, to politics intruding on the military – but they are anxious for the military to engage in politics." He urged his supporters, "Let us not heed these counsels of fear and suspicion.... Let our patriotism be reflected in the creation of confidence rather than crusades of suspicion" (Entire speech published verbatim in Rusher, pp. 121-123).

In 1965 a Republican leader told the *Arizona Republic* that 80 percent of all Birch Society members were "dedicated, patriotic and frightened Americans. More than 19 percent are nuts whose brains and judgment are warped. And the remaining people frighten me to death."

Many conservative Americans found the "crusade of suspicion" irresistible. Most Birch Society members, about 60,000 all told, lived in cozy suburbs in the south and southwest (Rusher, p, 118).

The Phoenix chapter of the Society was founded in 1960, and six more cropped up within two years. By 1965, there were 100 chapters in the state and some 2,000 members. Most of them lived in the suburbs around Phoenix.

They came in all ages, but one of the youngest and most receptive to the call was young Robbie Jay Matthews of Phoenix, a prototypical middle-class American kid who, as an adult, went on to muster a bund he called The Order, the neo-nazi cell that murdered radio talk show host Alan Berg in 1984.

Twenty years before, on October 25, 1964, Una Matthews, his mother, drew Robbie's attention to a tabloid insert in the *Arizona Republic* entitled, *The John Birch Society: A Report*. In *The Silent Brotherhood* (Signet, 1989), Kevin Flynn and Gary Gerhardt describe the momentous day that Robbie Matthews, age 12, became a fascist: "Una flipped through the magazine's pages, each marked 'advertisement' at the top.... The article described how the society was composed of local chapters with 10-20 members, usually formed by someone in the neighborhood who was concerned about communism. A full-time coordinator gave assistance and direction to the chapters."

"This group really wants to do something about it," Una Matthews told her son, who took the magazine to his room and studied it thoroughly. "He didn't understand everything, but he understood enough to become increasingly alarmed. These people he'd been hearing about, these Russian communists, wanted to take over the world." Young Matthews dwelt on the implications. He feared for his family. Reading: "How are we reacting to the realities of our world? What do we think of the steady gain of communism – of the millions killed, tortured and enslaved by this criminal conspiracy? Do we still laugh at Kruschev's claim that our children will live under communism? Do we shrug off Cuba? Will we shrug off Mexico? Do we watch with curiosity? De we pull down the curtains on these disturbing thoughts?"

Young Robbie Matthews, a future "man on horseback," clipped the coupon and sent the Birch Society $5.00 for a copy of Robert Welch's *Blue Book*, the group's manifesto.

"No more," Flynn and Gerhardt write, "would the world be just what he could see up and down West Lawrence Lane." (pp. 29-30).

CHAPTER TEN

ON A BAD CASE OF CRANIAL BLEEDING,

THE BIRTH OF CSC & THE COLLAPSE OF FANNIE MAE

"Shoot the Dissenters"

In September 2008, Wall Street was shaken to learn of the brain hemorrhage death of prominent business consultant Michael Hammer – one of the 25 "most influential" people in America, per Time magazine – while bicycling with a friend in Boston.

R.I.P. Michael Hammer (1948 - 2008)

Champion of 'Reengineering'
Saved Companies, Challenged Thinking

By CARI TUNA
Wall Street Journal

September 6, 2008; Page A12

In the early 1990s, as personal computers, the Internet and cellphones began to transform the business landscape, Michael Hammer rose to prominence as the champion of the decade's trendiest management buzzword: "reengineering."

Using new paradigms and technologies, companies were meant to redesign business processes from the ground up to meet goals faster and serve clients better.

Hammer and Company

Mr. Hammer, who died Thursday at age 60, gave the idea currency in an incendiary 1993 business best seller *Reengineering the Corporation: A Manifesto for Business Revolution*. The book sold over two million copies, stoking the growth of a multibillion-dollar reengineering movement and catapulting Mr. Hammer to the

197

forefront of management consultancy. In 1996, Time featured him on its first annual list of America's 25 most influential people, and *Forbes* in 2002 ranked *Reengineering the Corporation* the third most influential business book of the past two decades.

Hammer was idolized by the business press, but his prescription for reengineering the corporation "had a dark side" – like the industrial time studies of Arthur Koestler – as the streamlining of processes often went hand in hand with reductions in jobs.

"Often the term became jargon for mass layoffs. Mr. Hammer's rhetoric didn't help. It's basically taking an ax and a machine gun to your existing organization," he said in a 1994 *Computerworld* interview.

To *Forbes*: "On this journey we'll carry our wounded and shoot the dissenters."

A warm farewell from financial consultant Peter S. Cohan sheds light on the formation of Computer Sciences Corporation (CSC), the federal/military contractor vying with Blackwater for the Sleaziest-Business-of-the-Year Award. Cohan, writing at Bloggingstocks.com:

> As it turns out, I have a professional connection to Hammer and his co-author, James A. Champy. Hammer taught me at MIT – I took a course called Office Automation Systems from him in which he talked about the importance of imagining how a process would work if it could be reimagined from scratch. And Champy hired me to work for the firm he co-founded with several MIT Sloan School professors – Index Systems – which grew dramatically after the Reengineering book was published. Index was ultimately acquired by Computer Sciences Corporation.[1]

Was my own brain bleeding? Thought I'd been reading about an intellectual who revolutionized business management and had a "dark side." And now an even darker element entered the picture – CSC, the scandal-ridden corporate par-

1. (NYSE: CSC). http://www.bloggingstock.com/2008/09/05/reengineering-guru-dies/

ent of DynCorp, the private mercenary and child sex slave folk – and Index Systems.

This came personified in the form of Thomas P. Gerrity, the former dean and Joseph J. Aresty Professor of Management, Wharton School of Business at the University of Pennsylvania. Prior to Wharton, Gerrity was the chairman and CEO of the Index Group, the CSC subsidiary that grew out of Cohan's MIT project. Gerrity earned his S.B. and S.M. in EE from MIT in 1963 and 1964, respectively, attended Oxford University, was a Rhodes Scholar and received his Ph.D. from the MIT Sloan School of Management in 1970.

Mr. Gerrity also served as a member of the Board of Directors of Fannie Mae Corporation from September 1991 to December 2006, and as the chairman of the Audit Committee from January 1999 to May 2006. That's right, Fannie Mae – in the news 2010-11 after the controversial bailout.

Mr. Thomas P. Gerrity, we note, from CSC/Index, chaired the AUDIT committee at Fannie Mae … he was responsible for oversight. The brain lists…

Ow! – that cranial ache again – could it be that Michael Hammer was thinking about this when he keeled over on his bicycle and expired on the spot? Did a spreadsheet flash before his eyes?

Did he think of Mr. Gerrity and his shameful departure from Fannie Mae two years earlier, when he was forced out by a costly accounting scandal? The *Washington Post* reported:

Fannie to Settle Charges, Pay Fine
Some $400 Million in Penalties are Part of Agreement
By Kathleen Day and Annys Shin/WP
May 23, 2006; Page D01

Mortgage giant Fannie Mae will pay about $400 million in penalties under an agreement with two federal agencies to settle charges related to its $10.8 billion accounting scandal, sources said yesterday.

The settlement would end a nearly three-year investigation by the SEC and OFHEO into widespread accounting manipulation by the company – including the use of improper accounting techniques to maximize bonus pay for top executives. It would not cover potential SEC action against individuals involved in Fannie Mae's problems, nor does it end a criminal investigation by the Justice Department.

But for the company, it could mark a step toward resolving a controversy that has undermined its credibility as well as its stock price and has fueled efforts in the White House and Congress for stricter regulation.

The firm's accounting strategies smacked of Enron:

The company's troubles were first made public in 2004 after a preliminary probe by OFHEO alleged that Fannie manipulated earnings between 1998 and 2004 to smooth the growth of profits it reported to investors.... A separate probe, prepared for the Fannie Mae board by former senator Warren B. Rudman and released in February, concluded that the company manipulated earnings throughout the period under review and found that in one case it was done to maximize bonus payments...

Gerrity was perceived as a central player in the Fannie Mae scandal; so were other members of the board and they are interesting in their own right:

Last week, Fannie Mae said it will replace Thomas P. Gerrity as head of its audit committee at the end of the year. Gerrity ... has been audit committee chairman for seven years. Since the scandal broke in 2004, corporate governance watchdogs have urged Fannie Mae to replace its audit committee, which is responsible for overseeing the company's accounting and financial practices and the performance of its outside auditor. Most of the committee has turned over in the past two years. Xerox chairman and chief executive Anne M. Mulcahy left in September 2004. Then Thayer Capital Partners' Frederic V. Malek retired from the board at the end of last year. Presidential appointees William R. Harvey and Taylor C. Segue III were not reappointed...

Ultimately, federal charges against Gerrity et al. were dismissed. On August 1, 2007, the *Washington Post* reported:

A federal judge yesterday dismissed civil securities fraud charges against some current and former members of Fannie Mae's board, saying that investors had not presented specific enough allegations for those elements of their lawsuits to go forward. The charges were part of a tangle of litigation stemming from a multibillion-dollar accounting scandal at the government-chartered mortgage funding company. People who served on Fannie Mae's board remain defendants in lawsuits alleging a different offense – that they breached their duties....

The dismissed securities fraud charges involved directors who were on Fannie Mae's audit committee, including Thomas P. Gerrity, a professor and former dean at the Wharton School; Frederic V. Malek, a Washington financier; and Anne M. Mulcahy, chairman and chief executive of Xerox.[2]

Investors complained that the audit committee "failed miserably" in the performance of its duties. The allegations, however, "do not demonstrate the required state of mind of extreme recklessness," opined Judge Richard J. Leon, U.S. District Court for the District of Columbia. Judge Leon also tossed out charges against an insurance company, Radian Guaranty, who allegedly sold Fannie Mae a junk policy enabling Fannie Mae officers to manipulate earnings. Radian is "merely a third party alleged to have provided Fannie Mae with the means to misrepresent its finances," and was not responsible for corporate statements to investors, Leon wrote.

Frederic V. Malek is of particular interest here. He was campaign manager of the Bush-Quayle campaign in 1992, deputy national finance chairman for John McCain's presidential campaign.

And a Watergate holdover, a loyal Nixonite. Malek, per *Medical World News*, was "the son of a beer salesman in Berwyn, Illinois. He graduated from U.S. Military Academy in 1959. He served in Vietnam in the Special Forces, training South Vietnamese counterinsurgents. He left the Army in 1962 and married Marlene McArthur of San Francisco, and graduated from the Harvard Graduate School of Business Administration, and went to work at the management consultant firm, McKinsey & Co. He and several other consultants had plans to start their own firm, but one was 'drafted by Robert McNamara to help out at Defense.' ..." ("Is Health Planning Too Vital to be Left to MDs?" *Medical World News*, Jul. 31, 1970, pp. 16-18.)

2. http://securities.stanford.edu/newsarchive/2007/20070801_Dismissal103806_Hilzenrath.html

And there are his political bona fidés: Malek was Chairman of Triangle Corporation, Columbia, SC, 1967-1969. From 1969 to 1970 he was Deputy Under Secretary of the U.S. Department of Health, Education and Welfare; Special Assistant to President Richard Nixon, 1970-73; Deputy Director of the Committee to Re-Elect the President ("CREEP"), 1972; Deputy Director of the Office of Management and Budget, 1973-74; member of the White House Domestic Council, 1974-75; in 1975, he left government and was named Vice President of the Marriott Corporation.

The connections place him snugly in the Nixon camp:

> Malek's boss at the Office of Management and Budget in Aug. 1973 was Roy L. Ash, for whom the Ash Council was named. The Ash Council created the Environmental Protection Agency. Until 1972, Ash was the president of Litton Industries, one of whose numerous divisions, Litton Bionetics, was in the second year of a $10 million-plus contract to manage, operate and maintain the National Cancer Institute's Frederick Cancer Research Center at Fort Detrick, Maryland.[3]

Watergate:

> The Watergate scandal kept Nixon from fully carrying out his experiment in control, but his efforts were not forgotten. In fact, E. Pendleton James, who was in charge of Ronald Reagan's pre-inaugural talent search and then became assistant to the president for personnel, had worked under Fred Malek, Nixon's personnel chief. Malek was the author of the infamous 'Malek Manual,' a guide to political appointees, which emphasized a telling message: 'You cannot achieve management, policy or program control unless you have established political control.' ... Malek went on to describe techniques designed to 'skirt around the adverse action proceedings' required to proceed against civil servants in a legal manner. All were designed 'to remove undesirable employees from their positions.' ("The President and the Executive

---

3.(FASEB Newsletter, 1973 Aug. 6(6):2-3.)

Branch," by Joel D. Aberbach, UCLA Center for American Politics and Public Policy Occasional Paper Series 9 1-9.) William H. Taft IV was also a member of the Reagan transition team.[4]

Frederic V. Malek, GW Bush's crony, placed on the board of directors of a company controlled by The Carlyle Group as a favor to his father...

Did any of this flash through the late Michael Hammer's brain as it fatally hemorrhaged?

---

4. ("White House Transition Team," Washington Post, Feb. 18, 1980.)

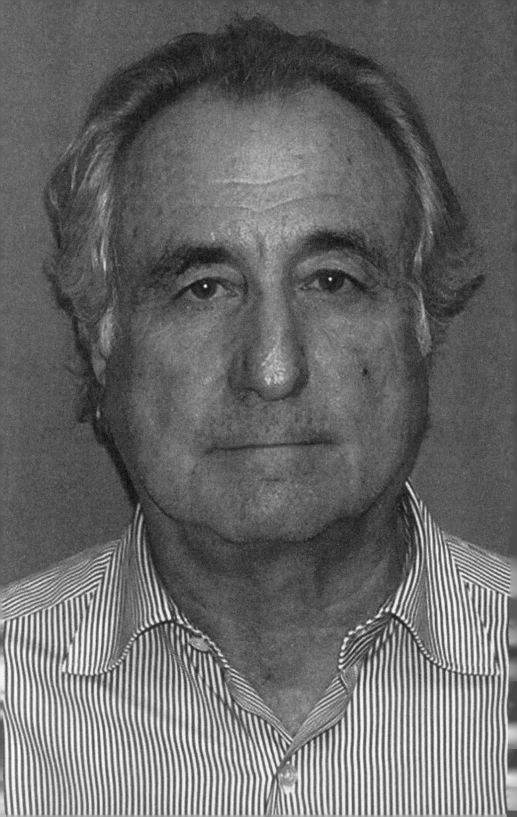

CHAPTER ELEVEN

ARMOUR RESIDENTIAL REIT
& WALL STREET'S NATIONAL SECURITY ROBBERBARONS

An investment consultant in Los Angeles informs us that Armour Residential Real Estate Investment Trust (ARR), a broker of mortgage-backed securities, "has routinely raised fresh capital by selling stock to new investors and then turned around and spent considerable sums on generous dividends for old and new investors alike. To some, this strategy actually looks like a glorified Ponzi scheme that could prove unsustainable in the end (with the dividend cut or even cancelled) in the end. Meanwhile, Armour Chairman Dan Staton also doubles as chairman of another company known as FriendFinder Networks [NASDAQ: FFN is the proprietor of an array of pornography sites, including Penthouse and bondage.com. FNN board chairman Marc Bell is also an Armour director] that has already seen its own stock collapse, plummeting from $10 to just 60 cents a share, this year. Could Armour face a looming disaster as well?"

ARR has been on the slide for the past two years. In 2010, the firm paid quarterly dividends. In Jan. 2011, ARR began monthly payouts, and the dividend was dropped by two thirds to 12 cents, then 11 cents in the third quarter. The firm is increasingly cash strapped, and its debt/equity ratio has been rising steadily for the past five years.

Odds are that Armour will inevitably fold under its own internal stresses, but not solely because the firm is engaged in a glorified Ponzi scheme, or even because it peddles the same mortgage-backed securities that brought about the 2008 recession.

"We Rob Banks"

ARR is following in the footsteps of the S&Ls in the '80s – many were looted by the CIA and the Mafia, as reported by Pizzo and Fricker, etal. in *Inside Job*, a book the corporate media did not find newsworthy – and Fannie Mae in the '90s. The presence of Nixon-aide/Marriott exec Fred Malek on Fannie Mae's auditing committee was a glaring red flag. The fall of the mortgage giant was not the result of poor judgment or incompetence; it was as deliberate as any Hole-in-the-Wall Gang bank heist.

For confirmation that a Ponzi scheme or corporate looting is afoot, one has to look no further than the audit committee – a select group of directors who fail miserably at spotting irregularities. These dancing partners are paid huge sums in inflated director salaries to look the other way. (In the past, Chicago's Arthur Andersen LLP, formerly on of the "Big Five" accounting firms, performed this invaluable service, but in 2002 lost its license to practice when its collaborative role in investment fraud became obvious in the case of Enron.)

Three board members make up the audit committee at Armour Residential REIT, and their bios are a travel guide to one of the darkest recesses of the national security underground:

- Stewart J. Paperin
- John "Jack" P. Hollihan, III
- Robert C. Hain

Dr. Stewart J. Paperin: CEO of Stephen Norris & Co. Capital Partners, also known as Steve Norris Partners, a private equity firm specializing in leveraged buyouts, may have a low name recognition score, but Stephen Norris was a co-founder of the Carlyle Group, the notorious investor in military contractors, haunt of the CIA's Frank Carlucci and William Barr, George Soros, James Baker III, GHW Bush, the aforementioned Fred Malek, NewsCorp director Saudi Prince Alwaleed bin Talal (Norris' close friend and investment partner in Euro Disney, Four Seasons Hotel and Citigroup), and other geopolitical heavyweights with intelligence and DoD ties.

Norris is also a former member of the Federal Retirement Thrift Investment Board, appointed by President GHW Bush in 1990.

From Dr. Paperin's bio at the Armour website: "In addition to his role with Stephen Norris & Co., Mr. Paperin has been a Director of Enterprise Acquisition Corp. since July 9, 2007 [Enterprise merged with ARR in 2009], and Executive Vice President of the Soros Foundation since 1996. From 1996 to July 2005, he was a Senior Advisor and Portfolio Manager for Soros Fund Management LLC. He has been Consultant to Soros Fund Management LLC since July 2005."

George Soros, Dr. Paperin's boss and an early Carlyle Group financier, is misunderstood by both the left and the right. His reputation as an open society philanthropist/progressive Hitlerite are cover stories. Beneath the veil of left-wing causes and media distractions, *Covert Action Quarterly* notes that Soros "thrusts himself upon world statesmen and they respond. He has been close to Henry Kissinger, Vaclav Havel and Poland's General Wojciech Jaruzelski."

When anti-globalization demonstrators marched in the frozen rain at the World Economic Forum in 2002, Soros was inside delivering an address: "As the police forced protesters into metal cages on Park Avenue, Soros was extolling the virtues of the 'Open Society' and joined Zbigniew Brzezinski, Samuel Huntington, Francis Fukuyama and others." Tellingly, one of the Soros foundations "runs CIA-created Radio Free Europe/Radio Liberty jointly with the U.S. and RFE/RL." Soros is a CIA collaborator, and the Soros Foundation is a front. One can only conclude that Dr. Paperin of the ARR audit committee, the right arm of George Soros, is also, without question, a CIA collaborator if not a full-fledged asset.

He was Financial Officer of Pepsico Corporation from 1980 to 1985 ...

To the national security elite born.

Pepsico: Journalist Alfred McCoy reported decades ago, in *The Politics of Heroin in Southeast Asia,* that the soft drink bottler, operated an opium refinery in Laos for the CIA during the Vietnam War period – with the lobbying assistance of Richard Nixon, no less. Ray Hunt, the son of domestic fascist H.L, Hunt, also sits on the Pepsico board. Pepsico was a driving force in the overthrow of Salvador Allendé and rise of Operation Condor. Reporter Greg Palast has noted in the *London Observer* that the coup plot "against Chile's President-elect Salvador Allende, using CIA sub-machine guns and ammo, was the direct result of a plea for action a month earlier by Donald Kendall, chairman of PepsiCo, in two telephone calls to the company's former lawyer, President Richard Nixon. Kendall arranged for the owner of the company's Chilean bottling operation to meet National Security Adviser Henry Kissinger on September 15. Hours later, Nixon called in his CIA chief, Richard Helms, and, according to Helms's handwritten notes, ordered the CIA to prevent Allende's inauguration."

John "Jack" P. Hollihan and Robert C. Hain: The other "watchdogs" on ARR's audit committee. Jack Hollihan is chairman of Litchfield Capital Holdings (ARR co-chair Scott J. Ulm was CEO of Litchfield from 2005 to 2009), recently gobbled up by Gramercy Capital, a trustee of the American Financial Realty Trust.

Jack Hollihan's career began in the 1970s as an attorney at Donovan Leisure Newton & Irvine. Donovan, Leisure was founded in 1929 by William J. "Wild Bill" Donovan, widely recognized as "the father of the CIA." Donovan formed the Office of Strategic Services (OSS) in 1942 to engage in spying and sabotage in Europe and Asia during WW II. Donovan himself hailed from Wall Street, and so did many of the operatives who served under his command. In 1947, when Donovan's OSS was restructured and renamed the Central Intelligence Agency under the direction of his protégé, Allen Dulles, Wall Street continued to serve as a teeming recruitment pool. Goldman Sachs CEO Lloyd Blankfein started out at Donovan Leisure. The list of notable alumni also includes CIA Director William Colby, former SEC chairman Roderick M. Hills, and RCA executive and Gulf Oil Director Samuel Murphy, Jr.

Before the firm folded in 1998, Donovan Leisure represented some of the most powerful CEOs and corporations in the country, including Walt Disney, General Electric, Kodak, Mobil Oil, American Cyanamid and American Home Products.

As noted, Hollihan went on to chair Litchfield Capital Management, a firm that recalls the name Josh Stampfli, who left Litchfield in 1999, joined Gale Technologies, an online brokerage that marketed Stampfli's Liquidity Engine technology, incorporating AI to radically expedite NASDAQ trade stocks at the rate of 300,000 transactions per day. When Gale went belly up in the 2000-2002 market decline, Stampfli was hired by Bernie Madoff, the big-ticket Ponzi swindler. It was an enduring relationship. On October 27, 2007, Madoff addressed a colloquium at New York's Philoctetes Center on the future of the stock market. Beside him sat technological wunderkind Josh Stampfli, director of Madoff's automated market division, creator of the Liquidity Engine. Together, they duped investors by claiming that the technology automated BLM Investment Securities LLC non-existent stock trades.

According to Madoff, Josh Stampfli conceived "the trading logic to manage position risk and handle the order flow inherent to the firm's business of providing liquidity to its customers." In 2010, after the fall of Madoff, Stampfli was hired by Credit Suisse to direct its Advanced Execution Services (AES) division, a leading marketer of electronic trading tools.

Jack Hollihan's bio boasts that he is "head of Global Project Finance ... for Morgan Stanley International," an investor in solar, wind and other emergent green technologies. The CIA wasn't far away. In fact, the executive director of GPF is Loren Ambinder, an alumnus of GE Finance and Millbank, Tweed, Hadley & McCloy LLP – another firm on intimate terms with Langley. Millbank Tweed's website notes, "since the office opened its doors in 1980, our partners have included federal cabinet-level secretaries and heads of the CIA and FBI, and others who have served in significant government posts." Former DCI's John J. McCloy and William Webster both hailed from Millbank Tweed.

Robert C. Hain, the third ARR director on the auditing committee, is a Hollihan partner at City Financial Investment Company Limited, and serves as chairman. Hain, an ARR director since 2009, has had seats on the boards of financial services, business, arts, health and social services organizations at the national and local levels in Toronto, Zurich, Winnipeg, Halifax and London. His close association to Hollihan assures that he is an insider, and represents no threat to ARR's financial shenanigans.

But the audit committee isn't the only "watchdog" at Armour with numerous of CIA ties. On September 30, 2011, ARR announced that it had appointed Deloitte & Touche LLP as "the Company's independent registered public accounting firm, replacing the Company's previous independent registered public accounting firm, EisnerAmper LLP."

Augusto Pinochet's Favorite Bank

A few of the symbiotic CIA connections lurking at Delloitte & Touche:

- D&T was the liquidator of BCCI, the Agency's key money laundering bank prior to its collapse.
- Mention of D&T evokes the name A.B. "Buzzy" Krongard, former CIA executive director and Blackwater board member, appointed by George Tenet on March 16, 2001. Krongard, per his corporate bio, was general counsel at the firm. He was general counsel of Deloitte Haskins & Sells, prior to its combination with Touche Ross and Co. in 1989, "responsible for all legal matters affecting a multi-billion-dollar international professional partnership. Previously, he was Associate General Counsel and a Member of Peat Marwick Mitchell, and an associate at Cravath Swaine & Moore [another firm often associated with the CIA] in its New York and Paris offices, where he specialized in corporate finance, mergers and acquisitions, SEC matters, and European financings." His Wikipedia entry notes that Krongard has been "a longtime consultant to DCIs."

- Deloitte & Touch did business with, and protected, Chilean dictator Augusto Pinochet (recalling the aforementioned role of PepsiCo in his rise to power). On August 23, 2009, the UK's *Independent* reported that D&T used simple ruses to disguise the fact that "the banks were dealing with the Pinochet family fortune. Accounts were opened which were designated by any combination of his Christian names or initials – Augusto Jose Ramon – and the surnames of his father, Pinochet, or his mother, Ugarte, and those of his wife, Lucia Hiriart Rodriguez. Some bankers preferred to call him Joe (from Jose), or APU (Augusto Pinochet Ugarte). The practice made the tracing of information about him as difficult as, say, looking for Griff Rhys Jones under 'Jones.'" Richard Evans, a former representative of D&T, was alleged by the *Brilac* report "to have acted in connection with Ashburton Trust, which was created by Riggs and whose beneficiaries included Pinochet's five children, who each had a 20 per cent share. Mr. Evans was also listed by *Brilac* as a director of Althorp Investment Trust, another repository for Pinochet family funds. It said he was active in promoting businesses in Argentina and was being investigated for money laundering. Deloitte spokesman Ignacio Tena said: "Deloitte & Touche Corporate Services was contracted by Riggs Bank and Trust Company (Bahamas) to render administrative services for Riggs and some of its clients. Riggs did the due diligence, and gave all the information related to its clients, in accordance with the usual commercial practice and the Bahamas' law."

ARR has no shortage of national security dancing partners. The CIA ties are numerous, and we haven't detailed all of them here. If the fall of the go-go thrifts in the '80s have taught us anything, it is that CIA reprobates are busily engaged in corporate looting. ARR appears to be but one current example of an unknown number of targeted Wall Street firms. Buyer beware.

CHAPTER TWELVE

GEORGE SCHULTZ,
INTERNATIONAL TERRORIST

As the Bush-Cheney bund bores deeper into the pages of historical infamy (and Obama appoints protegés of Kissinger, Scowcroft and Schultz to prolong ongoing covert ops atrocities), it is incumbent upon concerned residents of this great democracy to take stock of reality (elusive in this age of public diplomacy) and not forget the *dope* – the financial core of black operations waged by the intelligence sector's world-dominating "elite."

The Rockefellers used heroin to quell the Harlem riots in the 1930s, so there are multiple uses for the opiate, but mostly it brings in gobs of cash. So wouldn't you know that Bechtel, a recurring name in the history of corporate scandals to the present day, would have a place in this sordid history.

Drift back in time for a moment to the early 1970s, when the Nixon administration, like Bush's three decades on, teetered uncertainly on the brink. The central determinant of Nixon's ultimate downfall was Alexander Butterfield – a former spy stationed in Asia.

Butterfield, recall, made headlines when he casually announced that the president had recorded conversations in the oval office. That was the political death of Richard Nixon, who was badly kicked around, and not one reporter stopped to ponder why a spook in the White House would crucify his boss with this devastating revelation.

Butterfield gave away the store at another key point in history when he spilled the beans to *Wall Street Journal* reporter Jonathan Kwitny, author of *The Crimes of Patriots*. When asked about Bernie Houghton and other principals at Australia's Nugan Hand Bank, the CIA's cash cleaners, Butterfield gave him a few names that literally broke the bank.

Kwitny was referred to General Heine Aderholt, who ran covert operations throughout Asia with Iran-contra's John Singlaub, and was in a position to observe the actions of Maurice "Bernie" Houghton at Nugan Hand.

Houghton, it emerged, had been active in the opium trade in the Golden Triangle. Kwitny's investigation led to a legal claim letter signed by Tom Rahill, an American worker in Dhahrain, Saudi Arabia. According to this letter,

> Mr. Houghton's representatives would visit Aramco construction camps in Saudi Arabia shortly after each monthly payday. We investors would turn over Saudi riyals to be converted at the prevailing dollar exchange rate, and receive a Nugan Hand dollar certificate.... The monies, we were told, were to be deposited in the Nugan Hand Hong Kong branch for investments in various "secured" government bonds.

But Aramco wasn't the only company that turned Nugan Hand Bank into a burgeoning financial brokerage/crater.

"Other large U.S concerns are said by investors to have boosted Nugan Hand, and let salesmen hold meetings on company property. Among them were Bechtel, the giant international construction firm then guided by George Shultz and Caspar Weinberger, and University Industries, Inc. of San Diego." (University Industries is extant, now known as JWP West. The company's website reports that it was founded "in the mid-1960s as a water supplier to Long Island and Queens, New York [and] JWP transformed itself through acquisition. By the start of the 1980s, JWP was the nation's largest computer reseller and the biggest electrical and maintenance contractor. Essentially, clients use JWP to help increase productivity and decrease costs by upgrading their facilities through, for example, more efficient communication and computer systems. JWP designs, installs, and supports these technical systems." (For more, also see: Pollack, Andrew, "JWP Gains

Control of Businessland," *New York Times*, August 6, 1991, and Steinberg, Jacques, "Water Utility of a Thousand Faces," *New York Times*, November 2, 1991.)

Employees of Aramco, Bechtel, the largest engineering firm and third largest privately-held company in the United States, and University Industries officials actually confirmed Kwitny's allegations, to his complete surprise, with a bland "sounds like you've got quite a story there" were directed to Bernie Houghton, who talked them into investing in the bank at a promised return of 18%. Houghton only dealt in hard cash, and was seen leaving Bechtel with garbage bags stuffed full of paper money.

When the bank went bust, the employees lost their investments. The scheme made Enron's stock manipulations look like a putting green.

U of C political researcher Peter Dale Scott reports on the stunning hypocrisy of George Schultz, who does, however, make a valid point concerning drugs and world terrorism:

> President Reagan came to office with a mission: to roll back the frontiers of world communism, especially in the Third World. Almost from the start he singled out Nicaragua as a dangerous base of Soviet bloc operations in the Western Hemisphere. But with the American public's anticommunist sentiments dulled by a decade of détente and memories of Vietnam, how could his administration revive support for combating the Nicaraguan challenge to U.S. power and credibility?
>
> One answer was to invent a new threat, closely associated with communism and even more frightening to the public: narco-terrorism. The term, rarely well defined by its users, encompasses a variety of phenomena: guerrilla movements that finance themselves by drugs or taxes on drug traffickers, drug syndicates that use terrorist methods to counter the state's law enforcement apparatus, and state-sponsored terrorism associated with drug crimes. But in the hands of administration officials, the epithet served a more political than analytical purpose:

to capitalize on popular fear of terrorists and drug traffickers in order to mobilize support for foreign interventions against leftist regimes. As two private colleagues of Oliver North noted in a prospectus for a propaganda campaign to link the Sandinistas and drugs, "the chance to have a single issue which no one can publicly disagree with is irresistible."

Administration spokesmen drove the lesson home through sheer repetition. In January 1986, President Reagan said, "The link between the governments of such Soviet allies as Cuba and Nicaragua and international narcotics trafficking and terrorism is becoming increasingly clear. These twin evils – narcotics trafficking and terrorism – represent the most insidious and dangerous threats to the hemisphere today." A year and a half earlier, Secretary of State George Shultz decried the "complicity of communist governments in the drug trade," which he called "part of a larger pattern of international lawlessness by communist nations that, as we have seen, also includes support for international terrorism, and other forms of organized violence against legitimate governments."

The tell-tale silence of George Schultz on the complicity of right-wing governments in the international drug trade, a far more common alliance, are a dead give-away that something has gone chillingly awry in the so-called "Party of Lincoln."

Since 1997, Bechtel has poured $1.1 million into lobbying, a relatively small investment that has nevertheless managed to violate political campaign restrictions, as documented by the POGO Federal Contractor Misconduct Database. In exchange, Bechtel has received an excess of $41.3-billion in defense and federal contracts since FY 2000.

On May 5, 2003, *The New Yorker* reported that the bin Laden family hold "a ten million dollar stake in the Fremont Group, a San Francisco-based company formerly called Bechtel Investments, which was until 1986 a subsidiary of Bechtel." Riley Bechtel, a Fremont director, is chairman and CEO of the Bechtel Group, and was appointed to Bush's Export Council. Shultz is both a director of both Bechtel and the Fremont Group.

Revolving door conflicts-of-interest abound.

During the build-up to the Iraq invasion, for instance, Shultz served as chairman of the advisory board of the Committee for the Liberation of Iraq. Ironically, during Reagan's term, Secretary of State George Schultz supported the sale of arms and intelligence to Saddam Hussein. In 1988, the dictator, who rose to power with generous assistance from the CIA, gassed 5,000 Kurds. Undaunted, the administration valiantly fought legislation that would have imposed sanctions on Iraq. After the Kurd slaughter, Bechtel signed several contracts with Hussein – among them a proposal to erect an immense chemical plant near Baghdad.

The Corpwatch website has traced connections between Bechtel and the Iraq invasion. Justification for the war drew heavily on Schultz's policy formulation of pre-emptive war, otherwise known as the Bush Doctrine: "Bechtel employees like George Shultz not only used their political influence to help bring this war about, but key Bechtel board members and employees with advisory positions to the Bush Administration helped ensure that Bechtel would receive one of the most lucrative contracts… " for rebuilding a country that Bechtel had a hand in decimating. Within a month of the initial bombing campaign, Bechtel managed to skirt the usual bidding process, and was granted one of the largest of the rebuilding contracts. Worth $680 million, the contract included the assessment and repair of every significant component of Iraq's infrastructure, from power generation sites to water and sewage systems.

Back home, Bechtel has been the instigator of some of the most atrocious mishaps in the commercial nuclear power industry.

In 1974, Michigan's Consumers Energy sued the company for $300 million when the Palisades facility malfunctioned. The state settled for $14 million.

Three years later, in California, Bechtel's Humbold Bay reactor was shut down when it was discovered to be perched on an earthquake fault.

Also in 1977, at California's San Onofre Unit Number 2, Bechtel installed the reactor vessel *backwards*. The reactor has, to the present day, cursed Southern California Edison with design flaws. At one point, the utility planned on floating the reactor on a barge to the Barnwell nuke waste dump in South Carolina, but Charleston authorities refused permission to enter the port. Several San Onofre employees exposed to radiation have sued Bechtel after contracting cancer. The San Onofre site was shut down in January 2012 after a minor radiation leak was investigated, and found to have been caused by the degradation of steam generator tubes shortly after they'd been installed. Environmentalists contend that the plant cannot possibly be operated safely. On February 1, 2013, the San Diego Union-Tribune reported that Edison has spent "in excess of $300 million on replacement power and repairs at the plant, expenses it hopes to pass on to customers. Amid the outage, utility customers continue to pay at least $835 million in annual operations, maintenance and capital costs. The replacement steam generator project cost at least $670 million and is already being billed to ratepayers."

Bechtel also aggravated the situation at Fukushima. After the Japanese nuclear disaster, Enformable Nuclear News reported on January 9, 2013, "Bechtel was contracted by the United States government to send emergency water pump cranes to the crippled nuclear power plant in an attempt to keep the reactors from melting down, but due to a bizarre situation where the cost of the equipment of $750,000 suddenly rose to $9.6 million dollars, this action was delayed for weeks." So USAID searched for equipment elsewhere and found it at the Pentagon ... one water pumping system that "did not even get dispatched to Japan until March 21st." Five radiation scarred days later, two entire weeks after the tsunami struck, "the SDF was still training off-site on the Bechtel pumping system, but it was too late as explosions had already ripped through the buildings after the nuclear fuel overheated and melted."

There was, then, a high Roentgen dose of irony in nuke warnings issued by Hoover Institute scholar George P. Schultz,

GEORGE SCHULTZ, INTERNATIONAL TERRORIST

Sidney Drell and Steven P. Andreasen in the June 8, 2012 issue of *Science*: "In the 26 years since Chernobyl, the nuclear power industry has strengthened its safety practices, yet Fukushima demonstrates the fragility of the civil nuclear enterprise."

The authors revived protestations of the anti-nuclear movement 40 years earlier, raised the frightening possibility of fatal mishaps and miscalculations. They appealed to fears that nuclear materials could fall into the hands of terrorist organizations. The nuclear industry emerged victorious after the very same arguments – dismissed as onerous liberal scare-mongering at a time when the country sought alternatives to the escalating costs of petrol power – were first proposed. Schultz made millions of dollars on the construction of leaky nuclear generators. It's regrettable that Bechtel lobbied against the environmentalists who attempted to apply brakes to the industry with Schultz's own belated reasoning in the '70s, before Three Mile Island, Chernobyl and Fukushima. The world would be a much safer place to live in if he had made these "liberal" public pronouncements before profiting enormously by endangering us all with slipshod engineering.

CHAPTER THIRTEEN

CHRISTO-FASCISM WITHOUT TEARS:
RESPONSE TO EVANGELICAL WRITERS WHO DISTANCE THE CHURCH FROM THE NAZI PARTY

"The prophet seldom has any honor in his own country."
– Adolf Hitler

"Today I believe that I am acting in accordance with the will of the Almighty Creator: by defending myself against the Jew, I am fighting for the work of the Lord."
– Adolf Hitler

Point 24 of the *Nazi Progamme* in 1920s Germany stated that the only religion that the party officially denounced was "Jewish." "We demand liberty for all religious denominations in the State," he sermonized. The Nazi Party denounced "the Jewish-materialist spirit within and without us, and is convinced that our nation can achieve permanent health from within only on the principle: the common interest before self-interest."

Many faith-based historians of WW II have downplayed the role of religion in Hitler's Germany, most notably Richard Overy, author of *The Dictators*, cited by Christian researchers everywhere to reprimand those who suggest that the Nazi leader used religion as a vehicle of mass persuasion. Despite prestige appointments and numerous awards for scholarship, Overy, as a historian of Hitler's Germany, is not altogether honest. His contention that Hitler was hostile to capitalism, for instance, is a canard. Pay no heed to slippery conservative Christians who cite Richard Overy and his contention that Christianity was "in decline" and played no role in the rise of the Third Reich.

Overy's sourcing alone is a red flag. He relies heavily on the writing of Hermann Rauschning (a friend of Hitler who "defected" and sat out the war in the United States). questionable citations and deliberate misinterpretations of Nazi Party rhetoric are common.

One widely-repeated citation is made by Bruce Walker in an article posted on the Internet, "The Nazis and Christianity," published by *American Thinker*, a Christian site.

According to Walker, the decline of Christianity in Germany led directly to the rise of Nazism. Professor Henri Lichtenberger in his 1937 book *The Third Reich* describes the religious life of Weimar, where large cities were "spiritual cemeteries with almost no believers at all, except for those who were members of the clergy."

Seems to be history until one considers that Henri Lichtenberger, the French historian, was a fascist propagandist who idolized Friedrich Nietzsche and Richard Wagner, a mercenary with a pen recruited from ranks favoring a Franco-German intersect in the early '20s.

He was pro-Nazi. Lichtenberger's word on anything was determined by who paid him.

This is the caliber of "experts" that right-wing evangelical propagandists cite when making the claim that Nazi Germany was "secular." The bottom line is that, in private, Hitler found National Socialism and Christianity fundamentally incompatible because he believed that the latter – "an invention of the Jews" – had given rise to Bolshevism. Ironic, then, that before Hitler, Lenin became Christ ... in a true atheist state ... as reported by *Vision*, a quarterly academic print and online journal of news and analysis:

> As chairman of the Council of People's Commissars, Lenin soon became a dictator..... The use of traditional

religion played a part in securing popular support. Following an attempt to assassinate Lenin in 1918, his public persona was infused with religious verbal and visual imagery. Sociologist Victoria Bonnell notes that now the leader "was characterized as having the qualities of a saint, an apostle, a prophet, a martyr, a man with Christ-like qualities, and a 'leader by the grace of God.'" Posters showed Lenin like a saint in Russian iconic art....

Aspects of the political, social and religious fabric of the Russian Motherland provided many of the necessary conditions for Lenin's cult.... While Hitler and Stalin were deranged and profoundly evil, they were aided and abetted by masses of people who moved toward them as the leaders they desired. As we have noted before in this series, the symbiosis of leader and led cannot be ignored as we try to explain the bloodlust that characterizes the rule of many, if not all, false messiahs. Nor is exploitation of religious fervor ever far from the surface as leaders seek and maintain followers. Mussolini appealed to elements of traditional Catholic religion to create his fascist cult, and Hitler was well aware of religion's power to induce loyalty to a cause. It was no different in the atheistic Soviet Union for most of the last century.

Hitler's Religious Beliefs (Quotes from *Mein Kampf*)

Hitler evangelized: "I believe that I am acting in accordance with the will of the Almighty Creator: by defending myself against the Jew, I am fighting for the work of the Lord."

In his youth, Hitler attended Catholic Church and was exposed to the anti-Semitism of the prevailing religious culture. In *Mein Kampf* and in his speeches, Hitler appeared to be a fanatical believer in God. In one speech, he declared:

The world will not help, the people must help itself. Its own strength is the source of life. That strength the Almighty has given us to use; that in it and through it we may wage the battle of our life.... The others in the past

223

years have not had the blessing of the Almighty – of Him Who in the last resort, whatever man may do, holds in His hands the final decision. Lord God, let us never hesitate or play the coward, let us never forget the duty which we have taken upon us.... We are all proud that through God's powerful aid we have become once more true Germans.

On marriage: "A volkish state must therefore begin by raising marriage from the level of a continuous defilement of the race, and give it the consecration of an institution which is called upon to produce images of the Lord and not monstrosities halfway between man and ape." (*Mein Kampf*)

On race war: "But if out of smugness, or even cowardice, this battle is not fought to its end, then take a look at the peoples five hundred years from now. I think you will find but few images of God, unless you want to profane the Almighty." (Mein Kampf)

Hitler's Biblical beliefs show clearly where he got the notion for offensive action.

On liberty: "God does not make cowardly nations free." (Mein Kampf)

On Judaism: "Their whole existence is an embodied protest against the aesthetics of the Lord's image." (Mein Kampf)

A prophecy: "Their sword will become our plow, and from the tears of war the daily bread of future generations will grow." (Mein Kampf)

In a speech delivered on April 23, 1922, Hitler delivered a sermon:

My feelings as a Christian point me to my Lord and Savior as a fighter. It points me to the man who once in loneliness, surrounded only by a few followers, recognized these Jews for what they were and summoned men to fight against them. ... In boundless love as a Christian and as a man, I read through the passage which tells us how the Lord at last rose in His might and seized the scourge to drive out of the Temple the brood of vipers and adders. How terrific was His fight for the world against the Jewish poison.

On himself: "I am now as before a Catholic and will always remain so." (Hitler speech, 1941)

Anyone who dares to lay hands on the highest image of the Lord commits sacrilege against the benevolent creator of this miracle and contributes to the expulsion from paradise. (Mein Kampf)

"We were convinced that the people needs and requires this faith. We have therefore undertaken the fight against the atheistic movement, and that not merely with a few theoretical declarations: we have stamped it out." (Hitler speech, Berlin, October 31, 1933)

CHAPTER FOURTEEN

SATANIST MICHAEL AQUINO REVISITED

The uncanny attraction of the Third Reich – Nazi Germany – lies in the fact that it endorsed and practiced both dynamism and life-worship without end and to a world-shaking degree of success.

– Michael Aquino

To hear High Priest Michael Aquino tell it, his Temple of Set, a splinter group of San Francisco's Church of Satan, is no more sinister than the Order of Woodcraft Chivalry. Setianism, he insists, "is a legitimate and ethical religion, incorporated as such in California in 1975 and enjoying since that time full state and federal recognition as a religious institution."[1]   Aquino bristles at any suggestion of Satanism at the Temple of Set. The cult "does not believe in 'Satan' – our mythology is ancient-Egyptian, after all."[2] Yet he has described himself in Temple literature as the "Anti-Christ," and published essays on "Greater" and "Lesser" Black Magic.[3] Don Webb, a Temple priest, describes it as a "Satanic religion." The Setian, Webb writes, "chooses as role model a 'god against the gods.' We choose an archetype that corresponds with the disharmonizing part of our own psyches…. This role model is the 'Lord of this World,' who is rejected by the Right Hand

---

1. M. Aquino letter to A. Constantine, Sept. 27, 2000. Ibid.
2. *San Francisco Chronicle*, November 3, 1987, A-7.
3. In Webb's *"The Black Beyond Black: The Temple of Set."*

Path as the Prince of Darkness."⁴ Visitors to the Temple's web site are met by a blazing white pentagram, and the Temple answering machine has boasted that the caller has reached "the only international Satanic religious institution recognized by the government."⁵ So perhaps it's really about Satan, after all.

The decorated veteran of the Army's 306th Psychological Operations Battalion is as skilled in the art of black propaganda as he is black magic.

The Temple's ranking magus was born on October 16, 1946. He set out on the Left-Hand Path during the Vietnam War. Aquino joined the Church of Satan in the late 1960s, and was ordained a priest in Kentucky, where he was stationed on leave from the war. Aquino lectured on Satanism at the University of Louisville, and mustered a small coven for rites at his home.

In Southeast Asia, he engaged in tactical psyops, including the use of Hueys outfitted with ultra-high-decibel banks of loudspeakers.⁶

Dale Seago, a pilot assigned to the psyop crew, says they would "take them up above the cloud layer where they couldn't be seen, where the rotor blades couldn't be heard, but you could very clearly hear the broadcasts on the ground."⁷

Aquino prepared one blood-curdling tape exploiting Vietnamese-Buddhist burial customs. The local peasantry believed "the necessity of burying the body of the deceased because if they didn't do that the souls would be condemned to wander eternally tormented by demons," Seago says. Aquino's tape "began with this wailing Vietnamese funeral music and then phased into screaming, gradually getting louder." After an eternity, the screaming subsided into the moans of a dying Viet-Minh soldier, his body abandoned by comrades.

"It was chilling," Seago recalls, "and then finally you hear him being dragged away screaming by the demons." The psyops unit would "wait for a really severe thunderstorm and they would take the choppers up, go over the cloud layer, and through these

4. *San Francisco Chronicle*, June 24, 1994, p. D7.
5. Arthur Lyons, *Satan Wants You.*
6. *San Francisco Examiner* reporter's typewritten transcript.
7. Dale Seago interview, c. 1987.

buckets of rain and jagged lightning and thunder, you'd hear this stuff coming out of the sky. Apparently it was quite effective." Aquino "won a lot of notoriety for that in Vietnam."

Seago says that Aquino did not participate in much killing in 'Nam – not that it was an issue. "I remember a conversation I had with him once. Somehow the subject of killing came up – something I had never done – but the word he used to describe the experience was 'interesting.'" Aquino admitted that he had killed "once or twice," but "he found he had no particular emotional reaction to it."

Vietnamese houseboys, Seago says, "would have nothing to do with Aquino's quarters. He had a Baphomet plaque up on the wall, candles and a makeshift altar. He had a bit of a reputation as a magic man among the locals and nobody would go near him."

The Old Twisted Cross

Decades later, Michael Aquino is still, to most onlookers who are not his liturgical or military brethren, as popular as a phlegmatic leper. There are the Apocalyptic teachings, the coming forth by night: "For Mankind now hastens toward an annihilation which none but the Elect may hope to avoid ..." In his introduction to "The Order of the Vampire," Aquino writes that students will learn "invisibility."[8] His words, but Aquino now denies that the Temple has ever dabbled in such quackery: "We do not have any particular interest in 'invisibility.'"[9]

And there are the testimonials of former Setians, including H.J. Mowry, who left the Temple in 1995: "There's nothing innovative about Setianism. In fact, it's just one more 'traditional' herd-breeding religion ... I've discovered that Setians do little more than revel in self-deccit ... a mockery and a distortion of truth."[10]

Another Temple defector, Kevin Filan, says that he was blackmailed and coerced: "Aquino uses embarrassing infor-

---

8. *San Francisco Chronicle*, November 3, 1987.
9. Michael Aquino, November 27, 2000 letter to the author.
10. Temple of Set dissident's statement.

mation obtained while people are members of their cult to attempt to discredit or harass them later. This is among the most odious of their tactics. I was 'outed' and my workplace posted to the nets with the suggestion that people 'pay me a visit' in an attempt to silence my criticisms of their cult."[11]

Lillian Rosoff of San Bruno, California was granted a temporary restraining order against Aquino in 1999. She was harassed for two months, Rosoff complained to the San Mateo, California Superior Court. She complained that Aquino phoned her repeatedly in the early morning to pressure her to return to the Temple. Aquino once banged on the door of her home at 3 a.m. After ten minutes of this, he shouted that he "was tired of playing games with her," that she'd "better watch out for his next move," according to her affidavit. She had "an intense fear" of him, and "due to past experiences" did "not know how far the defendant [would] go."

Then there are reports of Aquino's interest in Nazi occultism, and the 1987 child molestation charges arising at the Presidio Child Development Center. The story took to front pages throughout northern California and soon dropped into the national news stream.

In Carmel, California, political conspiracy researcher Mae Brussell drew upon the local headlines for her weekly broadcast over KAZU-FM in Monterey. Topics of discussion for November 16, 1987: "SATAN, THE OCCULT, REICHSFUHRER SS HEINRICH HIMMLER, US DEFENSE DEPT., SAN FRANCISCO POLICE AND FEDERAL ATTORNEYS, DEFENSE INTELLIGENCE AGENCY, CHILD MOLESTATIONS AND RITUALS ON MILITARY & CIVILIANS, AND MIND CONTROL."

Mind control was a familiar theme to researchers of Nazism. Terminal mind control experiments were conducted in the concentration camps, and fully documented in the postwar period by the U.S. Naval Technical Mission. "Brainwashing with chemicals" at Auschwitz addressed the psychoactive effects of barbiturates and derivatives of morphine. Mescaline was studied at Dachau.

11. http://www.io.com/~ix/writing/setianetics.txt

Not that the American military hasn't curdled a few synapses in the name of "national security." The U.S. Navy undertook its own mescaline experimentation, motivated by the Technical Mission's Nazi report, and "Project Chatter," an interrogation study, was initiated in 1947.[12] The April 1972 issue of *Science Digest* describes the use of hypnosis to elicit multiple personality disorder in military test subjects. In this article, G.H Eastabrooks, a hypnotist and mind control pioneer, detailed covert operations concealed by a fog of induced amnesia. Intelligence data was retrieved by use of code words to trigger a pseudo-personality programmed to deliver it, leaving the host completely unaware of his role in the operation.[13]

"Michael Aquino was on television this week," Mae Brussell reported. "The police in San Francisco had taken some of his video tapes. He claimed they were mostly Carl Sagan's *Space*, but in there you could see a photograph of the Waffen SS, just one of his belongings in a place filled with swastikas and Nazis. And the news accounts told about the Nazi uniform."

The Pentagon at first denied that Aquino was even in the Army, then reversed itself and stood by Aquino and his top-security clearance. Brussell: "In 1981 he was a reserve attaché to the Defense Intelligence Agency, and a year later a student at the Foreign Services Institute, sponsored by the State Department. In 1981, [Reagan appointee] Daniel Graham – the head of 'Star Wars,' the 'high frontier' – was head of the Defense Intelligence Agency."[14]

Aquino (once a national commander of the Eagle Scouts Honor Society) sneers at the Nazi allegations. The Temple's "very minor interest" in Nazi occultism, he insists, "is every bit as responsible as that of Public Television documentaries on the topic."[15] Aquino has written that Nazism is "a very powerful area of magic ... unrealized by the profane?"[16] He has praised

---

12. Harry V. Martin and David Caul, *"Mind Control,"* 1995, http://www.sonic.net/sentinel/gvcon8.html
13. Summation in Colin Ross, MD letter to New Orleans therapist Valerie Wolfe.
14. Transcript of Mae Brussell broadcast, KAZU-FM, Pacific Grove, CA.
15. November 27, 2000 Aquino letter to the author.
16. Quoted in Rashke's *Painted Black*, p. 149.

the "unique quality" and "uncanny attraction of the Third Reich" in his introduction to the "Order of the Trapezoid." Occult "techniques perfected by the Nazis continue to be used/abused – generally in an ignorant and superficial fashion – by every country of the world in one guise or another."[17]

Carl Rashke, a professor of religious studies at the University of Denver, asks: "You can have the heart of Hitlerism without six million dead Jews?"[18]

In 1985, a small group defectors – including his brother-in-law William T. Butch and a ranking Setian – went on to establish a sect of their own, the Temple of Nepthys in Mill Valley, California, citing Aquino's "obsession" with Nazism as the deciding grievance.[19]

And the SS uniform? "I have never worn a Nazi uniform in my life, in or out of a parade," he informs us.[20] Most responsible clergymen do not have Nazi apparel hanging about the rectory. Perhaps he didn't actually wear the uniform (?).

There are questions about his bloodline. On November 23, 1987, a local televised interview with Aquino kicked off with a report that his mother "was engaged to a member of the Waffen SS." Aquino denies it. In 1929, after his mother, a sculptor, graduated from Stanford University, he wrote in response to the criticisms of a Temple defector, "she went to Germany to study as an apprentice to the famous sculptor Georg Kolbe."

Aquino neglects to mention that Georg Kolbe, according to the Wiesenthal Center, "adapted" to Nazi rule just fine. Ms. Ford-Aquino's mentor indulged his art throughout the Third Reich period, "cheap pathos largely geared to the Nazi mythology of the Nordic-Germanic 'master race.'" Kolbe's studio was "a favored venue for guided tours by members of the 'Strength through Joy' organization." An artist beloved by the Nazi Party, Kolbe died in Berlin in November 1947.[21]

---

17. Quoted in Michael Newton, *Raising Hell: An Encyclopedia of Devil Worship and Satanic Crime* (Avon Books, 1993), p. 18.
18. *Painted Black*, p. 154.
19. Newton and Lyons.
20. Aquino, November 27, 2000 letter to author.
21. Weisenthal Center: http://motlc.wiesenthal.org/pages/t040/t04015.html

While in Germany, Aquino explains, his mother "had a romance with a university student named Karl Eitel Roth, who was not a member of the Nazi Party (or the SS). In the late 1930s, my mother returned to the United States and married my father, who served as a sergeant in Patton's 43rd Cavalry in World War II and was decorated with the Purple Heart for wounds in action."

Michael Aquino insists that his father was not a Nazi, but his own literary efforts could have been written by Goebbels. In *The Crystal Tablet of Set*, he claimed that the genocidal Nazis – who believed in "total war" and performed hideous terminal medical experiments on captive "subhumans" in highly-efficient death camps – worshipped "life." (And Dr, Aquino is actually regarded as an "intellectual" in some quarters.) "The 'life,'" he explained, "is the life of the state, or more precisely the Volk (perhaps best translated as the 'soul of the people')."[22] National Socialists worshipped the soul of the Caucasian *volk*, perhaps, and indeed they constituted the life of the state ... but why is this admirable, and why is Aquino's respect for mass murderers not merely the blather of a twisted neo-Nazi?

His October 1982 "Stifling Air" rituals at Wewelsberg Castle, the haunt of Himmler's Waffen SS, certainly smudged Aquino's priestly polish. "I indeed performed a magical ritual in the Wewelsberg Castle in Westphalia," Aquino explains by e-mail, "but there was nothing in the least pro-Nazi about it. It was rather a ritual concerning the unique location of that particular castle at what certain occult lore terms 'the middle-point of the world.' That happens to be 'coincidentally' why Heinrich Himmler appropriated that same castle during the Nazi era. Its occult history and significance date back to 1604, which is, I think it is fair to say, pre-jackboot."[23]

On November 3, 1987, the *San Francisco Chronicle* offered another, more sinister perspective on Dr. Aquino's occult rituals at Wewelsberg: "Nazis considered the black arts and satan-

22. "Order of the Trapezoid Statement."
23. Newton, p. 18.

ic worship part of an ancient Germanic tradition. In his book *Crystal Tablet of Set*, [Aquino] writes that he performed the rituals to recreate an order of knighthood for followers of Satan."

True-crime reporter Michael Newton considers Aquino's public stance on the Reich "deliberately ambiguous," a tactical position.[24] (Set, the mythical Egyptian core of Aquino's religious beliefs, was the god of confusion, and the psyops veteran often taps the well to dilute criticism and frustrate the hounds nipping at his tail.)

American society, he opines, is already "engulfed by power-seeking disguised as altruistic politics and by propaganda disguised as information. There is no exception" – thus spake political science doctorate and psychological warfare veteran Michael Aquino, a commentary on domestic politics viewed from the darkest corner of the national security underground.[25]

Attic Expeditions

Michael Aquino claims to have reported directly to the Joint Chiefs of Staff.... Expert of psychological warfare, Aquino wanted to use satellites for brainwashing the US public.
– *S.F. Examiner*, November 2, 1987

Dale Seago: "I joined a psychological warfare unit in 1976 at Fort MacArthur in San Pedro. I was a Spec 4. Later I went to ROTC for two years and returned to the same psyops unit with Aquino as a second lieutenant.... Aquino split from the Church of Satan and formed the Temple of Set in 1975. He was already living in Santa Barbara and working at the psyops unit and I had not yet joined the cult. The unit was the 306th Psychological Operations Battalion, which dealt with psyops on a national policy level."[26]

The U.S. military was heavily represented at the Temple. William Butch, Aquino's brother-in-law, a former Pittsburgh police officer, was a naval reservist. Bruce Bibee, a former

24. Ibid.
25. Quote in Newton, pp. 18-19.
26. Seago interview transcript.

captain in Aquino's psyops unit in San Pedro, enlisted in the Temple. Captain Willie Browning was a military intelligence officer. Setian Dennis K. Mann was a reserve Army major in the intelligence field.[27] An Army CID investigative report filed with the San Francisco Police Department notes that an informal check of official records revealed that Mann and Browning were "Captains, Military Intelligence."[28] Black Ops. Aquino himself has served stints as a Green Beret, a liaison officer in NATO countries, and a consulting faculty member at the U.S. Army Command and General Staff.[29]

The promising young Satanist's military function in Vietnam was "human ecology' – a CIA code-word for behavior modification and mind control. Major Jack Downing, a self-professed "Man in Black," recalls, "I was working alongside the CIA as a consultant in psyops and as a specialist in 'human ecology.' That's a phrase that connotes different things, depending on the context, from the wholesome to the not-so-wholesome. In the capacity for which I was employed, it was a way of pinning down the psyche and behaviors of human beings in differing environments or under various circumstances." Human ecology applied "the observational principles of anthropologists and psychologists alongside the more manipulative techniques of advertisers, social engineers and 'golden age' brainwashers. It was, in retrospect, a very unorthodox and ethically questionable thing." Downing says, "we brought the MK [mind control] projects into the war. The extreme circumstances of warfare gave us excellent opportunities to observe the ways certain mind control technologies might work."[30]

Downing was in Germany utilizing "some of the findings we got." He set up "some things" at Army bases stateside. "At the time of my leaving, my role ... as human ecology expert was taken up by another officer, a Michael Aquino, who was trying out these [mind control] principles in the context of Anton LaVey's church."

27. Ibid.
28. Lt. Col. T.C. Jones, Army CID report, Investigative Policy and Studies Division.
29. *San Francisco Chronicle*, October 31, 1987.
30. Jach Downing interview transcript, November 1998.

Reports surfaced in the 1980s that Aquino plied his knowledge of mind control at the Temple of Set, as well.

He refers to the case that drew national media attention as the "Presidio Scam," but the Army's own evaluation weighed the ritual molestation charges and found them credible.

"Regarding children," Dale Seago says, "I don't know how he feels about them in general. I do know that he virtually hates his son, Dorien." Aquino has always felt that Dorien is not really his son "by his first wife, Janet. If he felt he could get away with it – and he probably didn't mean this literally – he would happily go into [Dorien's] room at night and smother him with pillows."

Ethical, responsible Michael Aquino was accused by the U.S. Army CID on August 11, 1989 of "Conspiracy, Kidnapping, Sodomy, Indecent Acts or Liberties With a Child, False Swearing, Intentional Noncompliance With Article 30 Uniform Code of Military Justice, Maltreatment of a Subordinate and Conduct Unbecoming an Officer," in connection with the Presidio charges. After the High Setian sued the Army to have his name stricken from the title block of the report, the court investigated and a decision was handed down by the Commanding General of the Army CID on September 28, 1990: "Plaintiff remains titled for Conspiracy, Kidnapping, Sodomy, Indecent Acts and False Swearing."[31]

Aquino's plea of innocence notwithstanding, there is little doubt that molestation occurred at the Presidio. An internal investigator told Diana Napolis, a San Diego County social worker, that "he believed at least 20 preschoolers had been molested." Even the FBI's Kenneth Lanning, a staunch ritual abuse debunker, has stated publicly that numerous children were sexually abused at the Child Development Center.[32]

The intelligence sector and its mind control cults have made extensive use of front organizations like the False Mem-

31. United States District Court for the Eastern District of Virginia, Alexandria division, Michael A. Aquino plaintiff, civil action v. no 90-1547-a, the honorable Michael P. W. Stone, Secretary of the Army, Department of the Army, Washington, D.C., defendant.

32. Diana Napolis Internet statement, 08 May 1997.

ory Syndrome Foundation (many of the professionals on the FMSF board have engaged in illicit classified mind control experiments, often involving children) and friendly contacts in the media to characterize ritual child abuse as an "urban legend" and "false memories" concocted by therapists to reap fraudulent medical insurance claims.

But *The Journal of Child Abuse & Neglect* reported in 1993 that most therapists are reluctant to treat ritual abuse survivors: "One of the first complications in the evaluation of ritualistic abuse cases is the frequent disbelief and skepticism on the part of professionals" encountering "the bizarre and extreme nature of the allegations." As therapists and police investigators gather reports of "ritualistic abuse from across the nation, and as adult and child victims disclose their experiences, evidence for the veracity of these cases accumulates." Another common deterrent to therapist involvement is fear instilled by "threats to evaluators ... communicated via the children or experienced directly. Even when no overt threat exists, the horrifying nature of the allegations can engender a fearful [avoidance] response on the part of clinicians."[33]

The confusion bred by underhanded "experts" with a monopoly on media access gave rise to widespread ignorance. The issue of ritual abuse (a form of mind control) has provoked widespread skepticism, fundamentalist religious hysteria, fear, and even some legitimate reporting here and there.

Material evidence of the abuse is critical but hard to come by. In the Presidio case, medical evidence supported the psychological evaluation of the children. Five or more of them had a sexually transmitted infection. "A stir was created when the media announced that several of the children had been diagnosed with chlamydia," Aquino has written. "However, the Army later announced the tests were unreliable. No retesting of the children was ever conducted. Chlamydia can be transmitted by direct contact with any mucous membrane. No testing of the children's parents for this disease was conducted."

33. Kelley, Brant and Waterman, "Sexual Abuse in Day Care Centers," *Child Abuse and Neglect*, Vol. 17, 1993, p. 84.

Jackals - The Stench of Fascism

Aquino claims to have medical records confirming that he has never had the disease.

There is no doubt that children at the center were infected. Contrary to Aquino's explanation, the Department of Health and Human Services reports that chlamydia, like HIV, is contracted NOT merely by contact with mucous membranes, but "during sexual intercourse via the exchange of bodily fluids through mucous membranes in the anus, mouth and genital areas."

Aquino's contention that the children were "not retested" raises questions. Several laboratory tests, according to the DHHS, are conducted to confirm the presence of chlamydial infection and distinguish it from gonorrhea. And once a child is on medication, another test is standard procedure to determine if the child is still infected. And "because there are often no symptoms for chlamydial infection, someone infected may unknowingly pass the bacteria to their SEXUAL partners."

Aquino has yet to explain how several children from the Presidio came to have sexual contact with the same infected pedophile outside the school. There is obviously a much higher probability that someone at the Presidio passed the disease through sexual contact.

Conspiracy Theory

Michael Aquino's claim to innocence didn't stanch the flow of headlines: "ARMY SAYS CONSTITUTION LETS SATANIST HOLD TOP SECRET JOB – PRESIDIO CARE CENTER FIRST TO FACE ARMY SCRUTINY – SATANISM LINKED TO SCORES OF S.F. CHILD ABUSE CASES – WORLDWIDE PROBE OF ARMY CENTERS – PENTAGON TACKLES PRESIDIO MOLEST CASE ..."

He has consistently claimed that the Army CID investigation was a conspiracy motivated by military intolerance of his religion. In response to Aquino's debunking: "This investigation was not a 'witch-hunt.' Plaintiff was not targeted because of his religious beliefs. In fact, as plaintiff repeatedly points out ... the Army has been aware of [Aquino's] religious beliefs throughout his career and has not interfered with his religious practices. The sole reasons for this investigation and the CID decision … are the facts that point to plaintiff's sexual abuse." Preschooler Kinsey Adams-Thompson, "in a completely public setting, identifies … a man who sodomized her" and forced her to "place her mouth on his penis."

Based on Aquino's "witch-hunt" thesis, one would have to accept "that there was a giant conspiracy between the parents, the daughter, the psychiatrist, the child psychiatrist that treated the girl, between the CID agents who investigated the case, between the military policemen and investigators … and between the officials in the Army Criminal Law Division who also reviewed the case."[34]

On May 31, 1991, Patrick Lisowski, an attorney representing the Army in Aquino's lawsuit, opined that it was only possible to buy his claims if one also believes that "a mother and a father instructed their daughter to fabricate this story of child molestation," then "pick out someone who they didn't like," and embedded "in her somehow the fact that this was the man" who molested her.

At various times, Aquino has suggested that Kinsey's therapist, her parents, the press, the police, the courts, the Army and private investigators, researchers, Temple of Set defectors, crime writers, everyone is "lying" about him, that he was in Washington, D.C. when the ritual molestations took place. "The San Francisco Police investigated," he explained in a public statement on June 7, 1999, and "verified that Lilith [Aquino] and I had been 3,000 miles away in Washington, D.C. – where I was on duty every single day." SFPD detectives closed the case. Charges were not filed.

But don't take his word as Gospel. Aquino left the Presidio in the summer of 1986. He was assigned to Washington, D.C., then St. Louis. But he was, according to Army investigators, "back in the Presidio in San Francisco during that summer." Aquino's alibi is a cracked goose egg.

Army files reveal that the San Francisco Police Department dropped the 1987-88 prosecution unjustifiably. The fed-

---

34. *Michael A. Aquino –v- Michael P.W. Stone*, "Hearing on Motions," May 31, 1991.

eral Court of Appeals for the Fourth Circuit found that the SFPD discontinued the investigation of Aquino and wife Lilith in September 1988 "for lack of sufficient evidence." The Army CID pressed on with the investigation, and in August 1989 issued a report concerning "the various child abuse and related criminal offenses investigated," and concluded that the police department's case was stymied "because all further leads involved adults who refused to cooperate."[35]

To silence the children, guns were reportedly pointed at their heads and family members were threatened.[36] True enough, some witnesses were not "cooperative" at all.

The Army CID maintains that the probe of Aquino and Gary Hambright, an employee of the center, "was not arbitrary or capricious. Kinsey made a certain, reliable identification of plaintiff in a non-suggestive setting, while shopping with her parents at the [Presidio] exchange. She exhibited the fear and terror that one expects upon recognition of a threat or source of harm. Her earlier statements to the child psychiatrist and her mother about 'Mikey' and 'Shamby,' persons until then unidentified, support the validity of the identification." Her description of Aquino and her "identification from a photo and video line-up also corroborate the identification at the PX. Kinsey identified plaintiff's house as the place where 'Mr. Gary' took her from the Child Development Center, and where she saw 'Mikey' in 'Army clothes' like her father's."

Kinsey Adams-Thompson described the blue-gray color of Aquino's house. Photos taken at Aquino's apartment "show masks, guns, toy animals and ceremonial items that are similar to things described by Kinsey and other children. A notebook from plaintiff's apartment contained the name "Mike Todo," and "Todo" was one of the persons present at "Mr. Gary's house." Why, you might get the idea that Aquino had committed the molestations, as charged. That Aquino told "a different version of the events is irrelevant," concluded the Army.

35. U.S. Court of Appeals document, Fourth Curcuit, Aquino v. Michael P. W. Stone, Secretary of the Army.
36. In Objective Evil: Satanic Cults in U.S. Intelligence, Roy Black, quoted in Cover-Up of the Century, by Daniel Ryder, 1994, p. 72.

When his military status was called into question on the Internet, he claimed in response that he is still an Army Reservist in good standing. Court documents tell another story. In 1990, an Army continuation board recommended terminating Aquino's service after conducting its own investigation of the ritual abuse charges, and he was processed out of the Army Active Reserves.[37]

Baudelaire pondered "the sorrows of Satan" in verse. Michael Aquino experienced those pangs first-hand.

The newspapers reported that Gary Hambright, a Baptist minister who died of AIDS, stood charged with molesting dozens of children. Parents sued the Army for an excess of $60 million, and in some instances monetary settlements with parents were reached. Gary Hambright left behind an obituary thick with references to "my Lord and Savior, Jesus Christ."[38]

On April 19, 1988, all ten charges against Hambright were dropped by U.S. Attorney Joseph Russionello, who admitted that there was clear and convincing evidence of child molestation but "insufficient evidence" to link those charged to the crimes. Parents immediately denounced Russioniello, who had demonstrated that "the federal system has broken down," and was unable "to protect the rights of citizens age three to eight." Russionello has been known to perform services for the intelligence sector. Jack Blum, a U.S. Senate investigator, testified before a Select Committee on October 23, 1996 that he returned $35,000 in cocaine profits seized in a trafficking bust to the Nicaraguan contras.[39]

And those accusatory headlines kept coming: "Satanic cult has bizarre links to Marin" (*Marin Independent Journal*, December, 6, 1987): "… Satanic church members, including a key figure in the Presidio child molestation case, have been linked to satanic cult activities in Marin County." William and

---

37. Fourth Circuit Court of Appeals.
38. *San Jose Mercury News*, January 5, 1990, Orange County Register, January 6, 1990, and http://www.skeptictank.org/hs/cabuse2.htm, "A Safe Haven for Pedophiles."
39. U.S. SENATE SELECT COMMITTEE ON INTELLIGENCE HEARING ON THE ALLEGATIONS OF CIA TIES TO NICARAGUAN CONTRA REBELS AND CRACK COCAINE IN AMERICAN CITIES, October 23, 1996.

Lynn Butch, the in-laws, were listed by the county clerk as "founders of two Marin satanic cult groups: Dark Star 9 Pylon and Meta Mates." It was reported that Aquino's portfolio included property in Marin and Sonoma inherited from his mother, "who died of cancer in San Francisco in 1985 ... a temple priestess. She left her son a $3.2 million estate, including a house ... leased by Project Care for Children and the Marin County Child Abuse Council..."

Lynn Butch, Lillith Aquino's sister, "is the daughter of Harry H. Johnson, a wealthy Mill Valley developer who was allegedly kidnapped in September by Kenneth R. Russo. Russo contends that Johnson swindled him out of more than $500,000 in a business deal."

Hell of a Note

Aquino made national headlines again in February 1997, when he and wife Lilith filed a lawsuit against ElectriCiti Inc., an Internet service provider, for its part in a "conspiracy" resulting in "negligence and infliction of emotional distress." Aquino's complaint concerned Diana "Curio" Napolis, a researcher on the Internet who "has been posting defamatory messages" about him to various Internet newsgroups. He complained that the ISP "has not only permitted Curio to continue the postings, but has actively assisted Curio in making these postings." He sought $250,000 in damages.[40]

Diana Napolis, for six years an investigative social worker for the San Diego County court system, is a licensed family therapist and a skilled investigator. Offended that the civil criminal justice system had failed to lock him up, "Curio" obtained declassified Army documents related to the Presidio child abuse charges and Aquino's processing out of the military and posted them on the Net. Aquino claimed that Napolis "has posted at least 1,800 derogatory and threatening messages on as many as 38 different newsgroups," *Web* magazine reported that September.

---

40. ElectriCiti statement, WWW, "Aquino vs ElectriCiti Inc., Your online freedom is threatened!" February 17, 1997.

But at least one of the "Curio" posts was fabricated: "I can find you [Aquino] whenever I want. And it soon will be much more than just finding for both your perv' wife and you." The threats were reported in the press far and wide ... but have never been documented – were, in fact, a figment of Aquino's fertile imagination. Napolis denies that she had anything to do with the message attributed to her, or that she has ever threatened the Satanist: "He cannot produce an authentic message, transmitted publicly or privately, with any such words written by me," she wrote in an Internet post. "Other Satanists have threatened him ... but I've never done it – it's not my style. In contrast, one of his cult members threatened to cannibalize me (I didn't take it seriously)."[41]

The Internet provider responded that the firm "does not know the identity of Curio, or even know if Curio is an ElectriCiti customer.... ElectriCiti does not have prior knowledge or interest in either the Aquinos, Curio, or any conflict between them."[42]

The case was thrown out of court on June 13, 1997 with "leave to amend."

"Apparently," Napolis explains, "Aquino wants to continue to lash out blindly and punish someone, anyone." He attempted to seal the court's file on the case. His appeal was thrown out "with prejudice." He can never file his "cyber-stalking" suit – a certain threat to first amendment rights on the Internet – again. Web activists everywhere exhaled a collective sigh of relief.

Curio and her file of government documents are not Aquino's only migraine. On July 7, 2000, Rusty Nelson, a photographer living in Omaha, Nebraska in the 1980s, stated in a spammed e-mail message that Lawrence King, an alleged participant in a local pedophile ring, passed a suitcase stuffed with bearer bonds to a familiar "dark villain" Dr. Michael Aquino, "earmarked for covert Contra operations."

John DeCamp, a veteran of the CIA's Phoenix Program in Vietnam and a Nebraska attorney representing some of the vic-

41. Diana Napolis newsgroup statement, "Aquino v. Curio."
42. Public ElectriCiti statement.

tims in the King case, observes that Nelson – a personal photographer in the employ of King, then a Republican Party scion and fund-raiser for Oliver North's Iran contra initiative – "was in a position to know." Bearer bonds, he says, "provide anonymity, the cornerstone of money-laundering. Money laundering is associated with three things: drugs, war and politics."

Aquino had a chance to respond to DeCamp's allegations when a northern California radio station attempted to schedule a debate between them. "He was going to go on," but "at the last minute, when he found out I was going to be on with him, refused." But the Temple of Set leader changed his mind and appeared on the program after all. DeCamp: "I had information that pretty much torpedoed his main claim that none of the charges against or his removal from [the Army] were ever proven." The Nebraska lawyer recalls that he was "able to blow him apart on the radio, and it ended on a hostile note."[43]

Accusations from survivors of ritual abuse and "Operation Monarch" mind control, a program that Aquino was reportedly involved in, have surfaced time and again in recent years and become a cause celebré of the Patriot right. Many of these accounts remain unverified. But these and the Presidio charges continue to hound Aquino. "What I have maintained," he insists, "and continue to maintain, was that the 'Satanic Ritual Abuse' myth that resulted in so many scares and scams in the 1980s was based on nothing more than a fictional idea planted by [Dr. Lawrence] Pazder in his … *Michelle Remembers* book."[44]

This account, mind you, is the word of a Satanic psyop agent from the same intelligence groups that recruited war criminals from Germany after WW II – Operation Paperclip, the recruitment of Nazi scientists, is still a program that warms beating hearts in the Pentagon. And all too often, mind control is the product of an alliance between the intelligence groups that Dr. Aquino represents so colorfully, and religious cults mustered or co-opted by the Department of Defense and CIA. Military intelligence involvement in a Satanic cult led by

43. Taped July 6 telephone interview with DeCamp.
44. Aquino e-mail to the author, September 2000.

a priest with a background in psychological operations does not appear in *Michelle Remembers*.

Survivors of ritual abuse trauma at the Presidio mirror scores of nearly identical cases that have surfaced across the country to haunt the victims for life ... only to be spun into non-existence by defense attorneys and an irresponsible press exerting an explosive and divisive influence on the communities affected. Jeannette Westbrook, a social worker who has served on the Kentucky Attorney General's Task Force on Child Sexual Abuse – and an RA survivor herself – notes that the convictions are entirely dependent upon tangible evidence, and when dealing with pre-school age children the determination of such basics as precise time, dates and setting of abuse is nearly impossible.

"You've got to be specific," she writes, to prosecute an RA case. "It's very, very difficult to know all of these things," but if child abuse advocates don't offer specific evidence, "you go in there, you get shot down," and the child is sadistically "revictimized over and over and over again."

Another factor is corruption. Before taking a case to court, Westbrook advises, it is necessary to investigate the police officers handling the case. "Find out what judge it's going to go before. There's never been a dichotomy as true as 'good-cop/bad-cop,'" and "you have to know who's playing what side of the fence."[45]

Diana Napolis has handled around 600 child abuse cases in the San Diego area. She has worked in the field for ten years: "I've seen all manner of atrocities committed against children and witnessed all types of adult games played to avoid culpability." She has also "seen the lack of resources allotted to adequately investigate, let alone alleviate child abuse at its most simplistic level."

Child sexual abuse, she says, "is rampant, one of the secrets in our society that nobody wants to hear about. After networking with many professionals around the country who worked in the trenches, I began to see a pattern of systematic harassment and threats." The press, Napolis says, "printed

45. Jeanette Westbrook at The Second Annual Ritual Abuse, Secretive Organizations and Mind Control Conference, August 14-15, 1999, DoubleTree Hotel in Windsor Locks, Connecticut.

their own one-sided version of events." A number of witnesses have "told me of threats they'd received, and related their frustration and serious concern." The Presidio case drew her interest "after meeting several parents and children who related their experiences. These people gave me newspaper articles and internal documents supporting claims that their children had been molested in the late 1980's, but there appeared to be no successful resolution for them other than a large out-of-court settlement with the Army. Some of these people are devastated to this day."

The devastation continues while protected perpetrators, including Dr. Aquino and the revisionist media-at-large, sing off-tune of innocence, drowning out the cries from scores of young victims.

CHAPTER FIFTEEN

OPERATION CONDOR:
9/11/1973 & 9/11/2001

The 9/11 attack was the parallel to the Pinochet coup.... Pinochet also imposed extraordinary police powers.... After 9/11, thousands of Arabs and Muslims were also rounded up by the US military and kept in prison in secret.... They were also tortured ... 9/11 was the equivalent of a coup for Bush. Its version of Operation Condor is being assembled in the Pentagon by Undersecretary of Defense Stephen Cambone and his military deputy, Lt. Gen. William G. Boykin...
– Maria Montelibre

In this world, in this strange world of covert overthrow of governments and clandestine armies and secret operations, the problem we're facing is that you are working with two realities: you're working with ... exchange of power, economic power, power over people, controlling their lives. In order to do that you disguise certain persons and send them into roles to influence. They become actors on a stage and they influence our minds in a way that is not real, but affect a reality that will touch us later."
– Mae Brussell, *Dialogue Assassination*, Broadcast No. 16, October 13, 1971

To Mussolini, *"fascismo,"* a word coined by the dictator, had dual meanings. It is rooted in the Latin "fasces," a strange-looking axe with poles strapped to it, but the term also meant: "Group."

Christopher Deliso at Antiwar.com found the 9/11 group when he poked into the Plame investigation, "a relay team of hawkish officials providentially placed throughout various government agencies." This serpentine network wound through the CIA, Pentagon, Office of Special Plans, State Department, DIA, NSA and other federal agencies. Deliso described operatives darkening the wings of the Libby investigation, but the same could be said of the 9/11 inquiry: the Bushite "relay team" performed "a handoff of information from the point of origin (the CIA) to the ultimate 'commissioners' of the inquiry." Given the "intra- and inter-factional nature of all of these agencies, it is understandable why the highest officials in the land jostled to get their 'people' strategically inserted throughout the departments, where they could garner inside information and hinder the objectives of their ostensibly direct employers whenever they conflicted with the goals of their real minders…"[1]

The "minders" were represented by George Schultz and a clutch of Hoover "scholars" at the Bush grooming sessions early in his first run for the White House. The Morgan, Rockefeller and Harriman syndicates, whose interests are served by think-tank sprawl, spruced him up, too. Skyscrapers and governments have crumbled beneath their feet. These are the Royals, and they set loose their hounds for the installation of a dictatorship in Chilé: Kissinger, Bush, Cheney, Rumsfeld, the CIA and a military junta on September 11, 1973 – "CIA acknowledges involvement in Allende's overthrow, Pinochet's rise," September 19, 2000 … "WASHINGTON (AP) – The CIA is acknowledging for the first time the extent of its deep involvement in Chile, where it dealt with coup plotters, false propagandists and assassins…"

Twenty-five years before the CIA's rare public confession, in a protracted plausible deniability phase, Howard Zinn went ahead and reported that Operation Condor, "the CIA action to overthrow Allende, was approved by the 40 Committee,

1. Christopher Deliso, "Lesser Neocons of L'Affaire Plame." http://www.antiwar.com/deliso/?articleid=8137.

whose chairman [was] Henry Kissinger. And it was Kissinger who recommended that Rockefeller head the commission to investigate the CIA."[2]

Rockefeller summed up the Commission report: "There are things that have been done which are in contradiction to the statutes, but in comparison to the total effort, they are not major."[3] The same could be said of the Corleone family.

How "in contradiction to the statutes" was Condor? So in contradiction that the river winding through Santiago was dammed with decapitated bodies.

How many statutes did that contradict?

Regime change has long been a staple of U.S. foreign policy. Exactly 28 years later, it happened again. But the strategy evolved with the times. The idea was not to merely impose military rule over a defenseless population, but to channel resources of government – its finances, military force, technology, personnel and secrets – their way.

Early jostling to insert the 9/11 relay team behind Bush resulted in the appointment of Donald H. Rumsfeld as Secretary of Defense.

Rumsfeld was among the central participants in Operation Condor I.

Latin America: Murder, Inc., a classified report prepared by the Senate Foreign Relations Committee Subcommittee on International Operations, revealed the origins of Condor. The title was an allusion to a confession from Lyndon Johnson a few months before his death: "We were running a Murder, Inc. in the Caribbean."

The report said that the U.S. had "joint operations between Argentina, Bolivia, Brazil, Chile, Paraguay and Uruguay. The joint operations were known as Operation Condor. These are special teams used to carry out [the] killing of enemies." Jack Anderson offered a blood-curdling glimpse of "Operation

2. Howard Zinn, "The CIA, Rockefeller, and the Boys in the Club," *Howard Zinn Reader*, 1975. http://www.thirdworldtraveler.com/Zinn/Rockefeller_BoysClub.html
3. Mae Brussell, "The Nazi Connection to the John F. Kennedy Assassination," http://www.maebrussell.com/Mae%20Brussell%20Articles/Nazi%20Connection%20to%20JFK%20Assass.html.

Condor, An Unholy Alliance" on August 3, 1979: "Assassination teams are centered in Chile. This international consortium is located in Colonia Dignidad, Chile. Founded by the SS, led by Franz Pfeiffer Richter, Adolf Hitler's thousand-year Reich may not have perished. Children are cut up in front of their parents, suspects are asphyxiated in piles of excrement or rotated to death over barbecue pits."

Colonel Otto Skorzeny, a postwar CIA recruit, codenamed the Battle of the Bulge Operation Greif – German for "Condor."

Another CIA recruit oversaw the Chilean incarnation of Condor. *Global Research* raked muck in the Agency's secret aviary:

> Henry Kissinger belongs in the dock alongside the Chilean dictator.... He remains a prominent figure in the affairs of the U.S. ruling establishment and is protected by the government. In 2002, the Bush administration attempted unsuccessfully to name this war criminal as the head of the 'independent' panel investigating the September 11, 2001 terrorist attacks on New York and Washington. George Bush senior should be the subject of an indictment for the role the CIA played under his direction in fostering and covering up for the assassination squads that roamed Latin America and, ultimately, the streets of Washington The most prominent figures in the Bush administration – Vice President Dick Cheney and Defense Secretary Donald Rumsfeld – are likewise implicated. Cheney was the White House chief of staff during the Condor Operation, while Rumsfeld was defense secretary, supervising US ties to the Latin American military.[4]

Rumsfeld cohort George Schultz struck up congenial business ties with the Pinochet regime, and learned a thing or two about fascist economics for grafting to domestic policies.

Independent Latin journalist Maria Montelibre writes, "General Pinochet's Labor Minister and Mining in those

---

4. "Arrest of Pinochet and the Condor Killers in the U.S.," December 19, 2004. http://www.globalresearch.ca/index.php?context=viewArticle&code=20041219&articleId=329

days, José Piñera, is a Harvard educated boy, friend of George Schultz, among others. Piñera is now head of the Cato Institute Privatization Project in the U.S., which supports and instigates Bush's privatization schemes."

"Piñera planned the Social Security privatization plan in Chile with Dictator Pinochet."[5]

Condor was raked up again by a reporter for Ireland's *Village Magazine* in 2004: "Extraordinary Rendition bears more than a passing resemblance to operation Condor, the 'multinational of terror' organized by six U.S.-backed Latin American dictatorships in the 1970s." The Latin American terror program crossed national borders. "Regimes swapped suspects and facilitated death squads and kidnap teams. Suspects were disappeared without a trace, held without due process and monitored by physicians during torture sessions."

The post-9/11, Condor-like rendition program was "first mooted inside the offices of US intelligence" at the behest of Donald Rumsfeld.[6]

Others noticed haunting parallels between Condor and Rumsfeld's "war on terror." An editorial appeared in *The Nation* in January 2005:

> Did anyone in the Bush White House cast an uneasy eye over the new indictment of Gen. Augusto Pinochet? It may seem over the top to mention that old buzzard in the same breath as an elected US President. But consider Task Force 6-26. It sounds like a relic of Pinochet's Operation Condor.... Task Force 6-26 is a secret unit composed mostly of U.S. Navy SEALs operating in Baghdad – its existence unacknowledged by the Pentagon. According to the Washington Post, a fact-finding mission for Army generals warned a year ago that Task Force 6-26 was running an off-the-books prison for detainees.[7]

---

5. Maria Montelibre, "Privatization of Social Security: First step towards fascism." http://www.elsemanario.net/print_col.php?cid=111

6. Michael McCaughan, "Shannon used as kidnap operation stop-over," *Village Magazine*, Ireland (October 2-8, 2004).

7. Anon., "Prosecuting US Torture," *The Nation*, January 3, 2005. http://www.thenation.com/doc/20050103/editors

But Rumsfeld coordinated with others in the District of Columbia, as William Blum notes: "1973, September 11, CHILE: President Allende overthrown by General Pinochet in a bloody coup in which *3000 Chileans are massacred*. The Rockefellers' ITT Corp., now run by John McCloy, donates $1 million to the coup effort, which is orchestrated by Henry Kissinger."[8]

The planning was conceived in pitiless detail by social engineers.

In the 1960s, Abt Associates – a consulting firm founded by Clark C. Abt, a German who migrated to the U.S. in 1937, earned a degree at MIT and joined Raytheon after the war – assisted the Pentagon and CIA with Project Camelot, a computer model for destabilizing foreign governments. Socialist scholar Guerry Hoddersen found that Abt Associates "developed a simulation game called Politica that drew information from a computer linking the files of the CIA, the Defense Intelligence Agency and the State Department. Politica was used in training Third World police," and predicting "which social forces could be mobilized against leftist governments."[9]

As early as 1965, the American Anthropological Association's executive board began to receive complaints concerning social engineering projects in developing nations. The DoD and CIA recruited anthropologists to assist in counterinsurgency operations, and from this program rose Project Camelot with its cynical code-name.

The Army, according to the AAA, "had a contract with American University to study sociopolitical factors that could lead to internal warfare in that country."[10]

A survey of Condor undertaken by an independent Virtual Truth Commission ("Telling the Truth for a Better America") exposed the "minders" of the coup:

---

8. Summation of William Blum's *Rogue State*. http://twincities.indymedia.org/newswire/display/19468/index.php
9. Guerry Hoddersen, "CAFTA: trade pact promises 'Brave New World' of misery and inequality," *Freedom Socialist*, vol. 25, no. 2, June-July 2004. http://www.social-ism.com/fsarticles/vol25no2/cafta.html
10. James N. Hill, "The Committee on Ethics: Past, Present, and Future," *Handbook on Ethical Issues in Anthropology*, AAA. http://www.aaanet.org/committees/ethics/ch2.htm

1976-OPERATION CONDOR, SOUTH AMERICAN AS-
SASSINATION CARTEL, THE YEAR GEORGE BUSH SR.
IS CIA DIRECTOR. In 1976, Nelson Rockefeller was Vice
President (to Ford), and his advisor Henry Kissinger was
Secretary of State. In this year Kissinger's puppet dictator
Pinochet, of Chile organized Operation CONDOR, to co-
ordinate death squad assassinations by the secret police of
the dictators of Chile, Brasil, Argentina, Uruguay, and Para-
guay. 30,000 leftists were assassinated/executed *disappeared*.
Many of the top ranking Nazi war criminals in South Amer-
ica are believed to have lived in Colonia Dignidad.

In 1993, a trove of documents called the "Archives of Terror" was discovered in Paraguay detailing Nazi war criminal
involvement in Operation Condor, and listing victims including Israeli agents who were trying to find Nazis for trial. It is
probable that George Bush and Henry Kissinger knew about
and directed Operation CONDOR.

General Pinochet was never ashamed of his pro-Nazi fe-
tish, preferring Nazi uniforms and marching music.

In 1985, Boris Weisfeiler, an American professor, was disappeared at Colonia Dignidad. Today, Dignidad, since rechristened
Villa Bavaria, is a prospering commune valued at $5-billion but
closed to the public and protected by the Chilean military. Gerhard Mücke, nicknamed "Uncle Mauk," presides over "Oktober-
fest" at Villa Bavaria. Mücke has testified that he was involved
in the burning of some 30 corpses with phosphorus to dispatch
evidence of mass murder under the Pinochet dictatorship[11]

Kissinger, not incidentally, was Bush's choice to head the
September 11th investigation. Paul Bremer III, a former director of Kissinger Associates, was Bush's appointed ruler of Iraq.[12]

---

11. *La Nación*, "Cómplices de Paul Schäfer siguen dirigiendo la Colonia Dignidad
acusan diputados," November 19, 2012.
12. Virtual Truth Commission, "Operation Condor." www.geocities.com~virtual-
truth/condor.htm Also see: Lucy Komisar, "Operation Condor and Pinochet," *Los
Angeles Times*, November 1, 1998.

Chapter Sixteen

THE TEXAS PACIFIC GROUP
AND THE SECRET HISTORY OF THE GEMPLUS SMART CARD

The Texas Pacific Group (TPG) is a nondescript title on a brass shingle gracing a wall in Fort Worth, Texas with a hidden subtext: "Cut-Throats, Spies & Brain Police LLC." TPG's holdings include companies most of us would recognize: MGM, Burger King, Ducati, America West and J. Crew.[1] TPG is often praised by the business press. Less publicity is lavished on an affiliated company, Aqua International. Details on Aqua's water privatization scheme turned up in a public report issued by the National Commission on Energy Policy – the direct successor to Dick Cheney's secret Energy Task Force.

An AP story on the commission's own web site notes that it advocates "expanded development of coal, natural gas and nuclear power."[2] Some members of the commission: Former CIA Director R. James Woolsey; Ralph Cavanagh (a proponent of "market-based solutions to environmental issues," widely blamed for creating the California energy crisis); Martin D. Zimmerman, a VP at Ford Motor Company; Frank Henry Habicht II, advisor to the energy and environment transition teams of the incoming Bush Administration in 2000, and former VP at William Ruckelshaus Associates; Marilyn Brown, director of the Oak Ridge National Laboratory in Tennessee; plus sundry industrial establishmentarians.

Aqua International CEO William Reilly, EPA director under GHW Bush, is a commission co-chair.

---

1. Hoover business directory: http://www.hoovers.com/texas-pacific-group/–ID__51545–/free-co-factsheet.xhtml
2. Josef Hebert, "Panel Says More Money Needed for Energy," AP, December 7, 2004. http://www.energycommission.org/site/page.php?mediacoverage=26

The report notes that the Texas Pacific Group, "along with OPIC, set up Aqua International and installed Reilly as its President and CEO in June 1997." The company "finances water privatization projects."

William Reilly was a TPG consultant from 1994 to 1997. In August 2002, Aqua International "assumed control of 49.4% of Jain Irrigation, based in Maharashtra, India. He sits on the DuPont board alongside Commissioner Archie W. Dunham, then the CEO of Conoco, a subsidiary of DuPont until 1998. When Conoco went its own way, Reilly was appointed as a director of ConocoPhillips. Since May 2000, Reilly has also been a director of Ionics, a company that invests in Third World water systems. In addition, Reilly is a board member of Eden Springs and chairman of the board at the World Wildlife Fund."

The WWF is a front for heavy industry that parades an environmental public interest group. It "rakes in millions from corporations," writes investigative reporter Jeffrey St. Clair ...

> ... including Alcoa, Citigroup, the Bank of America, Kodak, J.P. Morgan, the Bank of Tokyo, Philip Morris, Waste Management and DuPont. They even offer an annual conservation award funded by and named after the late oil baron J. Paul Getty. It hawks its own credit card and showcases its own online boutique. As a result, WWF's budget has swelled to over $100 million a year and it's not looking back. Where does all the money go? Most of it goes to pay for plush offices, robust salaries, and a tireless direct mail operation to raise even more money. WWF's CEO, the icy Kathryn S. Fuller, pulls in a cool $250,000 a year, including benefits. This is the remorseless logic of modern environmentalism, in which non-profits are more obsessed with fundraising than the corporations that they are supposed to be battling. Indeed, the relentless cash hunt leads them serenely right into corporate boardrooms, hands out, mouth gagged.[3]

3. Jeffrey St. Clair, "Panda Porn: The Marriage of WWF and Weyerhaeuser," *CounterPunch*, December 5, 2002.

256

The founder of the Texas Pacific Group is David Bonderman, a director of the World Wildlife Fund.[4] Bonderman was co-founder of the Halifax Group, formed in January 1999 with David W. Dupree, a former Carlyle Group director; William L. Rogers, founding partner of Colony Capital and the Robert M. Bass Group; also Thomas J. Barrack, chief executive of Colony and a former principal at Robert M. Bass. (Major Halifax Group investments include The World Bank, G.E. Capital, Mellon Ventures, Natexis, SunAmerica, Wells Fargo, Lexington Partners, Lerner Enterprises, and the Edward P. Bass/Lee Bass/Clark and Crow family offices.)[5]

Bonderman went to TPG in 1992 direct from the position of chief operating officer at the Bass Group, Inc., then based in Fort Worth, Texas. Prior to joining RMBG in 1983, Bonderman was a partner in the law firm of Arnold & Porter in Washington, D.C., where he specialized in corporate and antitrust litigation.

Bonderman serves on the board of Gemplus International S.A., a smart card developer.[6] And this is where the Texas Pacific Group shows its true colors.

The corporation's Internet hype makes no mention of the CIA or Nazi heavy industry:

> Leading the smart card industry, Gemplus was founded in 1988, at the very start of the development of smart card technology. They are now active around the world, with 58 sales and marketing offices, 6 research & development centers, 20 personalization facilities and 11 manufacturing sites. In total they said to have sold over 5.6 billion smart cards. And In 2005, Gemplus was named the industry leader for a seventh consecutive year with a 27% market share.

4. World Air Transport Summit website, "David Bonderman, Founding Partner, Texas Pacific Group." http://www.iata.org/events/agm/2006/speakers/david_bonderman.htm
5. http://www.thehalifaxgroup.com/advantages/advantages.htm
6. Press release, "Texas Pacific Group to Invest $300-$500 Million in Gemplus, Marking One of the Largest Private Equity Investments in Technology." http://www.prnewswire.co.uk/cgi/news/release?id=28118

The Quandt Family

On January 26, 2000, Gemplus announced the signing of a financial agreement with the Texas Pacific Group. The latter agreed to pour $300-$500 million into Gemplus: "Texas Pacific Group will join founder and chairman Marc Lassus, Gemplus employees and members of the Quandt Family of Germany, as one of the major shareholders of Gemplus." Terms of the contract were not disclosed to the public. "Gemplus will use the new capital to dramatically expand Gemplus' presence in the wireless communications, e-commerce, and Internet security markets."

The partnership was billed as one of the largest private equity investments in technology history. But there was no call for champagne at the next stockholder's meeting. The Quandts have well-deserved reputation for Nazi collaboration, as Jeffrey Myers, Department of History, Avila University, reports:

> With the rise of Hitler, the Quandts became enmeshed in the Nazi horror. The marriage of Gunther Quandt's ex-wife Magda to Joseph Goebbels initially linked the Quandt family to the Nazis, but Guenther Quandt and his sons all played significant independent roles in the Third Reich. Each eventually became a member of the Nazi party, and, more importantly, the Quandt firms of AFA and DWM (as well as the heavily Quandt-invested Daimler-Benz) utilized slave labor from the concentration camps of Hannover-Stcken, Mauthausen, and Sachsenhausen. In the immediate postwar period, the Quandts were subject to close scrutiny and heavy fines as a result of denazification. The family also faced the loss of factories due to wartime destruction and confiscation of properties in the Soviet zone. The Quandts' version of the Economic Miracle occurred largely thanks to the rearmament of West Germany in the mid-1950s, which made DWM and AFA profitable once again.[7]

7. Jeffrey Myers, "The Quandts: A Family History of German Big Business, 1871-2002," *Humanities and Social Sciences Online* (review of Rüdiger Jungbluth's *Die Quandts: Ihr leiser Aufstieg zur maechtigsten Wirtschaftsdynastie Deutschlands*. Frankfurt: Campus Verlag, 2002, ISBN 3-593-36940-0). http://www.h-net.org/reviews/showrev.cgi?path=70241129666606

The GPS Angle: Operation Condor, the Smart Card & the CIA's "Strategic Direction Initiative"

Gemplus history, like the Quandts', is steeped in mass murder ... Iran contra's Elliot Abrams and John Negroponte were apparently fond of Latin American Nazis. Toni Solo, an activist in Argentina, writes that said Nazis "refined their torment of Jewish victims back in Buenos Aires by torturing them beneath portraits of Adolf Hitler." Argentine paramilitary officers trained the Honduran army in "techniques of mass repression while John Negroponte was ambassador in the Honduran capital Tegucigalpa from 1981 to 1985. There he worked closely with Honduran armed forces chief Gustavo Alvarez Martinez to impose a 'national security' state on the Argentine model – that is, a police state based on extra-judicial murder."[8]

But funds for political murder didn't grow on trees. Solo observes: "Legal funds were hard to come by, illegal sources served, including drug proceeds and money siphoned through the fraudulent Bank of Commerce and Credit International, courtesy of links between George Bush, Sr., the Saudi royal family and the Bin Laden family."

BCCI collapsed after press reports tied the international bank to the Medellin cartel. "At this time, both Colombia and Taiwan also gave training. But the principal countries involved were Argentina and Israel, [which] set up a plant in Guatemala to manufacture Galil rifles. Under an agreement reached in October 1981, 200 Guatemalan army officers took anti-insurgency courses in Buenos Aires, including use of 'interrogation techniques.' Among their 'instructors' was Ricardo Cavallo. "Cavallo has been charged with involvement in 337 political kidnappings, 227 disappearances, and the theft of children of political prisoners."

Cavallo hailed from Operation Condor. "Cavallo and his colleagues, Jorge Radice, Jorge Acosta and others were tor-

8. Toni Solo, "Coming Soon to the United States? Plan Condor, the Sequel," *Dissident Voice*, September 27, 2003. http://www.dissidentvoice.org/Articles8/Solo_Condor-US.htm#Note12

turers in the Argentine armed forces." These Condors forced torture victims to sign legal documents "permitting them to dispose of their property, bank accounts and belongings." Cavallo collaborated with the Bolivian army under Luis Garcia Meza in the early '80s, "when Bolivia was virtually run by drug traffickers. With their illicit capital, Cavallo and his friends set up the security and data control businesses Martiel and Talsud in Argentina. They made deals with Seal Lock, an Argentine company representing U.S.-based Advantage Security systems. Martiel represented Casa de la Moneda of Brazil, CONSAD of Argentina, Ciccone Calcográfica and the French smart card firm Gemplus."

Talsud and Martiel were inseparable:

> Both worked on the deal to emit the New Zaire currency for CIA favorite President Mobutu in Zaire in 1993. In 1995, Bridas subsidiary TTI and Seal Lock helped Talsud secure lucrative deals in Argentina's Mendoza province. In 1996, Talsud got the contract to issue driving licenses in Argentina's Rioja province. Among Seal Lock's clients were the Argentine Ministry of Foreign Affairs, the Argentine Central Bank, The National Registry of Bolivia, Shell Paraguay and Israel's ZIM maritime line. Cavallo and his brother Oscar also set up a business in El Salvador called Sertracen, closely linked to the Salvadoran military. Sertracen issues driver and gun licenses in El Salvador.
>
> In August 1998, Cavallo entered Mexico as a tourist, miraculously managing to process his residency within a month. Within a year his Talsud company was bidding for the Mexican driver licensing authority (RENAVE), together with Gemplus and the Mexican company CIFRA. On September 7th 1999, they won the contract guaranteeing an estimated annual turnover of $400 million.

The Cavallo/RENAVE/Gemplus scandal was exposed by the Mexican press in 2003. The death count began…

Commerce Vice-Minister Raul Tercero signed off on the RENAVE deal. Tercero's body was found, throat cut, in a wooded region near Mexico City. In October 1998, during a bribery scandal tainting IBM, Marcel Cattaneo, "brother of the owner of Cavallo client CONSAD, was found hanging from a lamppost…. In June 1998, a friend of President Carlos Menem, leading businessman Alfredo Yabran, associated with De La Rue subsidiary Ciccone Calcografica, was found dead. In August … Jorge Estrada, Cavallo's former chief at the ESMA torture center and a shareholder in Martiel, was found dead, another apparent suicide."

The Texas Pacific Group came along in 2000 to invest in Luxembourg-based Gemplus and its smart card. The newswires documented significant changes in management and base of operations: "After the buyout, the new board made some odd decisions." First, all development and manufacture of Gemplus smart cards would be moved to the United States. This provoked widespread rage in France until the board of directors backed down.

In 2002, the board appointed a new President, "an American named Alex Mandl. Mandl resigned his position as a board member of In-Q-Tel," the CIA front applauded widely by American media, "to take his new job as GemPlus CEO."[9]

In-Q-Tel, of course, is a well-known CIA-sponsored commercial front. "The origins of the concept that has become In-Q-Tel," the company's site reports, "are traceable to Dr. Ruth David, a former CIA Deputy Director for Science and Technology."

This next step gives away the store: DCI George Tenet "had just launched his Strategic Direction Initiative that included technology as one of its areas for review. The study made a direct link between the Agency's future technology investments and *improving its information gathering and analysis capabilities.*"[10]

Stunning confession – straight from the In-Q-Tel site. It says that the machinations behind the acquisition of Gemplus were intended to bring the smart card under the control of Langley to advance the CIA's abilities to spy on us.

---

9. http://www.democraticunderground.com/
10. In-Q-Tel website.

A smart card, of course, is any pocket-sized slab of spun petroleum with embedded integrated circuits. Memory cards contain non-volatile data storage components and perhaps a fixed bit of security logic. Microprocessor cards contain memory circuits and microprocessors. They can range in complexity from simple identification codes to the equivalent of a miniature computer.

The smart card has been the source of widespread privacy concerns, as the *Toronto Star* reports:

> The Ontario government's plan to create smart cards to access a wide range of government services should be a red flag for anyone concerned about privacy, warn computer and privacy experts. David Jones, president of Electronic Frontier Canada, a group committed to protecting privacy and freedom of expression in cyberspace, says his worst fear is the creation of a "surveillance society." In a Big Brother world of electronic surveillance, "a government watches every aspect of your life constantly and cross-references all of the different interactions you've had with the government," says Jones, a professor of computer science at McMaster University.[11]

The shake-up at Gemplus continued:

CIA Controversy Mars New Gemplus CEO Appointment

Smart card vendor Gemplus International SA has finally appointed a new permanent CEO after a nine-month search, but the company's new leader, Alex Mandl, has immediately walked into controversy over his ties to the US Central Intelligence Agency. The Luxembourg-based company has been searching for a full-time CEO since it axed its former leader Antonio Perez in December 2001. The boardroom struggle also saw the ousting of the company's chairman Marc Lassus, and centered on a plan to move the company's headquarters from Paris to San Francisco.

A miserable nine months have followed, with the company cutting 1,000 jobs, accepting the resignation of its CFO and the writing down of 66.9m euros ($66.5m) from the value of a loan granted to Lassus to enable him to buy company shares.

11. Theresa Boyle, "Smart card chills privacy experts – 'Surveillance society' feared under provincial plan," *Toronto Star*, January 15, 2001.

The appointment of a new permanent CEO should have given the company cause for celebration, but has instead sparked new controversy. At least one board member, Ziad Takieddine, has expressed concern about Mandl's appointment, given his links with the CIA:

> Before accepting the role as Gemplus CEO, Mandl served on the board of trustees of In-Q-Tel, a non-profit organization sponsored by the CIA that invests in technological innovations that may aid national security. According to a Dow Jones report, several board members opposed Mandl's appointment on the grounds that his links with the CIA could undermine Gemplus's ability to sell smart card technologies in some countries. Among those who reportedly opposed Mandl's appointment is Gemplus's current chairman, Dominique Vignon. However, Mandl's appointment was carried by a majority of the company's board, and the support of the company's largest shareholder, Texas Pacific Group.[12]

RICO Republicans

The CIA was very bullish on the smart card despite occasional blowback:

Prosecutors: CIA agents left trail
Cellphone calls blew their cover
AP, July 28, 2005

ROME, Italy (AP) – It wasn't their lavish spending in luxury hotels, their use of credit cards or even frequent-flier miles that drew attention. Instead it was a trail of casual cellphone use that tripped up the 19 purported CIA operatives wanted by Italian authorities in the alleged kidnapping of a radical Muslim cleric. Italian prosecutors who have obtained arrest warrants for the 19 – none of whom are believed to be in Italy – presented evidence that the suspects used at least 40 Italian cell phones, some in their own names.

Experts say that either they were bumbling spies, or they acted with impunity because Italian officials had been

---

12. "CIA Controversy Mars New Gemplus CEO Appointment," Euro-Techforum newsletter, September 3, 2002. http://www.eurotechforum.com/pooled/articles/BF_NEWSART/view.asp?Q=BF_NEWSART_35838

> informed of their plan – a claim the government of Premier
> Silvio Berlusconi has publicly denied on several occasions…
>
> The wireless system used in Italy and most of the rest
> of Europe relies on a stamp-sized SMART CARD that is in-
> serted in the back of every handset. This removable "SIM"
> card stores an individual's phone number and other account
> data…

Despite the risks, the Agency was keen on smart card technology.

There was this press release on February 1, 2006: "New York, NY, and Ra'anana, Israel – SuperCom Ltd., a leading provider of smart card and electronic identification (e-ID) solutions, today announced that R. James Woolsey, former director of Central Intelligence and one of America's preeminent authorities on security issues, will be chairman of the company's newly created advisory board."[13]

The Woolsey appointment passed without comment, but the takeover of Gemplus provoked a full-blown international incident.

The French interpreted the Texas Pacific Group's advances on the smart card maker as a textbook case of economic warfare. Mark K. Jensen, an associate professor at Pacific Lutheran University, wrote in *Liberation* (a Parisian newspaper co-founded by Jean Paul Sartre, dismissed by *The Economist* as "the bible of today's armchair revolutionaries.") that Gemplus was the victim of corporate looting, "an attempt to strip it of its patents and transfer them to the United States through an American investment fund, Texas Pacific Group (TPG)." The U.S. was "behind in the area of *cartes puce*, a technology whose security applications have become a very sensitive matter."

The "hidden hand of the CIA [was] behind TPG's interests."

The buyout was conducted with the full compliance of Gemplus founder Marc Lassus, beset by "a series of strange decisions." The newly-installed American board members of the French corporation "first tried to move the company to the United States … after having earlier transferred part of the hu-

13. SuperCom release, "Former CIA Director Woolsey Named Chairman of SuperCom's New Advisory Board," February 1, 2006. http://www.supercomgroup.com/event_full.asp?info_id=658

man relations and legal affairs department to Geneva. After a year-and-a- half of mobilization by Gemplus's manager-share-holders, the TPG fund named a new boss, Alex Mandl," the aforementioned CIA In-Q-Tel director. "Even more bizarre, Mandl (still in charge, but having resigned from his term at In-Q-Tel amid the controversy) had omitted mentioning his former position in the CV he submitted to the board."[14]

Mandl also failed to mention in his resumé that TPG sprang from the same Dallas-Fort Worth area Republican organized crime net that has turned up periodically in many an investigation of corporate excesses, notably Darwin Deason and ACS, J. Livingston Kosberg and Gibraltar Savings, the Tom Delay mob, Swift Boat Veterans (the Wyly brothers psyop troupe).

David Bonderman, founder of TPG, was a struggling investor when the Bass brothers (stakes in Disney, Human Genome Sciences, Globalstar) – heirs to the oil wealth of Sid Richardson, their great-uncle – discovered him: "Lee Bass was immensely wealthy," the TPG web site reports, "but the 35-year-old was itching to aggrandize his already considerable fortune and to establish a name for himself.... He asked the 41-year-old Bonderman to lead the investment team he was gathering. Bonderman immediately agreed."

In 1983, on the day he wrapped up his last case at Arnold & Porter, "Bonderman packed his bags and moved to Fort Worth to spearhead the growth of the leveraged buyout (LBO) company Robert M. Bass Group."

Fort Worth residents fought a proposed federal highway through the city's historic district. Significantly, "the group was led by Robert Bass, one of four Fort Worth brothers whose inheritance from a wildcatter great-uncle had been built into a multibillion-dollar family fortune. Bonderman was hired to argue against the proposed highway and prevailed, impressing Bass a great deal and, unwittingly, steering his professional career in an entirely new direction..."[15]

14. Mark Jensen, "Europe fears aggressive U.S. takeovers in defense sector," *Liberation*, November 25, 2004. http://www.ufppc.org/content/view/1810/2
15. "Founder's Background," Texas Pacific Group Inc. site. http://www.fundinguniverse.com/company-histories/Texas-Pacific-Group-Inc-Company-History.html

The White House for Sale web site (http://www.white-houseforsale.org/) reports that Lee Bass ranked as G.W. Bush's fifth largest patron in his run for the presidency. "When Bush's ailing Harken Oil suspiciously won exclusive offshore drilling rights in Bahrain in 1990, the Basses bankrolled the venture. When Bush was governor in the late 1990s, several of his appointees to the University of Texas Board of Regents ... sat on the board of the newly-created University of Texas Investment Management Co. (UTIMCO), which oversees billions of dollars of endowment funds."

The *Houston Chronicle* notes that "UTIMCO's board doled out lucrative investment contracts to firms with close ties to Pioneer UTIMCO Chair Tom Hicks [vice chair of Clear Channel] or George W. Bush, including firms tied to Pioneers Lee Bass, Robert Grady [Carlyle Group] and Charles Wyly [Swift Boat Vets]."[16]

Hellman & Friedman (H&F), a TGP investment partner, was also immersed in CIA and Bush administration sleaze.

- Stanford University has a long history of collaboration with the CIA. Lloyd Dinkelspiel, H&F CEO Warren Hellman's uncle, was president of the Stanford Board of Trustees from 1953 to 1958.[17] (I.W. Hellman, his great-grandfather, was instrumental into turning Wells Fargo into a leading financial institution in California.)

- The firm owns 19.4 percent of the immense Axel Springer publishing empire, a CIA "Mockingbird" propaganda outlet.[18]

- When Michael J. Boskin (author of *Too Many Promises: The Uncertain Future of Social Security*), chairman

16. Demian Bulwa, "Warren's world," California Alumni site, December 2003. http://www.alumni.berkeley.edu/Alumni/Cal_Monthly/December_2003/Warrens_world.asp
17. For his relationship to Lloyd W. Dinkelspiel, see Carol Emert, "Warren Hellman, DEALMAKER," San Francisco Chronicle, May 13, 2001. http://www.sfgate.com/cgi-bin/article.cgi?file=/chronicle/archive/2001/05/13/BU220332.DTL. For the Dinkelspiel's position at Stanford, see university press release, June 14, 1993. http://www.stanford.edu/dept/news/pr/93/930614Arc3214.html
18. Alex Constantine, "And Now a Word from Our Sponsor – The CIA," Virtual Government, Feral House, 1996. On H&F's investment in Springer, see: http://pjsf.typepad.com/pjsf/2004/04/pocketful_of_no.html

of the President's Council of Economic Advisers under George H.W. Bush, returned to the Hoover Institute as a senior fellow, he received a teaching endowment from Tully M. Friedman, a managing partner of Hellman & Friedman.[19]

- Tully Friedman is a director of the American Enterprise Institute, a CIA/military intelligence front.[20]

- Warren Hellman (1934-2011), H&L founder, was named as an ex-officio member of California Governor Arnold Schwarzenegger's sinister Council of Economic Advisors in 2004, a panel that also included Warren Buffett and George Schultz.[21]

- Robert Dynes (hailing from AT&T Labs), president of the University of California and close friend of Randy "Duke" Cunningham, is married to physicist Frances Hellman, daughter of Warren Hellman.

    Hellman, the great-grandson of a Wells Fargo Bank founder, an heir to the Levi Strauss denim fortune, was "one of the richest and most powerful businessmen in the state." He had long been a fixture in "the secretive internal politics of the University of California [and] a frequent contributor to the campaigns of politicians like Assembly Speaker, later San Francisco mayor, Willie Brown, and Governors Pete Wilson and Gray Davis." The firm that survives him "manages billions of dollars for a host of investors, including the massive California Public Employees' Retirement System – CalPERS for short." Before his death in December 2011 of complications from treatment for leukemia, Hellman weathered "charges that campaign contributions he and other family members made to state officeholders were intended to induce the CalPERS board to steer additional investment business to Hellman's firm."[22]

---

19. Stanford University press release, "Economist Boskin to return to Stanford, Hoover Institution," September 24, 1993.
20. RightWeb. http://rightweb.irc-online.org/groupwatch/aei.html
21. Arnold Schwarzenegger web site. http://www.schwarzenegger.com/news.asp?id=1716
22. Matt Potter, "Buddied Up," *San Diego Reader*, March 23, 2006.

- In 2004, the *Mills College Weekly* reported, a consortium of national and student organizations from some 60 colleges and universities targeted an investment firm that Mills College had invested in "for being environmentally and socially irresponsible." This group pressured "Farallon Capital Management LLC, where Mills College has had up to 19 percent of its endowment invested, to disclose all of their investments, some of which have been questionable in the past." In 1986, Thomas F. Steyer, a Hellman & Freeman managing director, and Matthew Barger, deputy chair of the firm, "founded San Francisco-based Farallon with start-up capital provided by Hellman & Friedman ... co-founded by a former Chairman of Mills' Board of Trustees, Warren Hellman. Today, Farallon manages over $9.8 billion, making them the fourth largest private investment fund in the world." An investment the coalition found particularly offensive was Halliburton, "a company profiting from the war in Iraq, as well as other questionable investments in Indonesia, Argentina, and Russia. As recently as December 2003, Farallon held 140,000 shares in Halliburton, worth a total of $3,640,000 at the time of reporting." It wasn't the first such protest. From the mid-1980s to the early '90s, when Hellman was chairman of the board of trustees, "Mills students and faculty members marched, held sit-ins, signed petitions, and built and camped out in mock shanty towns, protesting the continued investment of millions of dollars in South Africa during apartheid. In 1984, *The Weekly* reported Mills had over $3 million in stocks invested in companies with direct investment in South Africa in 1984, and over $4 million by 1987."[23]

- "Hellman, jug-eared and wry," per a *San Francisco Chronicle* profile on May 13, 2001, "runs below the radar screen of many Bay Area residents. But few local

http://www.sdreader.com/php/cover.php?mode=print&id=20060323
23. Erica Gulseth, "Investment Firm with Ties to Mills Under Fire – Farallon Capital – criticized for poor environmental and social practices," Mills College Weekly, October 28, 2004. http://www.millsweekly.com/vnews/display.v ART/2004/10/28/41804a67aacc6%20

dealmakers can boast of anything approaching his impact on local politics, charities, the arts and business.....
Hellman studied economics at UC Berkeley and graduated from Harvard Business School in 1959. The first 13 years of his career were spent at Lehman Bros. in New York. Deal-driven and aggressive, 'Hurricane' Hellman, at 26, became Lehman's youngest partner ever. Ten years later, he was company president."[24]

Hellman didn't turn Lehman around himself, however. Chairman Peter G. Peterson – co-founder of the Blackstone Group, former chairman of the Federal Reserve Bank of New York (2000-04), CEO of Lehman Brothers, Kuhn, Loeb Inc., 1977-84, Secretary of Commerce under Nixon – had a hand in that.[25]

24. Carol Emcrt, "Warren Hellman, DEALMAKER," *San Francisco Chronicle,* May 13, 2001.
25. Bulwa. The Hellman-Lehman association began in 1870, when I.W. Hellman, Warren's great-grandfather, rode the transcontinental rail to New York and married German immigrant Esther Newgass. Esther's sister was the wife of Mayer Lehman, co-founder of Lehman brothers. For the arrival and early history of the Hellmans in America, see: http://66.102.7.104/search?q=cache:YpW9CJ0xreMJ:www.lajh.org/file_upload/DinkelspielFrances2004.pdf+I.W.+hellman+and+%22wells+fargo%22&hl=en&gl=us&ct=clnk&cd=19

CHAPTER SEVENTEEN

SMOKING OUT FOX NEWS
CORRESPONDENT MORT KONDRACKE'S DIA/PSYOPRoots

*If Fox, you know, was embarrassingly right-wing or some-
thing like that, it would be plain for all to see.*
                                        – Mort Kondracke

His Wikipedia biography perpetuates the myth: "After
college [1960], Kondracke joined the U.S. Army and
served in Washington, D.C. in the Counter Intelligence Corps while pursuing graduate work at Georgetown
University and working part time for the *Washington Star.*"

The Beltway Boy informs us candidly that he "served in
the Counter-Intelligence Corps." Kondracke left the CIC in
1963. The problem with this account: *Counter-intelligence became a function of Army Intelligence two years before the CIC
morphed into DIA.*

Wikipedia: "The Counter Intelligence Corps (CIC) was a
World War II and early Cold War intelligence agency within the
United States Army. Its role was taken over by the U.S. Army
Intelligence Corps in 1961. The proliferation of intelligence
agencies had meant needless duplication of effort and disputes
over responsibility, so in 1961 the CIC ceased to exist as an independent organization, as it and its Navy and Air Force equiv-
alents were combined into the Defense Intelligence Agency."

Mort Kondracke was a DIA agent, confirmed by a profile
attached to his personal papers at Dartmouth where he was an
undergraduate: "1960-1963 – Assigned to Army Intelligence,
Washington, D.C., worked part-time for the *Washington*

Star." He joined the CIC in 1960 when it was folded into the DIA. Kondracke knew this when he later claimed a military assignment to the CIC, a spin that morphs him from a snitch to a Cold War hero.

He didn't protect his country. He spied on it … while pursuing a graduate degree at Georgetown University *and* working part time for the *Washington Star*. The young spy juggled all of this without dropping a pin – full military service, Ivy League grad school studies – and he still had two, three days in the week left over for a part-time writing job.

And what did he do exactly as an active intelligence agent in the District of Columbia?

Kondracke: "When I was in the Army Counterintelligence Corps, there was a category of people called 'disaffected,' and we conducted security investigations on these people…"[1]

The political "analyst" pursued graduate studies in Washington, D.C., admittedly spying on the "disaffected." (In the context of his statement, he was referring to American soldiers who exhibited signs of losing it and turning violent, like the "fraggers" in Vietnam or Fort Hood's Nidal Hasan, but there is likely as much truth to this as there is to his claim that his mission was "counter-intelligence" because the DIA had a mission in the early '60s: surveillance and disruption of the Civil Rights movement.)

Did he sign a secrecy oath? It was a DIA dictate.

He couldn't actually talk to the world on cable about his assignments…. U.S. domestic and foreign policies, the Vietnam War, status quo racism…

Questions: *Who* classified people as disaffected and assigned Kondracke to spy on them? Could disaffected include political opposition to U.S. military or political or racial objectives at the time, perhaps on campus? Was his job at the *Star* cover for intelligence gathering in D.C.?

In the early '60s, the DIA was a political spying unit that specifically targeted racial integrationists on campus (see

1. http://newsbusters.org/blogs/brad-wilmouth/2009/11/17/olbermann-kristol-spit-ting-ft-hood-dead-hits-oreilly-calling-terroris#ixzz13yqkbVXf

Army Surveillance in America, 1775-1980, by Joan M. Jensen, pp. 238-39). This is beginning to sound a bit more like right-wing propagandist Mort Kondracke's bailiwick than the James Bond intrigues suggested by a "Counter-Intelligence Corps" agent of Cold War fame.

About that job at the *Washington Star*: The *Washington Times*, the rabidly right-wing propaganda sheet published by Sun Myung Moon, was founded a year after the *Washington Star* shut down. Many on the payroll at the Times are former employees of the *Star*. "Almost all had serious reservations" about the transition, laments Doug Lamborne, *Washington Times* sports editor and a former *Star* copy editor. "You'd have to be a brick not to go though some sort of moral convulsions. I lost five pounds the first week. We all had these twitchy sort of feelings: 'Is what we're doing right?'"

The *Star*'s editorial policy had always been considered, well, conservative. But there were limits ...

Propaganda ties: The *Washington Star* also gave us right-wing propagandist James J. Kilpatrick of *60 Minutes* fame. Fred Barnes, currently executive editor of the far-right *Weekly Standard* and a redundant presence on cable, covered the Supreme Court and the White House for the *Star* before moving to the Baltimore Sun in 1979.

The *Star*'s decline began in the 1950s because "the paper's general manager was *perceived* as *anti-Semitic*, which led to the loss of advertising revenue...."[2]

Hatred of Jews sank the *Star*.

The average anti-Semitic, "conservative," pro-military corporate publisher would have no problem providing journalistic cover for a young DIA agent.... Lord knows how many of the "disaffected" Kondracke spied on as a part-time reporter.

Years later...

Kondracke Advocates Ethnic Cleansing

Fox News contributor Mort Kondracke writes today that if President Bush's escalation policy doesn't work, his Plan B

2. http://everything2.com/title/The+Washington+Star

should be "winning dirty," which will likely involve "ethnic cleansing, atrocities against civilians and massive refugee flows…" No one has publicly advocated this Plan B, and I know of only one Member of Congress who backs it – and he wants to stay anonymous. But he argues persuasively that "it's the best alternative available if Bush's surge fails…" Kondracke says it's understandable that Sunnis suffer because "so far they've refused to accept that they're a minority. They will have to do so eventually, one way or another…"[3]

War Crimes Fine by Morton Kondracke

Morton Kondracke – "Obama Should Say 'No' to 'War Crimes' Probes of Bush Team"[4]

Kondracke Defends Rumsfeld
Iraq prison scandal not worth firing Rumsfeld
By Morton Kondracke
Chicago Sun-Times, *May 14, 2004*|

The abuse of Iraqi prisoners that is now coming to light was without a doubt despicable, abhorrent and illegal. But on the basis of known facts, these events do not justify the ouster of Defense Secretary Donald Rumsfeld or the political frenzy it has caused in Washington.[5]

Kondracke Denies that Waterboarding is Torture

Kondracke: Waterboarding "doesn't result in any lasting damage"

Summary: In a Fox News "All-Star" panel discussion, Morton Kondracke said of the interrogation technique known as waterboarding, "I'm sure it feels like torture, you know, it doesn't result in any lasting damage, but it feels like torture…."[6]

News Hounds: Torture? A-OK With the "All-Stars"

Kondracke's Power of Prophesy

Watching Mort Kondracke defend Republicans and predict gloom and doom for Democrats tonight it was impossible to

3.http://digg.com/politics/
4. http://www.caglepost.com/c/72/Morton+Kondracke.html
5. http://www.encyclopedia.com/doc/1P2-1531890.html
6. http://mediamatters.org/items/200710310004

guess that he had the slightest connection with the Democratic Party.... Kondracke claimed that the ethics charges involving DeLay and Frist would turn out to be nothing.... Then he reminded viewers that the Republicans are in power and the Bush poll numbers have risen to a 45% approval. Adding that this is only 2005, he hinted that the Party would recover by 2008 and there was little chance that Democrats could gain control in 2006. Fred Barnes chuckled and congratulated Kondracke with "an excellent job on your homework."[7]

Red-Baiting

From *The Nation*: "On The Beltway Boys, Morton Kondracke likened Nevada Democrats to Communist propagandists..."[8]

Healthscare: "Fox's Morton Kondracke (Beltway Boys, 6/24/07) warned of a slippery slope from single-payer care to a socialist dictatorship, saying that "Moore basically wants socialized everything and the movie neglects to tell you that Cuba is a dictatorship and an economic basket case." (That "basket case" grew at a rate of 9.5 percent in 2006, according to the CIA World Factbook.) ..."[9]

The "Anti-American Conspiracy"

Noam Chomsky on Kondracke's "enthusiasm for terrorist violence and illegal economic warfare":

The March 15 [NY Times Book Review] carries Morton Kondracke's review of Paul Hollander's Anti-Americanism view; the author and reviewer are loyal apologists for atrocities by the U.S. government and its clients. Kondracke applauds this worthy exposure of the crime of anti-Americanism, though he feels Hollander may go too far in citing benefits for the handicapped as an illustration of the leftist deviation of Congress...

Kondracke agrees that "the left gets more respect and attention in the news media than its ideas merit," and is "strongly influential" in colleges and the church. But all

7. http://www.newshounds.us/2005/10/01/mort_kondracke_democrats_are_in_an_ecstasy_of_indignation.php
8. http://www.thenation.com/doc/20070507/alterman
9. http://www.fair.org/index.php?page=3446)

is not lost: "There is not a single Marxist or 'anti-American' major daily newspaper (or even major newspaper columnist) in the country," and the dangerous "mainline churches" are losing membership. Fortunately, those with "a generally critical disposition toward existing social arrangements" are almost entirely barred, though we must keep up our guard in case the heresy finds a tiny outlet...

Kondracke is particularly outraged that even though "the Communist alternative has collapsed," the anti-Americans (by implication, pro-Communists) maintain their "permanently adversarial culture" and continue to "hate their nation." They "have not recanted," even though they have been proven "disastrously wrong" in their wild claims that the Sandinistas and other evil-doers "represented a bright future for mankind" – or, to replace raving by reality, that the Sandinistas might have offered hope for Nicaraguans. The criminals in this case include the World Bank, Central American Jesuits, the leading figure of Central American democracy, Jose Figueres, a great enthusiast for U.S. corporations and the CIA, indeed, a rather broad range. But that just shows how awesome the anti-American conspiracy is.[10]

Kondracke: McCain is "Truth-Teller" on Iraq war

During the "All-Star Panel" segment on the June 6 edition of Fox News Special Report with Brit Hume, Roll Call executive editor Morton Kondracke asserted that during the GOP presidential debates, Sen. John McCain "was the truth-teller about the war in Iraq."[11]

A Doctored Tape and Kondrake's Trademark "Spin"

After Fox edited out applause following Dr. Joseph Lowery's remarks at the Coretta Scott King funeral, Kondracke expressed surprise at the "muted" reaction of the audience:

... Fox News Special Report with Brit Hume showed an edited video clip of Rev. Joseph Lowery's remarks at

10. http://prernalal.com/scholar/Noam%20Chomsky%20%20The%20Propaganda%20System.pdf
11. *http://mediamatters.org/discuss/200706070011*

Coretta Scott King's funeral, during which he mentioned the failure to find weapons of mass destruction in Iraq. Lowery's remarks were greeted with 23 seconds of applause and a standing ovation, but the clip Fox News aired presented nine seconds of applause and little hint of the standing ovation without noting that the clip had been doctored. After seeing the clip, *Roll Call'*s Morton Kondracke concluded that the audience "wasn't exactly uproarious in its response" to Lowery.[12]

A well-spun punch-line: Kondracke is Fox News' Idea of a "liberal": "So-called liberal contributors, who are at best centrists, include NPR's Juan Williams and Mara Liasson and Roll Call's Morton Kondracke....[13] But most of us view him as a conservative: "John McLaughlin's The McLaughlin Group, which went on the air in 1981, is sponsored by a private corporation, General Electric, with two liberal journalists facing off against ... two conservatives such as Fred Barnes, Morton Kondracke or Pat Buchanon..."[14]

12. http://co-mm.org/items/200602090006
13. http://www.thenation.com/doc/20010312/eviatar
14. Laurence Jarvic, *PBS: Behind the Screen*, Forum Books, 1997.)

CHAPTER EIGHTEEN

SCIENTOLOGIST GRETA VAN SUSTEREN'S

JOE MCCARTHY CONNECTION, *MEIN KAMPF* & A CIA SHRINK IN THE FAMILY

*F*orbes ranks impish Fox News interviewer Greta Van Susteren among the world's 100 most powerful women. She also received Seton University's Sandra Day O'Connor Medal of Honor and the American Bar Association's Presidential Award for "Excellence in Journalism" in 2001.

Van Susteren set out on her career as a cable journalist in 1991 at CNN as a legal analyst assigned to the William Kennedy Smith trial. She was a commentator on the O. J. Simpson trial a few years later, and the exposure enhanced her reputation as a legal analyst. She subsequently moved on up to co-anchor, with political analyst Roger Cossack, *Burden of Proof*, and host of *The Point with Greta van Susteren*.

In 2002, she moved over to Fox News, and *On the Record with Greta Van Susteren*, the highest-rated cable news program in the 10 p.m. time slot. At Fox, she covered a number of high-profile court cases, including the Scott Peterson and Michael Jackson trials.

Van Susteren is a qualified legal analyst. She graduated from the University of Wisconsin in 1972 with a degree in economics, then entered the Georgetown Law School, earned a Juris Doctor degree in 1979, a Master of Laws degree three years later. While attending Georgetown, Van Susteren became the first Stuart Stiller Fellow at the university's Law Center. She was honored by Stetson Law School with an honorary doctorate degree. She was also an adjunct faculty member at Georgetown Law Center, 1984 to 1999.

Before her rise to cable television fame, she was a partner in her husband's Washington Beltway law firm: John Coale is a wealthy tort attorney whose clients include the victims of the Union Carbide disaster in Bhopal, and the 1996 ValuJet crash in the Everglades. Coale represented Lisa Marie Presley in her divorce from Michael Jackson.

Greta van Susteren's spiritual hankerings led her to Scientology: "She has tried to keep a rather low profile on the Scientology angle," notes the *St. Petersburg Times*.

Time Machine: The McCarthys & the Van Susterens
But involvement in a religion that professes belief in alien possession is not her only claim to TV infamy. Urban van Susteren, her father, was Senator Joseph McCarthy's campaign manager. The *Wisconsinology* website reports: "United States Marine Joseph R. McCarthy is the best man at the wedding of his best friend, the future Judge Urban Van Susteren of Appleton. The two men became friends at Marquette law school. Van Susteren would later manage Joe McCarthy's successful 1946 campaign against two term incumbent Robert LaFollette, Jr."

Van Susteren & *Mein Kampf*
Mein Kampf was reportedly the only book that Joseph McCarthy ever read. Urban Van Susteren once informed the press that the anti-communist zealot "never read books," with one exception: Hitler's *Mein Kampf*. McCarthy considered the screed to be a veritable handbook of tactical politics.

"Joe was fascinated by the strategy, that's all," explained Van Susteren. And who gave Gunner Joe a copy of this priceless political textbook?

> McCarthy's best friend, the man who loaned him a copy of *Mein Kampf*, was a fellow Wisconsin conservative, Urban Van Susteren. Progressives won't be surprised that Greta Van Susteren, a Fox News mainstay and Urban's daughter, grew

up in a home with a cherished edition of Hitler's famous template for fascist political organization and bigoted scapegoat.[1]

Urban Van Susteren had long been a close friend of McCarthy's. They studied law together, and Van Susteren served as a campaign strategist in McCarthy's successful 1946 run for the senate. McCarthy lived in the Van Susteren home when not in Washington, D.C., and as a result, young Greta was exposed to politics at a tender age.

Who Killed Senator Joe McCarthy?

Why, Urban van Susteren, of course. By 1956, the severity of McCarthy's alcoholism led to periodic hospitalization for detox. Jean, his wife, informed reporters in September that Joe was under observation at Bethesda Naval Hospital for treatment of a knee wounded at Guadalcanal. But in private, she implored friends to save Joe's life.

In *The Life and Times of Joe McCarthy,* Thomas Reeves recounts a 1995 visit to the Van Susteren's Appleton home: "One evening, after a full day of drinking, Joe began to experience delirium tremens in front of his wife and friends, crying out that snakes were leaping at him. Jean, in great anguish, soon confided to Urban Van Susteren that Joe's alcohol consumption had damaged his liver."

Van Susteren phoned the senator's doctor in Washington and was advised, "the liver condition was such that Joe would die in a short time unless he abstained from liquor completely. When Van Susteren confronted Joe about the matter the next morning.

"Joe flew into a rage. 'Kiss my ass,' he shouted."

Enraged, Van Susteren slammed "a bottle of whiskey in front of his old friend and told him to drink it and end things without further disgracing himself and his family."

Greta's Sister Lise Van Susteren and the CIA

Greta's sister, Lise Van Susteren, earned a medical doctorate in 1982 at the University of Paris, and interned

---

1. http://richc.myarchive.us/2005/11/mccarthyism-fallout/

at the Hospital St. Anne, Paris, at the American Hospital in the suburb of Neuilly, and at Hospital Tokoin in Lome, Togo. According to her bio, she was a resident in psychiatry at St. Elizabeth's Hospital in Washington, D.C., 1983-87. Lise Van Susteren was board certified in general psychiatry in 1989, and in forensic psychiatry in 1999. She was a staff psychiatrist, 1985-1991, at the Alexandria Mental Health Center in Virginia, and at the Springfield Mental Health Center in Springfield, Virginia, 1984-1989. Lise also worked "as a consultant to the Central Intelligence Agency, conducting psychological assessments of world leaders," according to her Wikipedia entry. "Lise's husband is Jonathan Kempner, president and CEO of the Mortgage Bankers Association, a trade association. She and Kempner have three daughters. Lise's mother-in-law, Helen Covensky, was a Holocaust survivor."

A Checkered Past (or Trolling for Survivors)

As a partner in John Coale's law firm, Greta Van Susteren was once a professional ambulance chaser. The firm found itself in trouble on two occasions for active soliciting, or 'ambulance chasing.' The second infraction was after the ValuJet disaster.

"Train wrecks, plane crashes, fires – you name it, the avuncular Coale has been there," the *St. Petersburg Times* reported on December 13, 1998, "trolling for business among grieving survivors."

Actor Tom Cruise, a fellow Scientologist, once weighed the notion of making a film about Coale's legal role in Bhopal.

Coale joined Scientology in the early 1980s. "I did a lot of drugs back in college," he acknowledges. "Into the '80s, I didn't do a lot of them, but I felt that I wanted to handle the problem, and Scientology handled it."

He brought his high-profile wife Greta into the Church.

Coale vs. the anti-Scientology Cult Awareness Network (CAN), from the *Times* profile: "In 1993, the husband-and-wife legal team played a small role in Scientology's campaign to take over the Cult Awareness Network, or CAN. Church-backed lawsuits bankrupted the organization, which helped people leave Scientology. Van Susteren and Coale represented an Ohio woman who sued a cult-deprogramming organization called Wellspring, whose executive director also sat on the CAN board. But their real target was CAN, which at the time was Scientology's public enemy No. 1."

The crowning disgrace from the perspective of CAN crusaders, according to L.A.'s weekly *New Times* on September 9, 1999, "occurred earlier this year in a Chicago courtroom. Already having vanquished CAN, appropriated its name, and moved its offices from Illinois to within blocks of Scientology headquarters in Hollywood, lawyers with ties to the church moved to take possession of 20 years' worth of CAN's highly sensitive case files." The files were loaded into some 150 boxes, included names and "detailed information on thousands of people The list of organizations targeted by the old CAN read like a who's who of fringe culture. Among them were the Ku Klux Klan and the Aryan Nations, dozens of obscure fundamentalist and evangelical Christian groups, the Church of Satan, the Unification Church of the Reverend Sun Myung Moon, followers of political extremist Lyndon LaRouche, and, of course, the Church of Scientology."

Van Susteren refuses to discuss the Church publicly and Scientology documents conceal her involvement. A Scientology pamphlet lists top contributors to a Clearwater, Florida construction project, and lists "Greta Conway" among them. Conway is Greta's middle name. Another publicity brochure lists "Mr. and Mrs. Coale" among Church donors.

But Coale insists that she isn't hiding anything. Religion, he observes in her defense, is a "personal" matter.

CHAPTER NINETEEN

TEA AND DISINFORMATION:
NPR PANDERS TO THE FAR-RIGHT

Since the emergence of the Tea Party, National Public Radio has given the jingoistic "patriots" a regular promo spot, *tsked* a few of their corporate sponsors, snickered at the occasional right-wing extremist (a universal mass media euphemism for "fascist"), but feigned not to know of the darkest strains of this toxic beverage, as if perpetually searching for words to describe it.

White supremacy isn't an issue at NPR.

But just look at the Tea Party's corporate funding: John M. Olin, the Bradley and Sloan Foundations, a maze of intelligence/ultra-conservative funding conduits, almost without exception. Funds for state propaganda from the American Enterprise Institute (a CIA/military intelligence front), the Heritage Foundation, on and on, warp the Middle Class; an onslaught of conservative mental programming that rivals the oily blather of Fox News.

"What does the Tea Party (or Parties) believe in?" asks a perky morning NPR voice, but no clear answers are forthcoming. Neither are serious criticisms found elsewhere in the media: ranking legislative candidate ties to neo-Nazis, the sharing of financiers with the ultra-conservative John Birch Society.

Instead, even NP's Robert Scheer, generally trusted by liberal listeners, seemingly hasn't heard of all that/Scheer has voiced his support of the Tea Party repeatedly because he shares "their anger at the banks." A plug. He goes so far as to praise Ron Paul. (And Scheer's unabashed admiration of

Reagan leaves one with no choice but to write him off as a hopeless crank.)

The neo-Nazi and Bircher connections are waved away as inconvenient distractions. "Over on the left," Bob Scheer admires them anyways.

NPR has been the Tea Party's national soapbox, a place to air unchallenged "astro-turf" claims, hide behind "Constitution" and "small government" ... and never explain what those code-words for fascism signify exactly to the often wealthy, "grass-roots" constituents of the far-right Teas.

Yet conservative media commentators, in a ploy intended to drive the media to the right, grind their teeth endlessly over "liberal bias" at NPR.

A UCLA Study Found NPR to be "to the Right of the *Washington Post*"

Excerpt: "All Programs Considered," by Bill McKibben,
***New York Review of Books*, November 11, 2010**

It seems churlish to criticize even mildly the flagship public radio news shows – their reliable excellence deserves lavish praise. In recent years, though, it's started becoming clearer that, for all their polish, the big shows like All Things Considered suffer from some of the same constraints that plague other parts of elite American journalism. They aim for a careful political balance – one academic study found their list of guests slightly to the right of the *Washington Post*, and "approximately equal to those of *Time*, *Newsweek*, and *U.S. News and World Report*." That's not a particularly interesting place to be, and it may explain why, especially in the Bush years, many left-of-center listeners defected to Amy Goodman's Democracy Now!, a highly professional but ideologically engaged daily hour on the Pacifica network. ....

Elitism and Right-Wing Bias

A 2004 study published by Fairness and Accuracy in Reporting found a cynical conservative bias at National Public Radio: "NPR's guest list shows the radio service relies on the same elite and influential sources that dominate mainstream commercial news, and falls short of reflecting the diversity of the American public."

UW survey: CNN, NPR spread Tea Party's message
By John Gastil

... Conservatives decry "National Liberal Radio" or, more plausibly, the leftward slant of MSNBC, whereas liberals mock the "fair and balanced" moniker of Fox News.

The first year of the Tea Party movement ... represents a new and vocally conservative actor that might tempt different media outlets to cover it in ways that reflect underlying biases.

To test for such prejudice, the University of Washington undergraduate students in my Political Deliberation course created a series of content analytic categories that they applied to a representative sampling of 55 news articles from April 2009 to April 2010.... Extracted from the websites of Fox News, NPR, and CNN, this sample is small, but some of its findings are striking. At the very least, a careful look at these articles suggests interesting differences – and surprising similarities – in how these outlets have covered the Tea Party.... Students calculated the number of lines in each article that suggested how the Tea Party was affecting each party, and from this, I calculated a simple index from minus 10 to plus 10 to measure the Tea Party's impact.

On balance, CNN's reporting suggested that the Tea Party would hurt the GOP a little (-5) but have no effect on the Democrats. NPR suggested it could hurt both parties (-6 for GOP, -4 for Dems), and Fox News' reporting suggested it would be a net benefit for the GOP (+5) and devastating for the Dems (-10).

Next, consider how the media report on the general public's sentiments toward the Tea Party. To date, every poll conducted has shown divided public opinion, with many Americans supporting the Tea Party and many others opposing it. Nonetheless, every one of the media outlets was more likely to include text indicating public support for the Tea Party than text indicating public opposition. NPR and Fox had roughly equal numbers, with three-quarters of their articles mentioning public support compared to only two-thirds noting opposition, whereas CNN devoted relatively few lines to either sentiment.

NPR stood out compared to CNN and Fox as the most likely to include in its stories the voices of ordinary citizens,

> along with Tea Party participants and organizers. NPR also showed the clearest imbalance in sourcing. These articles quoted seven Republicans for every Democrat...
>
> NPR [showed] the clearest imbalance in sourcing.... A quarter of the articles included Tea Party organizers compared to almost none featuring anti-Tea Party citizen demonstrators or activists.

Citing comments dating to the Nixon administration, the FAIR report said, "That NPR harbors a liberal bias is an article of faith among many conservatives. Despite the commonness of such claims, little evidence has ever been presented for a left bias at NPR."

NPR spokeswoman Jenny Lawhorn chirped: "This is America; any group has the right to criticize our coverage. That said, there are obviously a lot of intelligent people out there who listen to NPR day after day and think we're fair and in-depth in our approach."

CHAPTER TWENTY

SAN DIEGO SKYFALL:
JMI EQUITY, THE CIA, MAFIA & THE DARK SIDE OF DOUBLECLICK

JMI Equity, the San Diego Padres & the Mob

JMI Equity bills itself as "a growth equity firm focused on investing in growing software, internet, business services and healthcare IT companies." The firm's website fails to note its connections to European fascists and the intelligence underground, but one other criminal faction wields influence at JMI – the Mafia.

JMI was founded in 1992 by John Moores, owner of the San Diego Padrés. Moores' career is as littered with casualties as any in the venture capitalist field.

On January 27, 2000, the *San Diego Reader* was moved to ask, "ARE THE PADRES MARRIED TO THE MOB?" and it appeared to be the case. The scandal involved Metabolife Weight Loss Products founder Michael Ellis, then on probation for a prior conviction for the manufacture of methamphetamines in Rancho Santa Fe:

> "Metabolife has a close relationship with Padres owner John Moores, Next to Moores himself, the company was the largest contributor to the campaign in favor of Proposition C, the measure passed by voters in November to allow construction of a new taxpayer-subsidized baseball stadium for the Padres downtown. Moores spent more than $1 million of his own money to secure voter approval of the measure. Metabolife was the second-largest contributor, donating $50,000. Metabolife has other

ties to the team. It is reportedly a Padres 'corporate sponsor,' pays for radio spots featuring Padres announcer Ted Leitner endorsing its weight-loss product, and sponsors the 'Seventh Inning Stretch' during games. In May, the Union-Tribune reported that the company 'is also among the corporations angling to put its name on the new ballpark, a source close to the Padres confirmed.'"

Ellis picked a sustained legal fight flanked by entrepreneurs "with less than stellar reputations" who repeatedly kicked in Padré sponsorship fees in the six figures. They fought to keep Ellis' court file sealed, with no success. "When it was opened in November, it and related civil cases revealed that Ellis and his friend and codefendant Michael Blevins (who allegedly dealt marijuana and cocaine for 20 years) were allegedly promoting real estate deals on Otay Mesa done with cash the government said was from Blevins' drug trade. Blevins, who served three years in prison on the methamphetamine rap, and who a government agent claimed was once an associate of reputed Chicago mob boss Sam Sarcinelli, is also a founding partner of Metabolife."

The *Union-Tribune* reported in May 1999 that Metabolife was "closely associated with the ball club and is one of the team's 1999 corporate sponsors. It pays for Qualcomm Stadium signage that is visible on television, sponsors the 'Seventh Inning Stretch' during the game, and advertises on the Padres' radio broadcasts. In those commercials, Padres announcer Ted Leitner endorses Metabolife's herbal dietary supplement, 'It changed my life!'"

Moores' advisor on sponsorship deals was Jay Emmett, who lived in Manhattan and sat on the Padres' board. Emmett was president of the now-defunct Entertainment Sports International, Inc.

In the '80s, Emmett was a ranking executive at Warner Communications, proprietor of Warner Brothers Studios and sundry other entertainment assets. In September 1980, Emmett was indicted on bribery and racketeering charges "for his role in the infamous Westchester Premier Theatre scandal. The theater, built in the early 1970s on a dumping site near New York's Tappan Zee bridge, became noted as the place where

Frank Sinatra was photographed in 1976, beaming alongside New York's top Mafiosi, including Thomas Marson, Carlos Gambino, Jimmy 'the Weasel' Fratianno, and Paul Castellano."

In Master of the Game, Constance Bruck's 1994 biography of Time-Warner CEO Steve Ross, we learn: "the theater was *a Mafia front* from its inception."

Partners in the theater included Richard 'Nerves' Fusco of the Colombo crime family, and Gregory De Palma, a soldier for the Gambinos. "Later, Salvatore Cannatella, who, the government would allege, was connected to the Genovese family, would put $1.4 million into the theater and assume a dominant role." Besides performances by Sinatra, Bruck notes, the theater was the scene of all manner of rackets. "Skimming was incessant, with cash looted from the box office to pay back some of the 'shylock' money that had been used to start the theater and to line the pockets of those at the theater."

Sinatra, a ranking stockholder in Warner, "had been recruited to appear at the theater by Louis 'Louie Dones' Pacella, who worked for Frank 'Funzi' Tieri, head of the Genovese family." Jimmy Fratianno, a mobster turned federal informant, "implicated Sinatra in the theater's skimming operation. 'Fratianno told prosecutors that De Palma had paid Sinatra $50,000 or $60,000 in cash, in Las Vegas, to persuade him to play the theater in 1977.'"

Campaign contributions to Richard Nixon were also suspected. Mafioso Tony 'the Pro' Provenzano, an associate of a Warners executive, "in early 1973 collected about $500,000 in cash for Nixon and arranged to have it delivered to Charles Colson.... And Colson, during this period of time, was a highly paid consultant to WCI."

Emmett was hauled before the court in September, 1980. He agreed to a deal with prosecutors and pled guilty to two felony counts. Jay Emmett was summarily evicted from the Warner board of directors. "Emmett had been advised by Micky Rudin, Sinatra's agent and attorney, to assert his Fifth Amendment right against self-incrimination when called before the federal grand jury investigating the case, but had been told by Warner corporate counsel Arthur Liman to testify."

Liman, a partner at Paul, Weiss, Rifkind, Wharton & Garrison, had a rather large role in covering up the Iran contra affair, also the Attica riots. The *Infoplease* web site describes Liman as a "prominent legal strategist for tycoons and criminals."

When Emmett went shopping for legal counsel, Liman referred him to Edward Bennett Williams, "an ultra-connected [particularly at the CIA] Washington defense lawyer, as his attorney. Williams's client roster included Frank Sinatra, along with Teamsters Union head Jimmy Hoffa, Mafia godfather Frank Costello, and Sam "Momo" Giancana." Williams freed Giancana from prison "only to later see him gunned down in a bloody 1975 mob hit after he returned home to Chicago from an agreed-upon Mexican exile, prepared to testify to a congressional committee about what he knew about the CIA's purported role in the assassination of John F. Kennedy."

Williams had a protégé – Lawrence Lucchino, co-owner, with John Moores, of the Padres."

When Lucchino went looking for a team to invest in, he "was introduced to John Moores, who wanted to buy the Padres and build a new stadium."

Who is John Moores?

John Moores has a fat address book that the FBI needs to confiscate.

In 1993, a new baseball stadium (subsidized by the residents of Baltimore) was built for the Orioles. Peter Angelos, a local attorney who made his fortune in asbestos suits, Tom "Red Dawn" Clancy and other minority investors picked up the team for $173 million. Lucchino collected a tidy 11 percent commission.

In its 2000 exposé, the *San Diego Reader* recalled Lucchino's first meeting with the magnate. Moores was looking to buy the Padrés at the time. "Someone at Alex. Brown [brokerage] in Baltimore ... told him that he should hook up with me and that we should talk," Lucchino says. "I met with Moores and he turned out to be such a charming and attractive partner that it made my decision easy, and I chose to join with him and come [to San Diego]." By all accounts, Mafioso Jay Emmett was a key part of the deal.

As for the CIA, the interaction of the Agency with the organized sports world (a hive of organized crime) is not all that uncommon. The Cincinnati Reds, San Diego Padres, Houston Astros and Philadelphia Phillies are on very friendly terms with the Agency. As one web wag notes in his blog,

> It has now become public during investigations into the CIA practice of exporting torture known as 'extraordinary rendition' that Red Sox part owner Phillip H. Morse, a multimillionaire Florida businessman knowingly leased his private Gulfstream jet – complete with Red Sox decals – to The Company, who then kidnapped Abu Omar on the streets of Milan Italy in 2003 before sending him to Egypt where he was tortured horribly for more than a year. They hit him day and night. They made him listen to sounds at full blast, which was the reason why his hearing was impaired. They closed him in a sort of sauna and then in a refrigerator cell."[1]

John Moores' interaction with the Bush syndicate and CIA comes through his work at JMI Equity (the firm bears Moores' initials) in San Diego, one of the score of companies he has founded, including a dozen or so software concerns in Texas.

This curious episode, reported on September 6, 2005 by *Editor & Publisher*, is the sort of thing that may be not be of seismic importance, but is unforgettable:

Revealed: Rumsfeld at Padres Ball Game as New Orleans Sank

The seemingly carefree behavior of top Bush administration officials early last week, who stuck to their vacations as tens of thousands cried for help in New Orleans, gained

---

1. *Chicago Tribune*, June 25, 2005

another twist with revelations that Pentagon chief Donald Rumsfeld was taking in a ball game in San Diego last Monday night – about 24 hours after Katrina hit … Baseball Hall of Famer Dave Winfield wasn't the only VIP who joined Padres President John Moores in the owner's box last night at Petco Park. Secretary of Defense Donald H. Rumsfeld, here to join President Bush at the North Island Naval Air Station today, took in the game, too. Three weeks ago, Winfield stopped by the Pentagon with his family and later joined the Padres as they visited wounded soldiers at the Army's Walter Reed Hospital during a road trip. "Winfield was very moved by the experience," says his agent, Randy Grossman. "So he invited Rumsfeld to the Padres game. After the first few innings, the plan was to shift to dugout seats, for a closer look at the action."

And then there is the former chancellor of the University of California at San Diego, subsequently president of the University of California, Robert Dynes, close friend of Randy "Duke" Cunningham.

Matt Potter, writing in the *Reader* on March 23, 2006, reported that state senators "would soon question Dynes' leadership ability. In an era of state budget shortfalls, the University of California was in transition. Venture-capital financiers were taking over much of the university's research agenda, and administrators' bonuses, according to one state senator, reflected 'corporatization.' Dynes was well connected, with a wealthy wife and father-in-law [the late Warren Hellman] who was closely tied to California's financial establishment. Collaboration with industry was Dynes' vision for the university's future."

"Randy 'Duke' Cunningham was not alone in his fondness for Dynes. The San Diego establishment loved Dynes when he was UCSD chancellor. He had cozy relationships with Qualcomm's Irwin Jacobs and with Padres owner JOHN MOORES."

The *Union-Tribune* was enthusiastic about Dynes and the direction UCSD was taking: "Dynes, a physicist by training, keenly understands that close cooperation between academia and high-tech entrepreneurs is the surest way to accelerate the new economy," effused a December 2000 editorial.... "Dynes spent 22 years at AT&T Bell Laboratories before joining UCSD..."

Moores and the UC president were tight business associates: "In July 1999, according to a filing with the Securities and Exchange Commission, Regent Moores and Chancellor Dynes joined the board of Leap Wireless International, a company Qualcomm had spun off the previous year."

The fate of Leap Wireless doesn't bode well for its principals: "In April 2003, Leap, loaded up with more than $2.4 billion of debt, went bankrupt, blaming a downturn in the demand for its 'Cricket' flat-rate wireless services following the burst of the dot-com bubble. Critics claimed that the company had been badly mismanaged and the board of directors was A FRONT." That is, a front for the CIA and Mafia. And a judge at the bankruptcy court found that the company was "hopelessly insolvent." Stockholders were wiped out. Leap emerged from bankruptcy in August 2004, but by then both Dynes and Moores had fled the board.

From the original issue of Leap stock:

> Leap, headquartered in San Diego, Calif., is a customer-focused company providing innovative communications services for the mass market. Leap pioneered the Cricket Comfortable Wireless service that lets customers make all their local calls from within their local calling area and receive calls from anywhere for one low, flat rate. Leap has begun offering new services designed to further transform wireless communications for consumers. In March 2000, the company's stock traded for $100/share and it's now hovering around $1/share. Some of the investors may want to leap without wires.[2]

In October 1999, Warren Hellman's investment firm, Hellman & Friedman, in league with John Moores, shelled out an undisclosed sum to purchase a nascent South Carolina company called Blackbaud, Inc., a manufacturer of accounting software for nonprofits. Hellman's son Marco was the board chairman of Blackbaud.

2. www.scripophily.net/leapwirininc.html

In November 2004, Warren Hellman and John Moores purchased Vertafore, a software provider for insurers.

In July 2005, Hellman & Friedman, partnered with JMI Equity bought DoubleClick, Inc. from its stockholders for $1.1 billion.

DoubleClick was the most innocuous name listed among JMI holdings. It is, frankly, an inane name for a software company, shows no imagination at all. A simple search for "Double-Click and surveillance" (thought to be a sure washout, but come to learn they're in the business of "key spyware") produced – the very first listing – a fascinating set of letters, to wit:

> Dear Sir: In a press release issued today, your Chief Privacy Officer made the following statement: "DoubleClick is committed to executing its business in the most open manner possible." This claim is more suited to a Chief Propaganda Officer than a Chief Privacy Officer.
>
> I have repeatedly asked DoubleClick to show the 88 million Americans what is kept in DoubleClick's Abacus Direct database about them, and I have met with repeated refusal. How could keeping billions of records in secret electronic dossiers constitute executing business in "the most open manner possible?" This flagrant boasting about what is manifestly untrue is simply one of the worst examples of public relations pabulum I have ever seen outside the tobacco industry.
>
> The press release uses the phrase "fair information practices," but DoubleClick's own practices are nonconsensual, opaque and grossly unfair....
>
> On March 29 the Wall Street Journal reported that DoubleClick commissioned PricewaterhouseCoopers LLC to conduct a security audit of its computer systems.
>
> In the name of openness, I call on you to make that audit report public immediately...
>
> Sincerely,
>
> Jason Catlett
> President
> Junkbusters Corp.

DoubleClick was considered such a menace by the Denver-based Privacy Foundation that it listed the merger with Abacus among the top ten most important stories of the year 2000:

"The merger of database marketer Abacus Direct with online ad company DoubleClick hit front pages and sparked a federal investigation in January 2000 when it was revealed that the company had compiled profiles of 100,000 online users – without their knowledge – and intended to sell them. The resulting outcry stymied the plan, which was shelved later in the year as DoubleClick and combative chairman Kevin O'Connor endured the steep decline among Internet ad stocks. In the press and in the public square, the name 'DoubleClick' became synonymous with Internet privacy breaches..."

In 2002, the Electronic Privacy Information Center filed a series of class action lawsuits "against DoubleClick for violation of privacy relating to the company's cookie tracking practices." In fact, a number of organizations submitted complaints, including the Center for Democracy and Technology (CDT) and the American Civil Liberties Union (ACLU). The Global Internet Liberty Campaign calculates that *DoubleClick* "*may have tracked 90 million U.S. households.*" That's a few households.

Suffice it to say, John Moores' JMI Equity did have some interest in surveillance technology – a possible national security concern given his ties to LA COSA NOSTRA?

But with the surveillance angle established, we go to the next step – CIA connections to JMI Equity. Intelligence ties aren't ostensibly apparent, but JMI's website director bios offer a clue:

- **Harry Gruner, General Partner** – From 1986 to 1991, Mr. Gruner was employed by ALEX. BROWN serving as a Principal in the Corporate Finance Department of the Technology Group...

- **Brad Woloson, General Partner** – Mr. Woloson joined JMI in 1994.... In 1992, Mr. Woloson joined ALEX. BROWN as a Financial Analyst in the Technology Group...

- **Bob Smith, General Partner** – In 1999, Mr. Smith joined ABS Capital Partners, a $1.4 billion private equity firm, where he focused on mid- to later-stage software company investments. From 1994 until 1999, Mr. Smith was employed by ALEX. BROWN serving as a Vice President in their Technology Investment Banking Group...

- **Charles Noell, General Partner** – Mr. Noell was the investment banker for BMC Software, Inc. and in late 1991 was hired by Mr. Moores as President of JMI Services, Inc. Mr. Noell's responsibilities were to manage the Moores' family office and to organize a private equity initiative focused on software and business services. From 1987 to 1991, Mr. Noell served as Managing Director and Co-Head of ALEX. BROWN's Technology Group...

- **Paul Barber, General Partner** – From 1990 to 1998, Mr. Barber was employed by ALEX. BROWN serving as Managing Director and Head of the Software Investment Banking Practice, where he specialized in advising clients in the enterprise applications, systems management and electronic commerce markets. In 1989, Mr. Barber worked in Product Marketing at Microsoft Corporation. Mr. Barber began his business career working in investment banking at Merrill Lynch & Co.

Alex. Brown? The investment house that gave us A.B. "Buzzy" Krongard, also of In-Q-Tel fame, formerly "Number Three" at the CIA who resigned from AB about the time the WTC fell, dogged by reports of 9/11 inside trades.

These were just two of the CIA officers haunting the corridors of Deutsche-Alex. Brown.

The following comes by e-mail from a contact in the investment community (name withheld) bearing reverberations of Iran-contra (the name Poindexter), and the Bush syndicate theme resurfaces:

"Mayo [Shattuck, former CEO of Deutsche Banc-Alex. Brown] graduated from Williams in 1976, and from Stanford GSB in 1980. He worked for five years for my friend's Bain & Co in the S.F. office, then was recruited out in 1985 by Alex. Brown to head their S.F.-Menlo Park division – he took Microsoft public soon after.

"When I mentioned that the Fisher family had Mayo join them as an advisor to their very private Rosewood Venture Capital in the spring of 2001, I failed to mention this is the Fisher family of Gap, Inc. that was charged with racketeering and settled the case about a year after the attack (civil litigation)

"I want to also point out that Mayo doesn't mention his role with the Bronfmans below, but he has been the trustee of the Bronfman trust, therefore his signature appears on many documents filed by Seagram's with the SEC. It seems to me that Mayo thus may be CIA because Bronfman was MI6 (in addition to his very early role during WWII on Board of Economic Warfare with Nelson Rockefeller). And his former boss, Buzzy Krongard, went off to work for the CIA by 1998. The Rockefeller relationships endured, with Mayo and Steve as co-heads of the giant Deutsche Bank division.

"ALSO, in June 2001, Mayo and Steve were staying at Michael Smurfit's jewel of a resort, "K-Club" (Kildare Club) which is where certain Saudi royals were also staying in preparation for the running of the Irish Derby ... which occurred about June 30 or by the first week of July, somewhere in that range. At this time (and until sometime in 2002), Michael Smurfit's company in the U.S. (one of them) known as Jefferson Smurfit not only included the old Container Corp. of America, but Sequoia Pacific (Steve Bechtel's code) aka Sequoia Voting Systems, which produced rigged machines ordered destroyed by a Louisiana Federal Court Judge."

Then there is Mayo's involvement with Nuclear Energy Institute:

"Mayo A. Shattuck III, age 49, a director since May 1999, has been Chairman of the Board of Constellation Energy since July 2002 and President and Chief Executive Officer since November 2001. Mr. Shattuck has also been Chairman of the Board of Baltimore Gas and Electric Company since July 2002. He was Global Head of Investment Banking and Global Head of Private Banking for Deutsche Banc Alex. Brown from June 1999 to October 2001, and held various officer positions during that period. From 1997 to June 1999, Mr. Shattuck was Vice Chairman of Bankers Trust Corporation. He is also a director of Capital One Financial Corporation, Gap, Inc., the Edison Electric Institute, the Nuclear Energy Institute and the Institute of Nuclear Power Operations."[3]

Poindexter was reported to have met with Dick Cheney to help shape energy policy.

"Christian H. Poindexter, age 62, has been Chairman of the Board, Chief Executive Officer and a director of Constellation Energy since its inception in May 1999, and was President until October 2000. He held similar positions with Baltimore Gas and Electric Company, Constellation Energy's predecessor, since 1993. ... In addition, he is a trustee of Johns Hopkins University and a director of Johns Hopkins Medicine Board, U.S. Naval Academy Foundation, Mercantile Bankshares Corporation ...

"Mayo A. Shattuck III, age 46, a director since May 1999, has been Co-Chairman and Co-Chief Executive Officer of DB Alex. Brown, LLC and Deutsche Banc Securities, Inc. since June 1999. From 1997 to June 1999, he was Vice Chairman of Bankers Trust Corporation. From 1991 to 1997, Mr. Shattuck was President and Chief Operating Officer and a director of Alex. Brown Inc., which merged with Bankers Trust in September 1997. Mr. Shattuck also was a director of Constellation Enterprises, Inc. from March 1998 to May 1999, and a director of Constellation Holdings, Inc. from January 1994 to March 1998."[4]

3.http://www.sec.gov/Archives/edgar/data/
4. http://www.sec.gov/Archives/edgar/data/

The rest, of course, is international spyware blowback history:

Google Buys DoubleClick for $3.1 Billion
New York Times, **April 14, 2007**

Google reached an agreement today to acquire DoubleClick, the online advertising company, from two private equity firms for $3.1 billion in cash, the companies announced, an amount that was almost double the $1.65 billion in stock that Google paid for YouTube late last year. ...

Google dodges privacy settings, hides cookies in Safari for iPhone
MobileBurn, February 17, 2012

Google is caught up in what has the potential to be a rather large privacy scandal. The company has acknowledged using a hack in ads served by its Google Ads/DoubleClick service that allowed it to bypass a privacy setting in the iPhone and iPad's Safari browser. This hack allowed Google to place a cookie, a small bit of tracking code, in Safari when it normally wouldn't have been allowed. ...

What will the unauthorized cookies scandal cost Google?'
MobileBurn, February 21, 2012

The discovery that Google has been tracking the Web activity of iPhone and iPad users on Safari without permission has the company in hot water and could end up costing it, both in terms of its reputation as well as monetarily.

"There is a pattern to Google's continued collection of user data, and then claiming it was an error," said Jeffrey Chester, executive director of the Center for Digital Democracy, Washington. "There was Google WiSpy, then Buzz, and now Safari. Daily headlines of privacy violations are fueling calls for stronger regulation, especially from the EU," he said.

"Consumer confidence in Google, especially as it grows its mobile and location business, is being harmed. Why should a consumer trust that a Google Wallet won't share their financial data with others?"

This is just the latest scandal involving mobile and consumer privacy. Last week Apple was the focus of concern over how some mobile applications on iOS are collecting and keeping users' mobile contact lists...

TEFLON NAZIS

The warnings were posted prominently, like mortuary signage along Dead Man's Curve. In the early 1920s, when Hitler and the NSDAP swaggered out of Munich's beerhalls to proliferate, socialist German newspapers took notice and denounced the future dictator. The most determined and sustained attacks appeared in the *Munich Post* in the early '20s, and for 12 years, as Ron Rosenbaum notes in *Explaining Hitler,* "produced some of the sharpest, most penetrating insights into his character, his mind and method, then or since." Journalists at the Post were "the first to investigate him, the first to expose the seamy underside of his party, the murderous criminal behavior masked by its pretensions to being a political movement. They were the first to attempt to alert the world to the nature of the rough beast slouching towards Berlin."

Hitler delivered his first speech at a small, public meeting on October 6, 1919. His party held its initial mass gathering four months later, and, at Hitler's urging to employ "brute force" against the left-wing opposition, rapidly revealed themselves to be a party of murderous thugs

The *Munich Post* issued its first editorial admonition against Hitler's "mischief" in August, 1920. The "corrupt leader of the German fascists" was open to "bribery," and had demonstrated his cowardice during WW I. As a political leader, he was only worthy of ridicule.

But the pages of German socialism's leading house organ were soon filled with sober criticism of Hitler and the brutality of the NSDAP. In November, 1921, at the Munich Hofbrauhaus, Hitler confronted the opposition, a crowd that included members of Majority-Socialist Party, as the Social Democrats were then known. Objections to an attempt on the life of Erhard Auer, a journalist at the *Post*, incited a rumble. Socialists in attendance assaulted the Sturmabteilung (SA for short, anti-labor paramilitary "stormtroopers" underwritten by corporations to terrorize workers and farm laborers) contingent with their beer steins, but they were no match for the protean Nazi Party. In *Mein Kampf*, Hitler described the brawl as the SA's "baptism of fire."

Even Hitler's hidden financing — a touchy subject that he consistently dodged — was an issue early on. In August 1921, the *Post* published a pamphlet entitled, "Adolf Hitler, Traitor," raising questions about his financial underpinnings: "Just what does he do for a living?" Somehow, the struggling writer and artist from Bavaria could afford to drive expensive automobiles and smoke classy cigarettes.

Hitler repeatedly filed libel suits decided by Bavaria's nationalistic, right-wing judges, and collected damages. But the *Post* didn't back down — even after November 8, 1923, when the "schock troop" division of the SA splintered windows at the *Post* with their rifle butts, vandalized editorial offices and pressroom, assaulted anyone found on the premises and burned copies of the newspaper in the street while local police looked on.

The give-and-take between the *Munich Post* and Hitler continued, with a short intermission that began and ended with his imprisonment in 1927, until the '30s.

But the German polloi, increasingly aware of the newspaper's warnings, failed to respond.

Sara Twogood of the Oral History Project at UCSB notes: "At its annual convention in 1931, the SPD decided to concentrate its attention on the Nazi party and its increasing popularity, for in its eyes, 'Fascist participation in the government is a danger to be avoided at all costs.'" But Hitler's slouching toward political power was only enhanced by popular support.

"The *Post* accordingly increased its coverage on Hitler and the Nazis. In the final two years of the *Munich Post*, from 1931-1933, very seldom was an issue published that did not contain numerous attacks and reports of Hitler's party. These articles usually covered Nazi murders of political opponents, followed by coverage of the courtroom verdicts that allowed the murderers to get off free or charged with extreme lesser crimes instead." The majority of Germans shrugged off these reports and swarmed headlong toward the Holocaust and total war.

On December 9, 1931, the *Post* revealed Hitler's "secret plan for Germany." Rosenbaum writes that the series "foretold with astonishing precision all the successive stages and persecutions the Nazi Party was to take against the Jews in the period between 1933 and 1939," including "removal of the Jews from the courts, from the civil service, the professions; police surveillance and property; detention and expulsion of 'unwanted' Jews; Nuremberg-type laws against intermarriage and sexual and social intercourse," and "a final solution ... of the Jewish question." Hitler's secret plan "proposed to use the Jews in Germany for slave labor or for cultivation of the German swamps administered by a special SS division."

The *Post*'s clashes with Hitler continued until March 9, 1933, when the newspaper was banned. Throughout Germany, socialist newspapers were shut down. Again, the SA ransacked the offices of the*Post*. Its journalists and editors were hauled off to concentration camps.

Rosenbaum: "They were the first to sense the dimensions of Hitler's potential for evil — and to see the way the world ignored the desperate warnings in their work." Hitler's opposition "fought with their hearts and jeopardized their freedom and lives hoping the world would listen," risked "imprisonment and death, trying unsuccessfully to warn the world," but "even more disheartening is how successful Hitler was in erasing his first enemies, the *Munich Post*, from history and memory."

The editors at the *Post* had an American ally in Edgar Mowrer, a foreign correspondent for the *Chicago Daily News*. Mowrer covered WW I battles in France and Belgium, and in 1915 was sent to Italy, where he met Benito Mussolini. In 1923, Mowrer was assigned to Berlin. He devoted the next ten years to documenting Nazi crimes and was awarded a Pulitzer in 1933.

"Despite pressure to soften his tine," writes Allison Griner, a researcher at the Fellowships at Auschwitz for the Study of Professional Ethics, "Mowrer's writing remained critical of political attitudes both within and towards Germany. Mowrer was one of the first American journalists to use the word 'extermination' and to warn about Nazi's 'barbarous campaign' against the Jewish people. In 1933, his book *Germany Puts the Clock Back* was rushed to publication. In it, Mowrer documented the progression of Weimar Germany into the Nazi regime, foretelling some of Hitler's bellicose plans."

His warnings were frantic, but it wasn't only readers of the *Daily News* who remained unmoved by German "atrocity stories." Even many German Jews were unresponsive. Andrew Nagorski, author of *Hitlerland*, a book about American journalists in Nazi Germany, writes that Mowrer "kept advising Jews, 'Get out of Germany!' There's a scene in the book where Mowrer is having lunch with group of Jewish bankers in Germany, and it becomes clear that each of them has given some money to [the] Nazi Party at the urging of non-Jewish industrialists. They were told it would be a way of protecting themselves a bit, and they believed it. Just like a lot of Americans, the German Jews thought, 'This can't really be happening.'"

"Why did so few heed the warnings of Hitler's opponents?" asks Richard Weikart, a conservative professor of history at California State University, Stanislaus. With the exception of leftists and Jews, "most Germans ignored the warning signs. Their willingness to tolerate Hitler's initial program of political oppression, because it was directed primarily against leftists, made them defenseless once the oppression widened to include Jews, Gypsies, the handicapped and even Christian clergy. ... I wonder if we are often too quick to distance ourselves from Hitler, Stalin, and other ogres of their ilk, as though WE would never–even with unlimited power at our disposal–oppress or harm a fellow human being. Many "ordinary Germans" (and even many foreigners) assisted Hitler, after all, in carrying out his atrocities."

It is hard to rule out the sympathy-for-the-devil theory when reading some of the international press reports from the period. London's *Observer*, for instance, on March 20 1932 inferred that criticism of Hitler's race hatred inflated the threat:

"It must not be forgotten that the major part of the German Republican Press is in Jewish hands."

Even foreign leaders remained willfully ignorant. Historian Steven Kreis at the *Lectures on Twentieth Century Europe* website goes so far as to find them complicit, de facto Nazi collaborators: "Although most western statesmen had *sufficient warning* that Hitler was a threat to a general European peace, they failed to rally their people and take a stand until it was too late. In this respect, you could argue that the responsibility for World War Two ought to remain *on the shoulders of Britain, France and the United States.*"

Compare and contrast the yawns that permitted Hitler to ascend to the highest political office in Germany, and the wholesale fear and loathing incited by the Red Scare of the 1950s. The former ignored actual evidence of the actual threat posed by fascism. The latter was mass paranoid hysteria, a political fantasy generated by an exaggerated threat. Americans, like the Germans, have been living with the stench of fascism since the early '20s, when Henry Ford and Irenee DuPont first kicked in to advance the Nazi cause. During the war, some 2,000 corporations in the US collaborated with the Nazis to enhance their bottom lines. And that may help to explain why America ignored the real threat and overreacted to the imagined one. Psychologically, we are conditioned by every intimation and nerve impulse of military-industrial culture to accept the actual fascist extreme, and fear a Red Dawn fantasy.

This may explain why many Americans were comfortable voting for Nixon, napalm and all, but felt uneasy with dove Eugene McCarthy.

"We have met the enemy ..."

Anti-fascist warnings are still coming nearly a century after the emergence of Hitler. The humanitarian spirit that drove the editors of the *Munich Post* to oppose the senseless political violence propagated by the ruling class of Germany survives in this book to oppose the senseless political violence propagated by the ruling class of America's blighted democracy.